FOLLOWING
THE
EQUATOR

ecco travels

PROTECTING THE LADIES

FOLLOWING THE EQUATOR

A Journey Around the World

MARK TWAIN

Vol. I   Illustrated

THE ECCO PRESS

Originally published by P. F. Collier & Son Company, New York

THE ECCO PRESS
100 West Broad Street
Hopewell, New Jersey 08525

Published simultaneously in Canada by
Penguin Books Canada Ltd., Ontario
Printed in the United States of America

Library of Congress Cataloging-in-Publication Data

Twain, Mark, 1835–1910.
    Following the equator: A journey around the world /
by Mark Twain (Samuel L. Clemens).
        p.   cm.—(Ecco travels)
      Originally published: New York: P. F. Collier, 1897
      (v. 1: paper)
    1. Twain, Mark, 1835–1910—Journeys. 2. Voyages and travels.
I. Title. II. Series
    [G440.T95T93   1992]   910.4'1—dc20   91-34826
    ISBN 0-88001-518-7 (volume I)
    ISBN 0-88001-519-5 (volume II)

Designed by Nick Mazzella
The text of this book is set in Bembo

9 8 7 6 5 4 3 2 1

THIS BOOK IS AFFECTIONATELY INSCRIBED TO
MY YOUNG FRIEND HARRY ROGERS, WITH REC-
OGNITION OF WHAT HE IS, AND APPREHENSION
OF WHAT HE MAY BECOME UNLESS HE FORM
HIMSELF A LITTLE MORE CLOSELY UPON THE
MODEL OF

THE AUTHOR

Contents

CONTENTS

FOLLOWING
THE
EQUATOR

Chapter I

A man may have no bad habits and have worse.
—*Pudd'nhead Wilson's New Calendar.*

THE starting-point of this lecturing-trip around the world was Paris, where we had been living a year or two.

We sailed for America, and there made certain preparations. This took but little time. Two members of my family elected to go with me. Also a carbuncle. The dictionary says a carbuncle is a kind of jewel. Humor is out of place in a dictionary.

We started westward from New York in mid-summer, with Major Pond to manage the platform-business as far as the Pacific. It was warm work, all the way, and the last fortnight of it was suffocatingly smoky, for in Oregon and British Columbia the forest fires were raging. We had an added week of smoke at the seaboard, where we were obliged to wait awhile for our ship. She had been getting herself ashore in the smoke, and she had to be docked and repaired. We sailed at last; and so ended a snail-paced march across the continent, which had lasted forty days.

We moved westward about mid-afternoon over a rippled and sparkling summer sea; an enticing sea, a clean and cool sea, and apparently a welcome sea to all on board; it certainly was to me, after the distressful dustings and smokings and swelterings of the past weeks. The voyage would furnish a three-weeks holiday, with hardly a break in it. We had the whole Pacific Ocean in front of us, with nothing to do but do nothing and be comfortable. The city of Victoria was twinkling dim in the deep heart of her smoke-cloud, and getting ready to vanish; and now we closed the field-glasses and sat down on our steamer-chairs contented and at peace. But they went to wreck and ruin under us and brought us to shame before all the passengers. They had been furnished by the largest furniture-dealing house in Victoria, and were worth a couple of farthings a dozen, though they had cost us the price of honest chairs. In the Pacific and Indian Oceans one must still bring his own deck-chair on board or go without, just as in the old forgotten Atlantic times—those Dark Ages of sea travel.

Ours was a reasonably comfortable ship, with the customary sea-going fare—plenty of good food furnished by the Deity and cooked by the devil. The discipline observable on board was perhaps as good as it is anywhere in the Pacific and Indian Oceans. The ship was not very well arranged for tropical service; but that is nothing, for this is the rule for ships which ply in the tropics. She had an over-supply of cockroaches, but this is also the rule with ships doing business in the summer seas—at least such as have been long in service.

Our young captain was a very handsome man, tall and perfectly formed, the very figure to show up a smart uniform's finest effects. He was a man of the best intentions, and was polite and courteous even to courtliness. There was a soft grace and finish about his manners which made whatever place he happened to be in seem for the moment a drawing-room. He avoided the smoking-room. He had no vices. He did not smoke or chew tobacco or take snuff; he did not swear, or use slang, or rude, or coarse, or indelicate language, or make puns, or tell anecdotes, or laugh intemperately, or raise his voice above the moderate pitch enjoined by the canons of good form. When he gave an order, his manner modified it into a request. After dinner he and his officers joined the ladies and gentlemen in the ladies' saloon, and shared in the singing and piano-playing, and helped turn the music. He had a sweet and sympathetic tenor voice, and used it with taste and effect. After the music he played whist there, always with the same partner and opponents, until the ladies' bedtime. The electric lights burned there as late as the ladies and their friends might desire, but they were not allowed to burn in the smoking-room after eleven. There were many laws on the ship's statute-book, of course; but, so far as I could see, this and one other were the only ones that were rigidly enforced. The captain explained that he enforced this one because his own cabin adjoined the smoking-room, and the smell of tobacco smoke made him sick. I did not see how our smoke could reach him, for the smoking-room and his cabin were on the upper deck, targets for all the winds that blew; and besides there was no crack of communication between them, no opening of any sort in the solid intervening bulkhead. Still, to a delicate stomach even imaginary smoke can convey damage.

The captain, with his gentle nature, his polish, his sweetness, his moral and verbal purity, seemed pathetically out of place in his rude and autocratic vocation. It seemed another instance of the irony of fate.

He was going home under a cloud. The passengers knew about his trouble, and were sorry for him. Approaching Vancouver through a narrow and difficult passage densely befogged with smoke from the forest fires, he had had the ill luck to lose his bearings and get his ship on the rocks. A matter like this would rank merely as an error with you and me; it ranks as a crime with the directors of steamship companies. The captain had been tried by the Admiralty Court at Vancouver, and its verdict had acquitted him of blame. But that was insufficient comfort. A sterner court would examine the case in Sydney—the Court of Directors, the lords of a company in whose ships the captain had served as mate a number of years. This was his first voyage as captain.

The officers of our ship were hearty and companionable young men, and they entered into the general amusements and helped the passengers pass the time. Voyages in the Pacific and Indian Oceans are but pleasure excursions for all hands. Our purser was a young Scotchman who was equipped with a grit that was remarkable. He was an invalid, and looked it, as far as his body was concerned, but illness could not subdue his spirit. He was full of life, and had a gay and capable tongue. To all appearances he was a sick man without being aware of it, for he did not talk about his ailments, and his bearing and conduct were those of a person in robust health; yet he was the prey, at intervals, of ghastly sieges of pain in his heart. These lasted many hours, and while the attack continued he could neither sit nor lie. In one instance he stood on his feet twenty-four hours fighting for his life with these sharp agonies, and yet was as full of life and cheer and activity the next day as if nothing had happened.

The brightest passenger in the ship, and the most interesting and felicitous talker, was a young Canadian who was not able to let the whisky bottle alone. He was of a rich and powerful family, and could have had a distinguished career and abundance of effective help toward it if he could have conquered his appetite for drink; but he could not do it, so his great equipment of talent was of no use to him. He had often taken the pledge to drink no more, and was a good example of what that sort of unwisdom can do for a man— for a man with anything short of an iron will. The system is wrong in two ways: it does not strike at the root of the trouble, for one thing, and to make a *pledge* of any kind is to declare war against nature; for a pledge is a chain that is always clanking and reminding the wearer of it that he is not a free man.

I have said that the system does not strike at the root of the trouble, and I venture to repeat that. The root is not the *drinking*, but the *desire* to drink. These are very different things. The one merely requires will—and a great deal of it, both as to bulk and staying capacity—the other merely requires watchfulness—and for no long time. The desire of course precedes the act, and should have one's first attention; it can do but little good to refuse the act over and over again, always leaving the desire unmolested, unconquered; the desire will continue to assert itself, and will be almost sure to win in the long run. When the desire intrudes, it should be at once banished out of the mind. One should be on the watch for it all the time—otherwise it will get *in*. It must be taken in time and not allowed to get a lodgment. A desire constantly repulsed for a fortnight should die, then. That should cure the drinking-habit. The system of refusing the mere *act* of drinking, and leaving the *desire* in full force, is unintelligent war tactics, it seems to me.

I used to take pledges—and soon violate them. My will was not strong, and I could not help it. And then, to be tied in any way naturally irks an otherwise free person and makes him chafe in his bonds and want to get his liberty. But when I finally ceased from taking definite pledges, and merely resolved that I would kill an injurious desire, but leave myself free to resume the desire and the habit whenever I should choose to do so, I had no more trouble. In five days I drove out the desire to smoke and was not obliged to keep watch after that; and I never experienced any strong desire to smoke again. At the end of a year and a quarter of idleness I began to write a book, and presently found that the pen was strangely reluctant to go. I tried a smoke to see if that would help me out of the difficulty. It did. I smoked eight or ten cigars and as many pipes a day for five months; finished the book, and did not smoke again until a year had gone by and another book had to be begun.

I can quit any of my nineteen injurious habits at any time, and without discomfort or inconvenience. I think that the Dr. Tanners and those others who go forty days without eating do it by resolutely keeping out the desire to eat, in the beginning; and that after a few hours the desire is discouraged and comes no more.

Once I tried my scheme in a large medical way. I had been confined to my bed several days with lumbago. My case refused to improve. Finally the doctor said:

"My remedies have no fair chance. Consider what they have to fight, besides the lumbago. You smoke extravagantly, don't you?"

"Yes."

"You take coffee immoderately?"

"Yes."

"And some tea?"

"Yes."

"You eat all kinds of things that are dissatisfied with each other's company?"

"Yes."

"You drink two hot Scotches every night?"

"Yes."

"Very well, there you can see what I have to contend against. We can't make progress the way the matter stands. You must make a reduction in these things; you must cut down your consumption of them considerably for some days."

"I can't, doctor."

"Why can't you?"

"I lack the will-power. I can cut them off entirely, but I can't merely moderate them."

He said that that would answer, and said he would come around in twenty-four hours and begin work again. He was taken ill himself and could not come; but I did not need him. I cut off all those things for two days and nights; in fact, I cut off all kinds of food, too, and all drinks except water, and at the end of the forty-eight hours the lumbago was discouraged and left me. I was a well man; so I gave thanks and took to those delicacies again.

It seemed a valuable medical course, and I recommended it to a lady. She had run down and down and down, and had at last reached a point where medicines no longer had any helpful effect upon her. I said I knew I could put her upon her feet in a week. It brightened her up, it filled her with hope, and she said she would do everything I told her to do. So I said she must stop swearing and drinking and smoking and eating for four days, and then she would be all right again. And it would have happened just so, I know it; but she said she could not stop swearing and smoking and drinking, because she had never done these things. So there it was. She had neglected her habits, and hadn't any. Now that they would have come good, there were none in stock. She had nothing to fall back on. She was a sinking vessel, with no freight in her to throw overboard and lighten ship withal. Why, even one or two little bad habits could have saved her, but she was just a moral pauper. When she could have acquired them she was dissuaded by her parents, who were ignorant people though reared in the best society, and it was too late to begin now. It seemed such a pity; but there was no help for it. These things ought to be attended to while a person is young; otherwise, when age and disease come, there is nothing effectual to fight them with.

When I was a youth I used to take all kinds of pledges, and do my best to keep them, but I never could, because I didn't strike at the root of the habit—the *desire*; I generally broke down within the month. Once I tried limiting a habit. That worked tolerably well for a while. I pledged myself to smoke but one cigar a day. I kept the cigar waiting until bedtime, then I had a luxurious time with it. But desire persecuted me every day and all day long; so, within the week I found myself hunting for larger cigars than I had been used to smoke; then larger ones still, and still larger ones. Within the fortnight I was getting cigars *made* for me—on a yet larger pattern. They still grew and grew in size. Within the month my cigar had grown to such proportions that I could have used it as a crutch. It now seemed to me that a one-cigar limit was no real protection to a person, so I knocked my pledge on the head and resumed my liberty.

To go back to that young Canadian. He was a "remittance-man," the first one I had ever seen or heard of. Passengers explained the term to me. They said that dissipated ne'er-do-weels belonging to important families in England and Canada were not cast off by their people while there was any hope of reforming them, but when that last hope perished at last, the ne'er-do-weel was sent abroad to get him out of the way. He was shipped off with just enough money in his pocket—no, in the purser's pocket—for the needs of the voyage—and when he reached his destined port he would find a remittance awaiting him there. Not a large one, but just enough to keep him a month. A similar remittance would come monthly thereafter. It was the remittance-man's custom to pay his month's board and lodging straightway—a duty which his landlord did not allow him to forget—then spree away the rest of his money in a single night, then brood and mope and grieve in idleness till the next remittance came. It is a pathetic life.

We had other remittance-men on board, it was said. At least *they* said they were R. M.'s. There were two. But they did not resemble the Canadian; they lacked his tidiness, and his brains, and his gentlemanly ways, and his resolute spirit, and his humanities and generosities. One of them was a lad of nineteen or twenty, and he was a good deal of a ruin, as to clothes, and morals, and general aspect. He said he was a scion of a ducal house in England, and had been shipped to Canada for the house's relief, that he had fallen into trouble there, and was now being shipped to Australia. He said he had no title. Beyond this remark he was economical of the truth. The first thing he did in Australia was to get into the lockup, and the next thing he did was to proclaim himself an earl in the police court in the morning and fail to prove it.

Chapter II

When in doubt, tell the truth.
                    —Pudd'nhead Wilson's New Calendar.

ABOUT four days out from Victoria we plunged into hot weather, and all the male passengers put on white linen clothes. One or two days later we crossed the 25th parallel of north latitude, and then, by order, the officers of the ship laid away their blue uniforms and came out in white linen ones. All the ladies were in white by this time. This prevalence of snowy costumes gave the promenade deck an invitingly cool and cheerful and picknicky aspect.

From my diary:

There are several sorts of ills in the world from which a person can never escape altogether, let him journey as far as he will. One escapes from one breed of an ill only to encounter another breed of it. We have come far from the snake liar and the fish liar, and there was rest and peace in the thought; but now we have reached the realm of the boomerang liar, and sorrow is with us once more. The first officer has seen a man try to escape from his enemy by getting behind a tree; but the enemy sent his boomerang sailing into the sky far above and beyond the tree; then it turned, descended, and killed the man. The Australian passenger has seen this thing done to two men, behind two trees—and by the one arrow. This being received with a large silence that suggested doubt, he buttressed it with the statement that his brother once saw the boomerang kill a bird away off a hundred yards and *bring it to the thrower*. But these are ills which must be borne. There is no other way.

The talk passed from the boomerang to dreams—usually a fruitful subject, afloat or ashore—but this time the output was poor. Then it passed to instances of extraordinary memory—with better results. Blind Tom, the negro pianist, was spoken of, and it was said that he could accurately play any piece of music, howsoever long and difficult, after hearing it once; and that six months later he could accurately play it again, without having touched it in the interval. One of the most striking of the stories told was furnished by a gentleman who had served on the staff of the Viceroy of India. He read the details from his note-book, and explained that he had written them down, right after the consummation of the incident which they described, because he thought that if he did not put them down in black and white he might presently come to think he had dreamed them or invented them.

The Viceroy was making a progress, and among the shows offered by the Maharajah of Mysore for his entertainment was a memory-exhibition. The Viceroy and thirty gentlemen of his suite sat in a row, and the memory-expert, a high-caste Brahmin, was brought in and seated on the floor in front of them. He said he knew but two languages, the English and his own, but would not exclude any foreign tongue from the tests to be applied to his memory. Then he laid before the assemblage his program—a sufficiently extraordinary one. He proposed that one gentleman should give him one word of a foreign sentence, and tell him its place in the sentence. He was furnished with the French word *est*, and was told it was second in a sentence of three words. The next gentleman gave him the German word *verloren* and said it was the third in a sentence of four words. He asked the next gentleman for one detail in a sum in addition; another for one detail in a sum of subtraction; others for single details in mathematical problems of various kinds; he got them. Intermediates gave him single words from sentences in Greek, Latin, Spanish, Portuguese, Italian, and other languages, and told him their places in the sentences. When at last everybody had furnished him a single rag from a foreign sentence or a figure from a problem, he went over the ground again, and got a second word and a second figure and was told their places in the sentences and the sums; and so on and so on. He went over the ground again and again until he had collected all the parts of the sums and all the parts of the sentences—and all in disorder, of course, not in their proper rotation. This had occupied two hours.

The Brahmin now sat silent and thinking, awhile, then began and repeated all the sentences, placing the words in their proper order, and untangled the disordered arithmetical problems and gave accurate answers to them all.

In the beginning he had asked the company to throw almonds at him during the two hours, he to remember how many each gentleman had thrown; but none were thrown, for the Viceroy said that the test would be a sufficiently severe strain without adding that burden to it.

General Grant had a fine memory for all kinds of things, including even names and faces, and I could have furnished an instance of it if I had thought of it. The first time I ever saw him was early in his first term as President. I had just arrived in Washington from the Pacific coast, a stranger and wholly unknown to the public, and was passing the White

House one morning when I met a friend, a Senator from Nevada. He asked me if I would like to see the President. I said I should be very glad; so we entered. I supposed that the President would be in the midst of a crowd, and that I could look at him in peace and security from a distance, as another stray cat might look at another king. But it was in the morning, and the Senator was using a privilege of his office which I had not heard of—the privilege of intruding upon the Chief Magistrate's working-hours. Before I knew it, the Senator and I were in the presence, and there was none there but we three. General Grant got slowly up from his table, put his pen down, and stood before me with the iron expression of a man who had not smiled for seven years, and was not intending to smile for another seven. He looked me steadily in the eyes—mine lost confidence and fell. I had never confronted a great man before, and was in a miserable state of funk and inefficiency. The Senator said:

"Mr. President, may I have the privilege of introducing Mr. Clemens?"

The President gave my hand an unsympathetic wag and dropped it. He did not say a word, but just stood. In my trouble I could not think of anything to say, I merely wanted to resign. There was an awkward pause, a dreary pause, a horrible pause. Then I thought of something, and looked up into that unyielding face, and said timidly:

"Mr. President, I—I am embarrassed. Are you?"

His face broke—just a little—a wee glimmer, the momentary flicker of a summer-lightning smile, seven years ahead of time—and I was out and gone as soon as *it* was.

Ten years passed away before I saw him the second time. Meantime I was become better known; and was one of the people appointed to respond to toasts at the banquet given to General Grant in Chicago by the Army of the Tennessee when he came back from his tour around the world. I arrived late at night and got up late in the morning. All the corridors of the hotel were crowded with people waiting to get a glimpse of General Grant when he should pass to the place whence he was to review the great procession. I worked my way by the suite of packed drawing-rooms, and at the corner of the house I found a window open where there was a roomy platform decorated with flags, and carpeted. I stepped out on it, and saw below me millions of people blocking all the streets, and other millions caked together in all the windows and on all the housetops around. These masses took me for General Grant, and broke into volcanic explosions and cheers; but it was a good place to see the procession, and I stayed. Presently I heard the distant blare of military music, and far up the street I saw the procession come in sight, cleaving its way through the huzzaing multitudes, with Sheridan, the most martial figure of the War, riding at its head in the dress uniform of a Lieutenant-General.

And now General Grant, arm-in-arm with Major Carter Harrison, stepped out on the platform, followed two and two by the badged and uniformed reception committee. General Grant was looking exactly as he had looked upon that trying occasion of ten years before—all iron and bronze self-possession. Mr. Harrison came over and led me to the General and formally introduced me. Before I could put together the proper remark, General Grant said:

"Mr. Clemens, I am not embarrassed. Are you?"—and that little seven-year smile twinkled across his face again.

Seventeen years have gone by since then, and to-day, in New York, the streets are a crush of people who are there to honor the remains of the great soldier as they pass to their final resting-place under the monument; and the air is heavy with dirges and the boom of artillery, and all the millions of America are thinking of the man who restored the Union and the flag, and gave to democratic government a new lease of life, and, as we may hope and do believe, a permanent place among the beneficent institutions of men.

We had one game in the ship which was a good time-passer—at least it was at night in the smoking-room when the men were getting freshened up from the day's monotonies and dullnesses. It was the completing of non-complete stories. That is to say, a man would tell all of a story except the finish, then the others would try to supply the ending out of their own invention. When every one who wanted a chance had had it, the man who had introduced the story would give it its original ending—then you could take your choice. Sometimes the new endings turned out to be better than the old one. But the story which called out the most persistent and determined and ambitious effort was one which *had* no ending, and so there was nothing to compare the new-made endings with. The man who told it said he could furnish the particulars up to a certain point only, because that was as much of the tale as he knew. He had read it in a volume of sketches twenty-five years ago, and was interrupted before the end was reached. He would give any one fifty dollars who would finish the story to the satisfaction of a jury to be appointed by ourselves. We appointed a jury and wrestled with the tale. We invented plenty of endings, but the jury voted them all down. The jury was right. It was a tale which the author of it may possibly have completed satisfactorily, and if he really had that good fortune I would like to know what the ending was. Any ordinary man will find that the story's strength is in its middle, and that there is apparently no way to transfer it to the close, where of course it ought to be. In substance the storiette was as follows:

John Brown, aged thirty-one, good, gentle, bashful, timid, lived in a quiet village in Missouri. He was superintendent of the Presbyterian Sunday-school. It was but a humble distinction; still, it was his only official one, and he was modestly proud of it and was devoted to its work and its interests. The extreme kindliness of his nature was recognized by all; in fact, people said that he was made entirely out of good impulses and bashfulness; that he could always be counted upon for help when it was needed, and for bashfulness both when it was needed, and when it wasn't.

Mary Taylor, twenty-three, modest, sweet, winning, and in character and person beautiful, was all in all to him. And he was very nearly all in all to her. She was wavering, his hopes were high. Her mother had been in opposition from the first. But she was wavering, too; he could see it. She was being touched by his warm interest in her two charity protégés and by his contributions toward their support. These were two forlorn and aged sisters who lived in a log hut in a lonely place up a cross-road four miles from Mrs. Taylor's farm. One of the sisters was crazy, and sometimes a little violent, but not often.

At last the time seemed ripe for a final advance, and Brown gathered his courage together and resolved to make it. He would take along a contribution of double the usual size, and win the mother over; with her opposition annulled, the rest of the conquest would be sure and prompt.

He took to the road in the middle of a placid Sunday afternoon in the soft Missourian summer, and he was equipped properly for his mission. He was clothed all in white linen, with a blue ribbon for a necktie, and he had on dressy tight boots. His horse and buggy were the finest that the livery-stable could furnish. The lap-robe was of white linen, it was new, and it had a hand-worked border that could not be rivaled in that region for beauty and elaboration.

When he was four miles out on the lonely road and was walking his horse over a wooden bridge, his straw hat blew off and fell in the creek, and floated down and lodged against a bar. He did not quite know what to do. He must have the hat, that was manifest; but how was he to get it?

Then he had an idea. The roads were empty, nobody was stirring. Yes, he would risk it. He led the horse to the roadside and set it to cropping the grass; then he undressed and put his clothes in the buggy, petted the horse a moment to secure its compassion and its loyalty, then hurried to the stream. He swam out and soon had the hat. When he got to the top of the bank the horse was gone!

His legs almost gave way under him. The horse was walking leisurely along the road. Brown trotted after it, saying, "Whoa, whoa, there's a good fellow"; but whenever he got near enough to chance a jump for the buggy, the horse quickened its pace a little and defeated him. And so this went on, the naked man perishing with anxiety, and expecting every moment to see people come in sight. He tagged on and on, imploring the horse, beseeching the horse, till he had left a mile behind him, and was closing up on the Taylor premises; then at last he was successful, and got into the buggy. He flung on his shirt, his necktie, and his coat; then reached for—but he was too late; he sat suddenly down and pulled up the laprobe, for he saw some one coming out of the gate—a woman, he thought. He wheeled the horse to the left, and struck briskly up the cross-road. It was perfectly straight, and exposed on both sides; but there were woods and a sharp turn three miles ahead, and he was very grateful when he got there. As he passed around the turn he slowed down to a walk, and reached for his tr—too late again.

He had come upon Mrs. Enderby, Mrs. Glossop, Mrs. Taylor, and Mary. They were on foot, and seemed tired and excited. They came at once to the buggy and shook hands, and all spoke at once, and said, eagerly and earnestly, how glad they were that he was come, and how fortunate it was. And Mrs. Enderby said, impressively:

"It *looks* like an accident, his coming at such a time; but let no one profane it with such a name; he was sent—sent from on high."

They were all moved, and Mrs. Glossop said in an awed voice:

"Sarah Enderby, you never said a truer word in your life. This is no accident, it is a special Providence. He *was* sent. He is an angel—an angel as truly as ever angel was—an angel of deliverance. *I* say *angel*, Sarah Enderby, and will have no other word. Don't let any one ever say to me again, that there's no such thing as special Providences; for if this isn't one, let them account for it that can."

"I *know* it's so," said Mrs. Taylor, fervently. "John Brown, I could worship you; I could go down on my knees to you. Didn't something tell you—didn't you *feel* that you were sent? I could kiss the hem of your lap-robe."

He was not able to speak; he was helpless with shame and fright. Mrs. Taylor went on:

"Why, just look at it all around, Julia Glossop. *Any* person can see the hand of Providence in it. Here at noon what do we see? We see the smoke rising. I speak up and say, 'That's the Old People's cabin afire.' Didn't I, Julia Glossop?"

"The very words you said, Nancy Taylor. I was as close to you as I am now, and I heard them. You may have said hut instead of cabin, but in substance it's the same. And you were looking pale, too."

"Pale? I was that pale that if—why, you just compare it with this lap-robe. Then the next thing I said was, 'Mary Taylor, tell the hired man to rig up the team—we'll go to the rescue.' And she said, 'Mother, don't you know you told him he could drive to see his people, and stay over Sunday?' And it was just so. I declare for it, I had forgotten it. 'Then,' said I, 'we'll go afoot.' And go we did. And found Sarah Enderby on the road."

"And we all went together," said Mrs. Enderby. "And found the cabin set fire and burnt down by the crazy one, and the poor old things so old and feeble that they couldn't go afoot. And we got them to a shady place and made them as comfortable as we could, and began to wonder which way to turn to find some way to get them conveyed to Nancy Taylor's house. And I spoke up and said—now what did I say? Didn't I say, 'Providence will provide'?"

"Why sure as you live, so you did! I had forgotten it."

"So had I," said Mrs. Glossop and Mrs. Taylor; "but you certainly *said* it. Now wasn't that remarkable?"

"Yes, I said it. And then we went to Mr. Moseley's, two miles, and all of them were gone to the camp-meeting over on Stony Fork; and then we came all the way back, two miles, and then here, another mile—and Providence *has* provided. You see it yourselves."

They gazed at each other awe-struck, and lifted their hands and said in unison:

"It's per-fectly wonderful."

"And then," said Mrs. Glossop, "what do you think we had better do—let Mr. Brown drive the Old People to Nancy Taylor's one at a time, or put both of them in the buggy, and him lead the horse?"

Brown gasped.

"Now, then, that's a question," said Mrs. Enderby. "You see, we are all tired out, and any way we fix it it's going to be difficult. For if Mr. Brown takes both of them, at least one of us must go back to help him, for he can't load them into the buggy by himself, and they so helpless."

"That is so," said Mrs. Taylor. "It doesn't look—oh, how would this do!—one of us drive there *with* Mr. Brown, and the rest of you go along to my house and get things ready. I'll go with him. He and I together can lift one of the Old People into the buggy; then drive her to my house and—"

"But who will take care of the other one?" said Mrs. Enderby. "We mustn't leave her there in the woods alone, you know—especially the crazy one. There and back is eight miles, you see."

They had all been sitting on the grass beside the buggy

for a while, now, trying to rest their weary bodies. They fell silent a moment or two, and struggled in thought over the baffling situation; then Mrs. Enderby brightened and said:

"I think I've got the idea, now. You see, we can't *walk* any more. Think what we've done; four miles there, two to Moseley's, is six, then back to here—nine miles since noon, and not a bite to eat: I declare I don't see how we've done it; and as for me, I am just famishing. Now, somebody's got to go back, to help Mr. Brown—there's no getting around that; but whoever goes has got to ride, not walk. So my idea is this: one of us to ride back with Mr. Brown, then ride to Nancy Taylor's house with one of the Old People, leaving Mr. Brown to keep the other old one company, you all to go now to Nancy's and rest and wait; then one of you drive back and get the other one and drive *her* to Nancy's, and Mr. Brown walk."

"Splendid!" they all cried. "Oh, that will do—that will answer perfectly." And they all said that Mrs. Enderby had the best head for planning in the company; and they said that they wondered that they hadn't thought of this simple plan themselves. They hadn't meant to take back the compliment, good simple souls, and didn't know they had done it. After a consultation it was decided that Mrs. Enderby should drive back with Brown, she being entitled to the distinction because she had invented the plan. Everything now being satisfactorily arranged and settled, the ladies rose, relieved and happy, and brushed down their gowns, and three of them started homeward; Mrs. Enderby set her foot on the buggy step and was about to climb in, when Brown found a remnant of his voice and gasped out—

"Please, Mrs. Enderby, call them back—I am very weak; I can't walk, I can't indeed."

"Why, dear Mr. Brown! You *do* look pale; I am ashamed of myself that I didn't notice it sooner. Come back—all of you! Mr. Brown is not well. Is there anything I can do for you, Mr. Brown—I'm real sorry. Are you in pain?"

"No, madam, only weak; I am not sick, but only just weak—lately; not long, but just lately."

The others came back, and poured out their sympathies and commiserations, and were full of self-reproaches for not having noticed how pale he was. And they at once struck out a new plan, and soon agreed that it was by far the best of all. They would all go to Nancy Taylor's house and see to Brown's needs first. He could lie on the sofa in the parlor, and while Mrs. Taylor and Mary took care of him the other two ladies would take the buggy and go and get one of the Old People, and leave one of themselves with the other one, and—

By this time, without any solicitation, they were at the horse's head and were beginning to turn him around. The danger was imminent, but Brown found his voice again and saved himself. He said—

"But, ladies, you are overlooking something which makes the plan impracticable. You see, if you bring *one* of them home, and one remains behind with the other, there will be three persons there when one of you comes back for that other, for some one must drive the buggy back, and *three* can't come home in it."

They all exclaimed, "Why, sure-ly, that is so!" and they were all perplexed again.

"Dear, dear, what *can* we do?" said Mrs. Glossop; "it is the most mixed-up thing that ever was. The fox and the goose and the corn and things—oh, dear, they are nothing to it."

They sat wearily down once more, to further torture their tormented heads for a plan that would work. Presently Mary offered a plan; it was her first effort. She said:

"I am young and strong, and am refreshed, now. Take Mr. Brown to our house, and give him help—you see how plainly he needs it. I will go back and take care of the Old People; I can be there in twenty minutes. You can go on and do what you first started to do—wait on the main road at our house until somebody comes along with a wagon; then send and bring away the three of us. You won't have to wait long; the farmers will soon be coming back from town now. I will keep old Polly patient and cheered up—the crazy one doesn't need it."

This plan was discussed and accepted; it seemed the best that could be done, in the circumstances, and the Old People must be getting discouraged by this time.

Brown felt relieved, and was deeply thankful. Let him once get to the main road and he would find a way to escape.

Then Mrs. Taylor said:

"The evening chill will be coming on, pretty soon, and those poor old burnt-out things will need some kind of covering. Take the lap-robe with you, dear."

"Very well, Mother, I will."

She stepped to the buggy and put out her hand to take it—

That was the end of the tale. The passenger who told it said that when he read the story twenty-five years ago in a train he was interrupted at that point—the train jumped off a bridge.

At first we thought we could finish the story quite easily, and we set to work with confidence; but it soon began to appear that it was not a simple thing, but difficult and baffling. This was on account of Brown's character—great generosity and kindliness, but complicated with unusual shyness and diffidence, particularly in the presence of ladies. There was his love for Mary, in a hopeful state but not yet secure—just in a condition, indeed, where its affair must be handled with great tact, and no mistakes made, no offense given. And there was the mother—wavering, half willing—by adroit and flawless diplomacy to be won over, now, or perhaps never at all. Also, there were the helpless Old People yonder in the woods waiting—their fate and Brown's happiness to be determined by what Brown should do within the next two seconds. Mary was reaching for the lap-robe; Brown must decide—there was no time to be lost.

Of course none but a happy ending of the story would be accepted by the jury; the finish must find Brown in high credit with the ladies, his behavior without blemish, his modesty unwounded, his character for self-sacrifice maintained, the Old People rescued through him, their benefactor, all the party proud of him, happy in him, his praises on all their tongues.

We tried to arrange this, but it was beset with persistent and irreconcilable difficulties. We saw that Brown's shyness would not allow him to give up the lap-robe. This would offend Mary and her mother; and it would surprise the other ladies, partly because this stinginess toward the suffering Old People would be out of character with Brown, and partly because he was a special Providence and could not properly act so. If asked to explain his conduct, his shyness would not allow him to tell the truth, and lack of invention and practice would find him incapable of contriving a lie that would wash. We worked at the troublesome problem until three in the morning.

Meantime Mary was still reaching for the lap-robe. We gave it up, and decided to let her continue to reach. It is the reader's privilege to determine for himself how the thing came out.

Chapter III

It is more trouble to make a maxim than it is to do right.
                —Pudd'nhead Wilson's New Calendar.

O N the seventh day out we saw a dim vast bulk standing up out of the wastes of the Pacific and knew that that spectral promontory was Diamond Head, a piece of this world which I had not seen before for twenty-nine years. So we were nearing Honolulu, the capital city of the Sandwich Islands—those islands which to me were Paradise; a Paradise which I had been longing all those years to see again. Not any other thing in the world could have stirred me as the sight of that great rock did.

In the night we anchored a mile from shore. Through my port I could see the twinkling lights of Honolulu and the dark bulk of the mountain-range that stretched away right and left. I could not make out the beautiful Nuuana valley, but I knew where it lay, and remembered how it used to look in the old times. We used to ride up it on horseback in those days—we young people—and branch off and gather bones

From note-book.

The man that invented the cuckoo
clock is ~~dead~~ no more. ~~This is old news but~~
~~good.~~

~~As news, this is a little stale~~ old, ~~but~~
~~some news is better~~ old ~~than~~ not at all.
~~As news, this is a little old, but~~
~~better late than never.~~

~~As news this is a little old, for it~~
~~happened 64 years ago, but it~~
~~is not the newest~~ always ~~news that is the best.~~ most interesting
The man that invented the cuckoo
clock is no more. It is old news,
but there is nothing else the
matter with it.

~~Occasionly~~

It is more ~~diffi~~ trouble to ~~con~~;
~~struct~~ make a maxim than it is to
do right.

in a sandy region where one of the first Kamehameha's battles was fought. He was a remarkable man, for a king; and he was also a remarkable man for a savage. He was a mere kinglet and of little or no consequence at the time of Captain Cook's arrival in 1777; but about four years afterward he conceived the idea of enlarging his sphere of influence. That is a courteous modern phrase which means robbing your neighbor—for your neighbor's benefit; and the great theater of its benevolences is Africa. Kamehameha went to war, and in the course of ten years he whipped out all the other kings and made himself master of every one of the nine or ten islands that form the group. But he did more than that. He bought ships, freighted them with sandalwood and other native products, and sent them as far as South America and China; he sold to his savages the foreign stuffs and tools and utensils which came back in these ships, and started the march of civilization. It is doubtful if the match to this extraordinary thing is to be found in the history of any other savage. Savages are eager to learn from the white man any new way to kill each other, but it is not their habit to seize with avidity and apply with energy the larger and nobler ideas which he offers them. The details of Kamehameha's history show that he was always hospitably ready to examine the white man's ideas, and that he exercised a tidy discrimination in making his selections from the samples placed on view.

A shrewder discrimination than was exhibited by his son and successor, Liholiho, I think. Liholiho could have qualified as a reformer, perhaps, but as a king he was a mistake. A mistake because he tried to be both king *and* reformer. This is mixing fire and gunpowder together. A king has no proper business with reforming. His best policy is to keep things as they are; and if he can't do that, he ought to try to make them worse than they are. This is not guesswork; I have thought over this matter a good deal, so that if I should ever have a chance to become a king I would know how to conduct the business in the best way.

When Liholiho succeeded his father he found himself possessed of an equipment of royal tools and safeguards which a wiser king would have known how to husband, and judiciously employ, and make profitable. The entire country was under the one scepter, and his was that scepter. There was an Established Church, and he was the head of it. There was a Standing Army, and he was the head of that; an Army of one hundred and fourteen privates under command of twenty-seven Generals and a Field Marshal. There was a proud and ancient Hereditary Nobility. There was still one other asset. This was the *tabu*—an agent endowed with a mysterious and stupendous power, an agent not found among the properties of any European monarch, a tool of inestimable value in the business. Liholiho was headmaster of the tabu. The tabu was the most ingenious and effective of all the inventions that had ever been devised for keeping a people's privileges satisfactorily restricted.

It required the sexes to live in separate houses. It did not allow people to eat in either house; they must eat in another place. It did not allow a man's women-folk to enter his house. It did not allow the sexes to eat together; the men must eat first, and the women must wait on them. Then the women could eat what was left—if anything was left—and wait on themselves. I mean, if anything of a coarse or unpalatable sort was left, the women could have it. But not the good things, the fine things, the choice things, such as pork, poultry, bananas, cocoanuts, the choicer varieties of fish, and so on. By the tabu, all these were sacred to the men; the women spent their lives longing for them and wondering what they might taste like; and they died without finding out.

These rules, as you see, were quite simple and clear. It was easy to remember them; and useful. For the penalty for infringing any rule in the whole list was *death*. Those women easily learned to put up with shark and taro and dog for a diet when the other things were so expensive.

It was death for any one to walk upon tabu'd ground; or defile a tabu'd thing with his touch; or fail in due servility to a chief; or step upon the king's shadow. The nobles and the king and the priests were always suspending little rags here and there and yonder, to give notice to the people that the decorated spot or thing was tabu, and death lurking near. The struggle for life was difficult and chancy in the islands in those days.

Thus advantageously was the new king situated. Will it be believed that the first thing he did was to destroy his Established Church, root and branch? He did indeed do that. To state the case figuratively, he was a prosperous sailor who burnt his ship and took to a raft. This Church was a horrid thing. It heavily oppressed the people; it kept them always trembling in the gloom of mysterious threatenings; it slaughtered them in sacrifice before its grotesque idols of wood and stone; it cowed them, it terrorized them, it made them slaves to its priests, and through the priests to the king. It was the best friend a king could have, and the most dependable. To a professional reformer who should annihilate so frightful and so devastating a power as this Church, reverence and praise would be due; but to a king who should do it, could properly be due nothing but reproach; reproach softened by sorrow; sorrow for his unfitness for his position.

He destroyed his Established Church, and his kingdom is a republic to-day, in consequence of that act.

When he destroyed the Church and burned the idols he did a mighty thing for civilization and for his people's weal— but it was not "business." It was unkingly, it was inartistic. It made trouble for his line. The American missionaries arrived while the burned idols were still smoking. They found the nation without a religion, and they repaired the defect. They offered their own religion and it was gladly received. But it was no support to arbitrary kingship, and so the kingly power began to weaken from that day. Forty-seven years later, when I was in the islands, Kamehameha V. was trying to repair Liholiho's blunder, and not succeeding. He had set up an Established Church and made himself the head of it. But it was only a pinchbeck thing, an imitation, a bauble, an empty show. It had no power, no value for a king. It could not harry or burn or slay, it in no way resembled the admirable machine which Liholiho destroyed. It was an Established Church without an Establishment; all the people were Dissenters.

Long before that, the kingship had itself become but a name, a show. At an early day the missionaries had turned it into something very much like a republic; and here lately the business whites have turned it into something exactly like it.

In Captain Cook's time (1778), the native population of the islands was estimated at 400,000; in 1836 at something short of 200,000; in 1866 at 50,000; it is to-day, per census, 25,000. All intelligent people praise Kamehameha I. and Liholiho for conferring upon the people the great boon of civilization. I would do it myself, but my intelligence is out of repair, now, from overwork.

When I was in the islands nearly a generation ago, I was acquainted with a young American couple who had among their belongings an attractive little son of the age of seven— attractive but not practicably companionable with me, because he knew no English. He had played from his birth with the little Kanakas on his father's plantation, and had preferred their language and would learn no other. The family removed to America a month after I arrived in the islands, and straightway the boy began to lose his Kanaka and pick up English. By the time he was twelve he hadn't a word of Kanaka left; the language had wholly departed from his tongue and from his comprehension. Nine years later, when he was twenty-one, I came upon the family in one of the lake towns of New York, and the mother told me about an adventure which her son had been having. By trade he was now a professional diver. A passenger-boat had been caught in a storm on the lake, and had gone down, carrying her people with her. A few days later the young diver descended, with his armor on, and entered the berth-saloon of the boat, and stood at the foot of the companionway, with his hand on the rail, peering through the dim water. Presently something touched him on the shoulder, and he turned and found a dead man swaying and bobbing about him and seemingly inspecting him inquiringly. He was paralyzed with fright. His entry had disturbed the water, and now he discerned a number of dim corpses making for him and wagging their heads and swaying their bodies like sleepy people trying to dance. His senses forsook him, and in that condition he was drawn to the surface. He was put to bed at home, and was soon very ill. During some days he had seasons of delirium which lasted several hours at a time; and while they lasted he talked *Kanaka* incessantly and glibly; and Kanaka only. He was still very ill, and he talked to me in that tongue; but I did not understand it, of course. The doctor books tell us that cases like this are not uncommon. Then the doctors ought to study the cases and find out how to multiply them. Many languages and things get mislaid in a person's head, and stay mislaid for lack of this remedy.

Many memories of my former visit to the islands came up in my mind while we lay at anchor in front of Honolulu that night. And pictures—pictures—pictures—an enchanting procession of them! I was impatient for the morning to come.

When it came it brought disappointment, of course. Cholera had broken out in the town, and we were not allowed to have any communication with the shore. Thus suddenly did my dream of twenty-nine years go to ruin. Messages came from friends, but the friends themselves I was not to have any sight of. My lecture-hall was ready, but I was not to see that, either.

Several of our passengers belonged in Honolulu, and these were sent ashore; but nobody could go ashore and return. There were people on shore who were booked to go with us to Australia, but we could not receive them; to do it would cost us a quarantine-term in Sydney. They could have escaped the day before, by ship to San Francisco; but the bars had been put up, now, and they might have to wait weeks before any ship could venture to give them a passage any whither. And there were hardships for others. An elderly lady and her son, recreation-seekers from Massachusetts, had wandered westward, further and further from home, always intending to take the return track, but always concluding to go still a little further; and now here they were at anchor before Honolulu—positively their last westward-bound indulgence—they had made up their minds to that—but where is the use of making up your mind in this world? It is usually a waste of time to do it. These two would have to stay with us as far as Australia. Then they could go on around the world, or go back the way they had come; the distance and the accommodations and outlay of time would be just the same, whichever of the two routes they might elect to take. Think of it: a projected excursion of five hundred miles gradually enlarged, without any elaborate degree of intention, to a possible twenty-four thousand. However, they were used to extensions by this time, and did not mind this new one much.

And we had with us a lawyer from Victoria, who had been sent out by the Government on an international matter, and he had brought his wife with him and left the children at home with the servants—and now what was to be done? Go ashore amongst the cholera and take the risks? Most certainly not. They decided to go on, to the Fiji Islands, wait there a fortnight for the next ship, and then sail for home. They couldn't foresee that they wouldn't see a homeward-bound ship again for six weeks, and that no word could come to them from the children, and no word go from them to the children in all that time. It is easy to make plans in this world; even a cat can do it; and when one is out in those remote oceans it is noticeable that a cat's plans and a man's are worth about the same. There is much the same shrinkage in both, in the matter of values.

There was nothing for us to do but sit about the decks in the shade of the awnings and look at the distant shore. We lay in luminous blue water; shoreward the water was green— green and brilliant; at the shore itself it broke in a long white ruffle, and with no crash, no sound that we could hear. The town was buried under a mat of foliage that looked like a cushion of moss. The silky mountains were clothed in soft, rich splendors of melting color, and some of the cliffs were veiled in slanting mists. I recognized it all. It was just as I had seen it long before, with nothing of its beauty lost, nothing of its charm wanting.

A change had come, but that was political, and not visible from the ship. The monarchy of my day was gone, and a republic was sitting in its seat. It was not a material change. The old imitation pomps, the fuss and feathers, have departed, and the royal trade-mark—that is about all that one could miss, I suppose. That imitation monarchy was grotesque enough, in my time; if it had held on another thirty years it would have been a monarchy without subjects of the king's race.

We had a sunset of a very fine sort. The vast plain of the sea was marked off in bands of sharply contrasted colors; great stretches of dark blue, others of purple, others of polished bronze; the billowy mountains showed all sorts of dainty browns and greens, blues and purples and blacks, and the rounded velvety backs of certain of them made one want to stroke them, as one would the sleek back of a cat. The long, sloping promontory projecting into the sea at the west turned dim and leaden and spectral, then became suffused with pink— dissolved itself into a pink dream, so to speak, it seemed so airy and unreal. Presently the cloud-rack was flooded with fiery splendors, and these were copied on the surface of the sea, and it made one drunk with delight to look upon it.

From talks with certain of our passengers whose home was Honolulu, and from a sketch by Mrs. Mary H. Krout, I was able to perceive what the Honolulu of to-day is, as compared with the Honolulu of my time. In my time it was a beautiful little town, made up of snow-white wooden cottages deliciously smothered in tropical vines and flowers and trees and shrubs; and its coral roads and streets were hard and smooth, and as white as the houses. The outside aspects of the place suggested the presence of a modest and comfortable prosperity—a general prosperity—perhaps one might strengthen the term and say universal. There were no fine houses, no fine furniture. There were no decorations. Tallow candles furnished the light for the bedrooms, a whale-oil lamp furnished it for the parlor. Native matting served as carpeting. In the parlor one would find two or three lithographs on the walls—portraits as a rule: Kamehameha IV., Louis Kossuth, Jenny Lind; and maybe an engraving or two: "Rebecca at the Well," "Moses Smiting the Rock," "Joseph's Servants Finding the Cup in Benjamin's Sack." There would be a center-table with books of a tranquil sort on it: *The Whole Duty of Man*, Baxter's *Saints' Rest*, Fox's *Martyrs*, Tupper's *Proverbial Philosophy*, bound copies of *The Missionary Herald* and of Father Damien's *Seaman's Friend*. A melodeon; a music-stand, with "Willie, We Have Missed You," "Star of the Evening," "Roll on, Silver Moon," "Are We Most There?" "I Would Not Live Always," and other songs of love and sentiment, together with an assortment of hymns. A what-not with semi-globular glass paper-weights, inclosing miniature pictures of ships, New England rural snow-storms, and the like; sea-shells with Bible texts carved on them in cameo style; native curios; whale's tooth with full-rigged ship carved on it. There was nothing reminiscent of foreign parts, for nobody had been abroad. Trips were made to San Francisco, but that could not be called going abroad. Comprehensively speaking, nobody traveled.

But Honolulu has grown wealthy since then, and of course wealth has introduced changes; some of the old simplicities have disappeared. Here is a modern house, as pictured by Mrs. Krout:

> Almost every house is surrounded by extensive lawns and gardens inclosed by walls of volcanic stone or by thick hedges of the brilliant hibiscus.
>
> The houses are most tastefully and comfortably furnished; the floors are of hard wood covered either with rugs or with fine Indian matting, while there is a preference, as in most warm countries, for rattan or bamboo furniture; there are the usual accessories of bric-à-brac, pictures, books, and curios from all parts of the world, for these island-dwellers are indefatigable travelers.
>
> Nearly every house has what is called a *lanai*. It is a large apartment, roofed, floored, open on three sides, with a door or a draped archway opening into the drawing-room. Frequently the roof is formed by the thick interlacing boughs of the *hou* tree, impervious to the sun and even to the rain, except in violent storms. Vines are trained about the sides—the stephanotis or some one of the countless fragrant and blossoming trailers which abound in the islands. There are

also curtains of matting that may be drawn to exclude the sun or rain. The floor is bare for coolness, or partially covered with rugs, and the *lanai* is prettily furnished with comfortable chairs, sofas, and tables loaded with flowers, or wonderful ferns in pots.

The *lanai* is the favorite reception-room, and here at any social function the musical program is given, and cakes and ices are served; here morning callers are received, or gay riding parties, the ladies in pretty divided skirts, worn for convenience in riding astride—the universal mode adopted by Europeans and Americans, as well as by the natives.

The comfort and luxury of such an apartment, especially at a seashore villa, can hardly be imagined. The soft breezes swept across it, heavy with the fragrance of jasmine and gardenia, and through the swaying boughs of palm and mimosa there are glimpses of rugged mountains, their summits veiled in clouds, of purple sea with white surf beating eternally against the reefs—whiter still in the yellow sunlight or the magical moonlight of the tropics.

There: rugs, ices, pictures, *lanais*, worldly books, sinful bric-à-brac fetched from everywhere. And the ladies riding astride. These are changes, indeed. In my time the native women rode astride, but the white ones lacked the courage to adopt their wise custom. In my time ice was seldom seen in Honolulu. It sometimes came in sailing-vessels from New England as ballast; and then, if there happened to be a man-of-war in port and balls and suppers raging by consequence, the ballast was worth six hundred dollars a ton, as is evidenced by reputable tradition. But the ice-machine has traveled all over the world, now, and brought ice within everybody's reach. In Lapland and Spitzbergen no one uses native ice in our day, except the bears and the walruses.

The bicycle is not mentioned. It was not necessary. We know that it is there, without inquiring. It is everywhere.

But for it, people could never have had summer homes on the summit of Mont Blanc; before its day, property up there had but a nominal value. The ladies of the Hawaiian capital learned too late the right way to occupy a horse—too late to get much benefit from it. The riding-horse is retiring from business everywhere in the world. In Honolulu a few years from now he will be only a tradition.

We all know about Father Damien, the French priest who voluntarily forsook the world and went to the leper island of Molokai to labor among its population of sorrowful exiles who wait there, in slow-consuming misery, for death to come and release them from their troubles, and we know that the thing which he knew beforehand would happen, did happen: that he became a leper himself, and died of that horrible disease. There was still another case of self-sacrifice, it appears. I asked after "Billy" Ragsdale, interpreter to the Parliament in my time—a half-white. He was a brilliant young fellow, and very popular. As an interpreter he would have been hard to match anywhere. He used to stand up in the Parliament and turn the English speeches into Hawaiian and the Hawaiian speeches into English with a readiness and a volubility that were astonishing. I asked after him, and was told that his prosperous career was cut short in a sudden and unexpected way, just as he was about to marry a beautiful half-caste girl. He discovered, by some nearly invisible sign about his skin, that the poison of leprosy was in him. The secret was his own, and might be kept concealed for years; but he would not be treacherous to the girl that loved him; he would not marry her to a doom like his. And so he put his affairs in order, and went around to all his friends and bade them good-by, and sailed in the leper ship to Molokai. There he died the loathsome and lingering death that all lepers die.

In this place let me insert a paragraph or two from *The Paradise of the Pacific* (Rev. H. H. Gowen):

Poor lepers! It is easy for those who have no relatives or friends among them to enforce the decree of segregation to the letter, but who can write of the terrible, the heartbreaking scenes which that enforcement has brought about?

A man upon Hawaii was suddenly taken away after a summary arrest, leaving behind him a helpless wife about to give birth to a babe. The devoted wife with great pain and risk came the whole journey to Honolulu, and pleaded until the authorities were unable to resist her entreaty that she might go and live like a leper with her leper husband.

A woman in the prime of life and activity is condemned as an incipient leper, suddenly removed from her home, and her husband returns to find his two helpless babes moaning for their lost mother.

Imagine it! The case of the babies is hard, but its bitterness is a trifle—less than a trifle—less than nothing—compared to what the mother must suffer; and suffer minute by minute, hour by hour, day by day, month by month, year by year, without respite, relief, or any abatement of her pain till she dies.

One woman, Luka Kaaukau, has been living with her leper husband in the settlement for twelve years. The man has scarcely a joint left, his limbs are only distorted ulcerated stumps, for four years his wife has put every particle of food into his mouth. He wanted his wife to abandon his wretched carcass long ago, as she herself was sound and well, but Luka said that she was content to remain and wait on the man she loved till the spirit should be freed from its burden.

I myself have known hard cases enough: of a girl, apparently in full health, decorating the church with me at Easter, who before Christmas is taken away as a confirmed leper; of a mother hiding her child in the mountains for years so that not even her dearest friends knew that she had a child alive, that he might not be taken away; of a respectable white man taken away from his wife and family, and compelled to become a dweller in the Leper Settlement, where he is counted dead, *even by the insurance companies.*

And one great pity of it all is, that these poor sufferers are innocent. The leprosy does not come of sins which they committed, but of sins committed by their ancestors, who *escaped* the curse of leprosy!

Mr. Gowen has made record of a certain very striking circumstance. Would you expect to find in that awful Leper Settlement a custom worthy to be transplanted to your own country? They have one such, and it is inexpressibly touching and beautiful. When death sets open the prison door of life there, the band salutes the freed soul with a burst of glad music!

Chapter IV

SAILED from Honolulu. From diary:

Sept. 2. Flocks of flying-fish—slim, shapely graceful, and intensely white. With the sun on them they look like a flight of silver fruit-knives. They are able to fly a hundred yards.

Sept. 3. In 9° 50′ north latitude, at breakfast. Approaching the equator on a long slant. Those of us who have never seen the equator are a good deal excited. I think I would rather see it than any other thing in the world. We entered the "doldrums" last night—variable winds, bursts of rain, intervals of calm, with chopping seas and a wobbly and drunken motion to the ship—a condition of things findable in other regions sometimes, but present in the doldrums always. The globe-girdling belt called the doldrums is twenty degrees wide, and the thread called the equator lies along the middle of it.

Sept. 4. Total eclipse of the moon last night. At seven-thirty it began to go off. At total—or about that—it was like a rich rosy cloud with a tumbled surface framed in the circle and projecting from it—a bulge of strawberry-ice, so to speak. At half-eclipse the moon was like a gilded acorn in its cup.

Sept. 5. Closing in on the equator this noon. A sailor explained to a young girl that the ship's speed is poor because we are climbing up the bulge toward the center of the globe; but that when we should once get over, at the equator, and start downhill, we should fly. When she asked him the other day what the foreyard was, he said it was the front yard, the open area in the front end of the ship. That man has a good deal of learning stored up, and the girl is likely to get it all.

Afternoon. Crossed the equator. In the distance it looked like a blue ribbon stretched across the ocean. Several passengers kodak'd it. We had no fool ceremonies, no fantastics, no horse-play. All that sort of thing has gone out. In old times a sailor, dressed as Neptune, used to come in over the bows, with his suite, and lather up and shave everybody who was crossing the equator for the first time, and then cleanse these unfortunates by swinging them from the yard-arm and ducking them three times in the sea. This was considered funny. Nobody knows why. No, that is not true. We do know why. Such a thing could never be funny on land; no part of the old-time grotesque performances gotten up on shipboard to celebrate the passage of the line could ever be funny on shore—they would seem dreary and witless to shore people. But the shore people would change their minds about it at sea, on a long voyage. On such a voyage, with its eternal monotonies, people's intellects deteriorate; the owners of the intellects soon reach a point where they almost seem to prefer childish things to things of a maturer degree. One is often surprised at the juvenilities which grown people indulge in at sea, and the interest they take in them, and the consuming enjoyment they get out of them. This is on long voyages only. The mind gradually becomes inert, dull, blunted; it loses its accustomed interest in intellectual things; nothing but horse-play can

rouse it, nothing but wild and foolish grotesqueries can enter-
tain it. On short voyages it makes no such exposure of itself;
it hasn't time to slump down to this sorrowful level.

The short-voyage passenger gets his chief physical exercise out of "horse-billiards"—shovel-board. It is a good
game. We play it in this ship. A quarter-master chalks off a
diagram like this—on the deck.

The player uses a
cue that is like a
broom-handle with a
quarter-moon of wood
fastened to the end of
it. With this he shoves
wooden disks the size
of a saucer—he gives
the disk a vigorous
shove and sends it fif-
teen or twenty feet
along the deck and
lands it in one of the
squares if he can. If it
stays there till the in-
ning is played out, it
will count as many
points in the game as
the figure in the square
it has stopped in repre-
sents. The adversary
plays to knock that
disk out and leave his
own in its place—par-

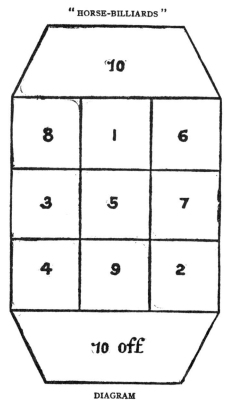

" HORSE-BILLIARDS "

DIAGRAM

ticularly if it rests upon the 9 or 10 or some other of the high
numbers; but if it rests in the "10-off" he backs it up—lands
his disk behind it a foot or two, to make it difficult for its

owner to knock it out of that damaging place and improve his record. When the inning is played out it may be found that each adversary has placed his four disks where they count; it may be found that some of them are touching chalk-lines and not counting; and very often it will be found that there has been a general wreckage, and that not a disk has been left within the diagram. Anyway, the result is recorded, whatever it is, and the game goes on. The game is one hundred points, and it takes from twenty minutes to forty to play it, according to luck and the condition of the sea. It is an exciting game, and the crowd of spectators furnish abundance of applause for fortunate shots and plenty of laughter for the other kind. It is a game of skill, but at the same time the uneasy motion of the ship is constantly interfering with skill; this makes it a chancy game, and the element of luck comes largely in.

We had a couple of grand tournaments, to determine who should be "Champion of the Pacific": they included among the participants nearly all the passengers, of both sexes, and the officers of the ship, and they afforded many days of stupendous interest and excitement, and murderous exercise—for horse-billiards is a physically violent game.

The figures in the following record of some of the closing games in the first tournament will show, better than any description, how very chancy the game is. The losers here represented had all been winners in the previous games of the series, some of them by fine majorities:

Chase,	102	Mrs. D.,	57	Mortimer,	105	The Surgeon,	92
Miss C.,	105	Mrs. T.,	9	Clemens,	101	Taylor,	92
Taylor,	109	Davies,	95	Miss C.,	108	Mortimer,	55
Thomas,	102	Roper,	76	Clemens,	111	Miss C.,	89
Coomber,	106	Chase,	98				

And so on; until but three couples of winners were left. Then I beat my man, young Smith beat his man, and Thomas beat his. This reduced the combatants to three. Smith and I took the deck, and I led off. At the close of the first inning I was 10 worse than nothing and Smith had scored 7. The luck continued against me. When I was 57, Smith was 97—within 3 of out. The luck changed then. He picked up a 10-off or so, and couldn't recover. I beat him.

The next game would end tournament No. 1.

Mr. Thomas and I were the contestants. He won the lead and went to the bat—so to speak. And there he stood, with the crotch of his cue resting against his disk while the ship rose slowly up, sank slowly down, rose again, sank again. She never seemed to rise to suit him exactly. She started up once more; and when she was nearly ready for the turn, he let drive and landed his disk just within the left-hand end of the 10. [*Applause.*] The umpire proclaimed "a good 10," and the game-keeper set it down. I played: my disk grazed the edge of Mr. Thomas's disk, and went out of the diagram. [*Applause.*]

Mr. Thomas played again—and landed his second disk alongside of the first, and almost touching its right-hand side. "Good 10." [*Great applause.*]

I played, and missed both of them. [*No applause.*]

Mr. Thomas delivered his third shot and landed his disk just at the right of the other two. "Good 10." [*Immense applause.*]

There they lay, side by side, the three in a row. It did not seem possible that anybody could miss them. Still I did it. [*Immense silence.*]

Mr. Thomas played his last disk. It seems incredible, but he actually landed that disk alongside of the others, and just to the right of them—a straight solid row of four disks. [*Tumultuous and long-continued applause.*]

Then I played my last disk. Again it did not seem possible that anybody could miss that row—a row which would have been fourteen inches long if the disks had been clamped to-gether; whereas, with the spaces separating them they made a longer row than that. But I did it. It may be that I was getting nervous.

I think it unlikely that that inning has ever had its parallel in the history of horse-billiards. To place the four disks side by side in the 10 was an extraordinary feat; indeed, it was a kind of miracle. To miss them was another miracle. It will take a century to produce another man who can place the four disks in the 10; and longer than that to find a man who can't knock them out. I was ashamed of my performance at the time, but now that I reflect upon it I see that it was rather fine and difficult.

Mr. Thomas kept his luck, and won the game, and later the championship.

In a minor tournament I won the prize, which was a Waterbury watch. I put it in my trunk. In Pretoria, South Africa, nine months afterward, my proper watch broke down and I took the Waterbury out, wound it, set it by the great clock on the Parliament House (8.05), then went back to my room and went to bed, tired from a long railway journey. The parliamentary clock had a peculiarity which I was not aware of at the time—a peculiarity which exists in no other clock, and would not exist in that one if it had been made by a sane person; on the half-hour it strikes the succeeding *hour*, then strikes the hour *again* at the proper time. I lay reading and smoking awhile; then, when I could hold my eyes open no longer and was about to put out the light, the great clock began to boom, and I counted—ten. I reached for the Water-bury to see how it was getting along. It was marking nine-thirty. It seemed rather poor speed for a three-dollar watch, but I supposed that the climate was affecting it. I shoved it half an hour ahead, and took to my book and waited to see what would happen. At ten the great clock struck ten *again*.

I looked—the Waterbury was marking half past ten. This was too much speed for the money, and it troubled me. I pushed the hands back a half-hour, and waited once more; I had to, for I was vexed and restless now, and my sleepiness was gone. By and by the great clock struck eleven. The Waterbury was marking ten-thirty. I pushed it ahead half an hour, with some show of temper. By and by the great clock struck eleven again. The Waterbury showed up eleven-thirty, now, and I beat her brains out against the bedstead. I was sorry next day, when I found out.

To return to the ship.

The average human being is a perverse creature; and when he isn't that, he is a practical joker. The result to the other person concerned is about the same: that is, he is made to suffer. The washing down of the decks begins at a very early hour in all ships; in but few ships are any measures taken to protect the passengers, either by waking or warning them, or by sending a steward to close their ports. And so the deck-washers have their opportunity, and they use it. They send a bucket of water slashing along the side of the ship and into the ports, drenching the passenger's clothes, and often the passenger himself. This good old custom prevailed in this ship, and under unusually favorable circumstances, for in the blazing tropical regions a removable zinc thing like a sugar-shovel projects from the port to catch the wind and bring it in; this thing catches the wash-water and brings it in; too—and in flooding abundance. Mrs. I., an invalid, had to sleep on the locker-sofa under her port, and every time she over-slept and thus failed to take care of herself, the deck-washers drowned her out.

And the painters, what a good time they had! This ship would be going into dock for a month in Sydney for repairs; but no matter, painting was going on all the time somewhere or other. The ladies' dresses were constantly getting ruined, nevertheless protests and supplications went for nothing. Sometimes a lady, taking an afternoon nap on deck near a ventilator or some other thing that didn't need painting, would wake up by and by and find that the humorous painter had been noiselessly daubing that thing and had splattered her white gown all over with little greasy yellow spots.

The blame for this untimely painting did not lie with the ship's officers, but with custom. As far back as Noah's time it became law that ships must be constantly painted and fussed at when at sea; custom grew out of the law, and at sea custom knows no death; this custom will continue until the sea goes dry.

Sept. 8—Sunday. We are moving so nearly south that we cross only about two meridians of longitude a day. This morning we were in longitude 178 west from Greenwich, and 57 degrees west from San Francisco. To-morrow we shall be close to the center of the globe—the 180th degree of west longitude and 180th degree of east longitude.

And then we must drop out a day—lose a day out of our lives, a day never to be found again. We shall all die one day earlier than from the beginning of time we were foreordained to die. We shall be a day behindhand all through eternity. We shall always be saying to the other angels, "Fine day to-day," and they will be always retorting, "But it isn't to-day, it's to-morrow." We shall be in a state of confusion all the time and shall never know what true happiness is.

Next Day. Sure enough, it has happened. Yesterday it was September 8th, *Sunday*; to-day, per the bulletin-board at the head of the companionway, it is September 10th, *Tuesday*. There is something uncanny about it. And uncomfortable. In fact, nearly unthinkable, and wholly unrealizable, when one comes to consider it. While we were crossing the 180th meridian it was *Sunday* in the stern of the ship where my family were, and *Tuesday* in the bow where I was. They were there eating the half of a fresh apple on the 8th, and I was at the same time eating the other half of it on the 10th—and I could notice how stale it was, already. The family were the same age that they were when I had left them five minutes before, but I was a day older now than I was then. The day they were living in stretched behind them half-way round the globe, across the Pacific Ocean and America and Europe; the day I was living in stretched in front of me around the other half to meet it. They were stupendous days for bulk and stretch; apparently much larger days than we had ever been in before. All previous days had been but shrunk-up little things by comparison. The difference in temperature between the two days was very marked, their day being hotter than mine because it was closer to the equator.

Along about the moment that we were crossing the Great Meridian a child was born in the steerage, and now there is no way to tell which day it was born on. The nurse thinks it was Sunday, the surgeon thinks it was Tuesday. The child will never know its own birthday. It will always be choosing first one and then the other, and will never be able to make up its mind permanently. This will breed vacillation and uncertainty in its opinions about religion, and politics, and business, and sweethearts, and everything, and will undermine its principles, and rot them away, and make the poor thing characterless, and its success in life impossible. Every one in the ship says so. And this is not all—in fact, not the worst. For there is an enormously rich brewer in the ship who said as much as ten days ago that if the child was born on his birthday he would give it ten thousand dollars to start its little life with. His birthday was Monday, the 9th of September.

If the ships all moved in the one direction—westward, I mean—the world would suffer a prodigious loss in the matter of valuable time, through the dumping overboard on the

Great Meridian of such multitudes of days by ships' crews and passengers. But, fortunately, the ships do not all sail west, half of them sail east. So there is no real loss. These latter pick up all the discarded days and add them to the world's stock again; and about as good as new, too; for of course the salt-water preserves them.

Chapter V

Noise proves nothing. Often a hen who has merely laid an egg cackles as if she had laid an asteroid.
—Pudd'nhead Wilson's New Calendar.

*W*EDNESDAY, Sept. *11*. In this world we often make mistakes of judgment. We do not, as a rule, get out of them sound and whole, but sometimes we do. At dinner yesterday evening—present, a mixture of Scotch, English, American, Canadian, and Australasian folk—a discussion broke out about the pronunciation of certain Scottish words. This was private ground, and the non-Scotch nationalities, with one exception, discreetly kept still. But I am not discreet, and I took a hand. I didn't know anything about the subject, but I took a hand just to have something to do. At that moment the word in dispute was the word *three*. One Scotchman was claiming that the peasantry of Scotland pronounced it *three*, his adversaries claimed that they didn't—that they pronounced it *thraw*. The solitary Scot was having a sultry time of it, so I thought I would enrich him with my help. In my position I was necessarily quite impartial, and was equally as well and as ill equipped to fight on the one side as on the other. So I spoke up and said the peasantry pronounced the word *three*, not *thraw*. It was an error of judgment. There was a moment of astonished and ominous silence, then weather ensued. The storm rose and spread in a surprising way, and I was snowed under in a very few minutes. It was a bad defeat for me—a kind of Waterloo. It promised to remain so, and I wished I had had better sense than to enter upon such a forlorn enterprise. But just then I had a saving thought—at least a thought that offered a chance. While the storm was still raging, I made up a Scotch couplet, and then spoke up and said:

"Very well, don't say any more. I confess defeat. I thought I knew, but I see my mistake. I was deceived by one of your Scotch poets."

"A *Scotch* poet! Oh, come! Name him."

"*Robert Burns.*"

It is wonderful the power of that name. These men looked doubtful—but paralyzed, all the same. They were quite silent for a moment; then one of them said—with the reverence in his voice which is always present in a Scotchman's tone when he utters the name:

"Does Robbie Burns say—*what* does he say?"

"This is what he says:

"There were nae bairns but only three—
Ane at the breast, twa at the knee."

It ended the discussion. There was no man there profane enough, disloyal enough, to say any word against a thing which Robert Burns had settled. I shall always honor that great name for the salvation it brought me in this time of my sore need.

It is my belief that nearly any invented quotation, played with confidence, stands a good chance to deceive. There are people who think that honesty is always the best policy. This is a superstition; there are times when the appearance of it is worth six of it.

We are moving steadily southward—getting further and further down under the projecting paunch of the globe. Yesterday evening we saw the Big Dipper and the north star sink below the horizon and disappear from our world. No, not "we," but they. They saw it—somebody saw it—and told me about it. But it is no matter, I was not caring for those things. I am tired of them, anyway. I think they are well enough, but one doesn't want them always hanging around. My interest was all in the Southern Cross. I had never seen that. I had heard about it all my life, and it was but natural that I should be burning to see it. No other constellation makes so much talk. I had nothing against the Big Dipper—and naturally couldn't have anything against it, since it is a citizen of our own sky, and the property of the United States—but I did want it to move out of the way and give this foreigner a chance. Judging by the size of the talk which the Southern Cross had made, I supposed it would need a sky all to itself.

OUT OF REPAIR

But that was a mistake. We saw the Cross tonight, and it is not large. Not large, and not strikingly bright. But it was low down toward the horizon, and it may improve when it gets up higher in the sky. It is ingeniously named, for it looks just as a cross would look if it looked like something else. But that description does not describe; it is too vague, too general, too indefinite. It does after a fashion suggest a cross—a cross that is out of repair—or out of drawing; not correctly shaped. It is long, with a short cross-bar, and the cross-bar is canted out of the straight line.

It consists of four large stars and one little one.

The little one is out of line and further damages the

shape. It should have been placed at the intersection of the stem and the cross-bar. If you do not draw an imaginary line from star to star it does not suggest a cross—nor anything in particular.

One must ignore the little star, and leave it out of the combination—it confuses everything. If you leave it out, then you can make out of the four stars a sort of cross—out of true; or a sort of kite—out of true; or a sort of coffin—out of true.

Constellations have always been troublesome things to name. If you give one of them a fanciful name, it will always refuse to live up to it; it will always persist in not resembling the thing it has been named for. Ultimately, to satisfy the public, the fanciful name has to be discarded for a common-sense one, a manifestly descriptive one. The Great Bear remained the Great Bear—and unrecognizable as such—for thousands of years; and people complained about it all the time, and quite properly; but as soon as it became the property of the United States, Congress changed it to the Big Dipper, and now everybody is satisfied, and there is no more talk about riots. I would not change the Southern Cross to the Southern Coffin, I would change it to the Southern Kite; for up there in the general emptiness is the proper home of a kite, but not for coffins and crosses and dippers. In a little while, now—I cannot tell exactly how long it will be—the globe will belong to the English-speaking race; and of course the skies also. Then the constellations will be reorganized, and polished up, and renamed—the most of them "Victoria," I reckon, but this one will sail thereafter as the Southern Kite, or go out of business. Several towns and things, here and there, have been named for her Majesty already.

In these past few days we are plowing through a mighty Milky Way of islands. They are so thick on the map that one would hardly expect to find room between them for a canoe;

yet we seldom glimpse one. Once we saw the dim bulk of a couple of them, far away, spectral and dreamy things; members of the Horne—Alofa and Fortuna. On the larger one are two rival native kings—and they have a time together. They are Catholics; so are their people. The missionaries there are French priests.

From the multitudinous islands in these regions the "recruits" for the Queensland plantations were formerly drawn; are still drawn from them, I believe. Vessels fitted up like old-time slavers came here and carried off the natives to serve as laborers in the great Australian province. In the beginning it was plain, simple man-stealing, as per testimony of the missionaries. This has been denied, but not disproven. Afterward it was forbidden by law to "recruit" a native without his consent, and governmental agents were sent in all recruiting vessels to see that the law was obeyed—which they did, according to the recruiting people; and which they sometimes didn't, according to the missionaries. A man could be lawfully recruited for a three years' term of service; he could volunteer for another term if he so chose; when his time was up he could return to his island. And would also have the means to do it; for the government required the employer to put money in its hands for this purpose before the recruit was delivered to him.

Captain Wawn was a recruiting shipmaster during many years. From his pleasant book one gets the idea that the recruiting business was quite popular with the islanders, as a rule. And yet that did not make the business wholly dull and uninteresting; for one finds rather frequent little breaks in the monotony of it—like this, for instance:

> The afternoon of our arrival at Leper Island the schooner was lying almost becalmed under the lee of the lofty central portion of the island, about three-quarters of a mile from the

shore. The boats were in sight at some distance. The recruiter-boat had run into a small nook on the rocky coast, under a high bank, above which stood a solitary hut backed by dense forest. The government agent and mate in the second boat lay about four hundred yards to the westward.

Suddenly we heard the sound of firing, followed by yells from the natives on shore, and then we saw the recruiter-boat push out with a seemingly diminished crew. The mate's boat pulled quickly up, took her in tow, and presently brought her along-side, all her own crew being more or less hurt. It seems the natives had called them into the place on pretense of friendship. A crowd gathered about the stern of the boat, and several fellows even got into her. All of a sudden our men were attacked with clubs and tomahawks. The recruiter escaped the first blows aimed at him, making play with his fists until he had an opportunity to draw his revolver. "Tom Sayers," a Maré man, received a tomahawk blow on the head which laid the scalp open but did not penetrate his skull, fortunately. "Bobby Towns," another Maré boatman, had both his thumbs cut in warding off blows, one of them being so nearly severed from the hand that the doctors had to finish the operation. Lihu, a Lifu boy, the recruiter's special attendant, was cut and pricked in various places, but nowhere seriously. Jack, an unlucky Tanna recruit, who had been engaged to act as boatman, received an arrow through his forearm, the head of which—a piece of bone seven or eight inches long—was still in the limb, protruding from both sides, when the boats returned. The recruiter himself would have got off scot-free had not an arrow pinned one of his fingers to the loom of the steering-oar just as they were getting off. The fight had been short but sharp. The enemy lost two men, both shot dead.

The truth is, Captain Wawn furnishes such a crowd of instances of fatal encounters between natives and French and English recruiting crews (for the French are in the business for the plantations of New Caledonia), that one is almost persuaded that recruiting is not thoroughly popular among the islanders; else why this bristling string of attacks and blood-curdling slaughter? The captain lays it all to "Exeter Hall influence." But for the meddling philanthropists, the native fathers and mothers would be fond of seeing their children carted into exile and now and then the grave, instead of weeping about it and trying to kill the kind recruiters.

Chapter VI

He was as shy as a newspaper is when referring to its own merits.
                    —Pudd'nhead Wilson's New Calendar.

CAPTAIN Wawn is crystal-clear on one point. He does not approve of missionaries. They obstruct his business. They make "Recruiting," as he calls it ("Slave-Catching," as *they* call it in their frank way) a trouble when it ought to be just a picnic and a pleasure excursion. The missionaries have their opinion about the manner in which the Labor Traffic is conducted, and about the recruiter's evasions of the law of the Traffic, and about the Traffic itself: and it is distinctly uncomplimentary to the Traffic and to everything connected with it, including the law for its regulation. Captain Wawn's book is of very recent date; I have by me a pamphlet of still later date—hot from the press, in fact—by Rev. Wm. Gray, a missionary; and the book and the pamphlet taken together make exceedingly interesting reading, to my mind.

Interesting, and easy to understand—except in one detail, which I will mention presently. It is easy to understand why the Queensland sugar-planter should want the Kanaka recruit: he is cheap. Very cheap, in fact. These are the figures paid by the planter: £20 to the recruiter for getting the Kanaka—or "catching" him, as the missionary phrase goes; £3 to the Queensland government for "superintending" the importation; £5 deposited with the government for the Kanaka's passage home when his three years are up, in case he shall live that long; about £25 to the Kanaka himself for three years' wages and clothing; total payment for the use of a man three years, £53; or, including diet, £60. Altogether, a hundred dollars a year. One can understand why the recruiter is fond of the business; the recruit costs him a few cheap presents (given to the recruit's relatives, not to the recruit himself), and the recruit is worth £20 to the recruiter when delivered in Queensland. All this is clear enough; but the thing that is not clear is, what there is about it all to persuade the recruit. He is young and brisk; life at home in his beautiful island is one lazy, long holiday to him; or if he wants to work he can turn out a couple of bags of copra per week and sell it for four or five shillings a bag. In Queensland he must get up at dawn and work from eight to twelve hours a day in the cane-fields—in a much hotter climate than he is used to—and get less than four shillings a week for it.

I cannot understand his willingness to go to Queensland. It is a deep puzzle to me. Here is the explanation, from the planter's point of view; at least I gather from the missionary's pamphlet that it is the planter's:

When he comes from his home he is a savage, pure and simple. He feels no shame at his nakedness and want of adornment. When he returns home he does so well dressed, sporting a Waterbury watch, collars, cuffs, boots, and jewelry. He takes with him one or more boxes[1] well filled with clothing, a

[1]"Box" is English for trunk.

57

musical instrument or two, and perfumery and other articles of luxury he has learned to appreciate.

For just one moment we have a seeming flash of comprehension of the Kanaka's reason for exiling himself: he goes away to acquire *civilization*. Yes, he was naked and not ashamed, now he is clothed and knows how to be ashamed; he was unenlightened, now he has a Waterbury watch; he was unrefined, now he has jewelry, and something to make him smell good; he was a nobody, a provincial, now he has been to far countries and can show off.

It all looks plausible—for a moment. Then the missionary takes hold of this explanation and pulls it to pieces, and dances on it, and damages it beyond recognition.

Admitting that the foregoing description is the average one, the average sequel is this: The cuffs and collars, if used at all, are carried off by youngsters, who fasten them round the leg, just below the knee, as ornaments. The Waterbury, broken and dirty, finds its way to the trader, who gives a trifle for it; or the inside is taken out, the wheels strung on a thread and hung around the neck. Knives, axes, calico, and handkerchiefs are divided among friends, and there is hardly one of these apiece. The boxes, the keys often lost on the road home, can be bought for 2s. 6d. They are to be seen rotting outside in almost any shore village on Tanna. (I speak of what I have seen.) A returned Kanaka has been furiously angry with me because I would not buy his trousers, which he declared were just my fit. He sold them afterward to one of my Aniwan teachers for 9d. worth of tobacco—a pair of trousers that probably cost him 8s. or 10s. in Queensland. A coat or shirt is handy for cold weather. The white handkerchiefs, the "senet" (perfumery), the umbrella, and perhaps the hat, are kept. The boots have to take their chance, if they do not happen to fit the copra trader. "Senet" on the hair, streaks of paint on the face, a dirty white handkerchief round the neck, strips of turtle-shell in the ears, a belt, a sheath and knife, and an umbrella constitute the rig of the returned Kanaka at home the day after landing.

A hat, an umbrella, a belt, a neckerchief. Otherwise stark naked. All in a day the hard-earned "civilization" has melted away to this. And even these perishable things must presently go. Indeed, there is but a single detail of his civilization that can be depended on to stay by him: according to the missionary, he has learned to swear. This is art, and art is long, as the poet says.

In all countries the laws throw light upon the past. The Queensland law for the regulation of the Labor Traffic is a confession. It is a confession that the evils charged by the missionaries upon the traffic had existed in the past, and that they still existed when the law was made. The missionaries make a further charge: that the law is evaded by the recruiters, and that the Government Agent sometimes helps them to do it. Regulation thirty-one reveals two things: that sometimes a young fool of a recruit gets his senses back, after being persuaded to sign away his liberty for three years, and dearly wants to get out of the engagement and stay at home with his own people; and that threats, intimidation, and force are used to keep him on board the recruiting ship, and to hold him to his contract. Regulation thirty-one forbids these coercions. The law requires that he shall be allowed to go free; and another clause of it requires the recruiter to set him ashore—per boat, because of the prevalence of sharks. Testimony from Rev. Mr. Gray:

There are "wrinkles" for taking the penitent Kanaka. My first experience of the Traffic was a case of this kind in 1884. A vessel anchored just out of sight of our station, word was brought to me that some boys were stolen, and the relatives wished me to go and get them back. The facts were, as I found, that six boys had recruited, had *rushed* into the boat, the Government Agent informed me. They had all "signed"; and, said the Government Agent, "on board they shall remain." I was assured that the six boys were of age and willing to go. Yet on getting ready to leave the ship I found four of the lads ready to come ashore in the boat! This I forbade. One of them jumped into the water and persisted in coming ashore in my boat. When appealed to, the Government Agent suggested that we go and leave him to be picked up by the ship's boat, a quarter-mile distant at the time!

The law and the missionaries feel for the repentant recruit—and properly, one may be permitted to think, for he is only a youth and ignorant and persuadable to his hurt—but sympathy for him is not kept in stock by the recruiter. Rev. Mr. Gray says:

> A captain many years in the traffic explained to me how a penitent could be taken. "When a boy jumps overboard we just take a boat and pull ahead of him, then lie between him and the shore. If he has not tired himself swimming, and passes the boat, keep on heading him in this way. The dodge rarely fails. The boy generally tires of swimming, gets into the boat of his own accord, and goes quietly on board."

Yes, exhaustion is likely to make a boy quiet. If the distressed boy had been the speaker's son, and the captors savages, the speaker would have been surprised to see how differently the thing looked from the new point of view; however, it is not our custom to put ourselves in the other person's place. Somehow there is something pathetic about that disappointed young savage's resignation. I must explain, here, that in the traffic dialect, "boy" does not always mean boy; it means a youth above sixteen years of age. That is by Queensland law the age of consent, though it is held that recruiters allow themselves some latitude in guessing at ages.

Captain Wawn of the free spirit chafes under the annoyance of "cast-iron regulations." They and the missionaries have poisoned his life. He grieves for the good old days, vanished to come no more. See him weep; hear him cuss between the lines!

> For a long time we were allowed to apprehend and detain all deserters who had signed the agreement on board ship, but the "cast-iron" regulations of the Act of 1884 put a stop to that, allowing the Kanaka to sign the agreement for three years' service, travel about in the ship in receipt of the regular rations, cadge all he could, and leave when he thought fit, so long as he did not extend his pleasure trip to Queensland.

Rev. Mr. Gray calls this same restrictive cast-iron law a "farce." "There is as much cruelty and injustice done to natives by acts that are legal as by deeds unlawful. The regulations that exist are unjust and inadequate—unjust and inadequate they must ever be." He furnishes his reasons for his position, but they are too long for reproduction here.

However, if the most a Kanaka advantages himself by a three-years course in civilization in Queensland is a necklace and an umbrella and a showy imperfection in the art of swearing, it must be that *all* the profit of the traffic goes to the white man. This could be twisted into a plausible argument that the traffic ought to be squarely abolished.

However, there is reason for hope that that can be left alone to achieve itself. It is claimed that the traffic will depopulate its sources of supply within the next twenty or thirty years. Queensland is a very healthy place for white people—death-rate 12 in 1,000 of the population—but the Kanaka death-rate is away above that. The vital statistics for 1893 place it at 52; for 1894 (Mackay district), 68. The first six months of the Kanaka's exile are peculiarly perilous for him because of the rigors of the new climate. The death-rate among the new men has reached as high as 180 in the 1,000. In the Kanaka's native home his death-rate is 12 in time of peace, and 15 in time of war. Thus exile to Queensland— with the opportunity to acquire civilization, an umbrella, and a pretty poor quality of profanity—is twelve times as deadly for him as war. Common Christian charity, common human- ity, does seem to require, not only that these people be re- turned to their homes, but that war, pestilence, and famine be introduced among them for their preservation.

Concerning these Pacific isles and their peoples an elo- quent prophet spoke long years ago—five and fifty years ago. In fact, he spoke a little too early. Prophecy is a good line of business, but it is full of risks. This prophet was the Right Rev. M. Russell, LL.D., D.C.L., of Edinburgh:

> Is the tide of civilization to roll only to the foot of the Rocky Mountains, and is the sun of knowledge to set at last in the waves of the Pacific? No; the mighty day of four thou- sand years is drawing to its close; the sun of humanity has performed its destined course; but long ere its setting rays are extinguished in the west, its ascending beams have glittered on the isles of the eastern seas. . . . And now we see the race of Japhet setting forth to people the isles, and the seeds of another Europe and a second England sown in the region of the sun. But mark the words of the prophecy: "He shall dwell in the tents of Shem, and Canaan shall be his servant." It is not said Canaan shall be his *slave*. To the Anglo-Saxon race is given the scepter of the globe, but there is not given either the lash of the slave-driver or the rack of the executioner. The East will not be stained with the same atrocities as the West; the frightful gangrene of an ethralled race is not to mar the

destinies of the family of Japhet in the Oriental world; humanizing, not destroying, as they advance; uniting with, not enslaving, the inhabitants with whom they dwell, the British race may [etc., etc.].

And he closes his vision with an invocation from Campbell:

> Come, bright Improvement! on the car of Time,
> And rule the spacious world from clime to clime.

Very well, Bright Improvement has arrived, you see, with her civilization, and her Waterbury, and her umbrella, and her third-quality profanity, and her humanizing-not-destroying machinery, and her hundred-and-eighty death-rate, and everything is going along just as handsome!

But the prophet that speaks last has an advantage over the pioneer in the business. Rev. Mr. Gray says:

> What I am concerned about is that we as a Christian nation should wipe out these races to enrich ourselves.

And he closes his pamphlet with a grim Indictment which is as eloquent in its flowerless straightforward English as is the hand-painted rhapsody of the early prophet:

> My indictment of the Queensland Kanaka Labor Traffic is this:
> 1. It generally demoralizes and always impoverishes the Kanaka, deprives him of his citizenship, and depopulates the islands fitted to his home.
> 2. It is felt to lower the dignity of the white agricultural laborer in Queensland, and beyond a doubt it lowers his wages there.

3. The whole system is fraught with danger to Australia and the islands on the score of health.

4. On social and political grounds the continuance of the Queensland Kanaka Labor Traffic must be a barrier to the true federation of the Australian colonies.

5. The Regulations under which the Traffic exists in Queensland are inadequate to prevent abuses, and in the nature of things they must remain so.

6. The whole system is contrary to the spirit and doctrine of the Gospel of Jesus Christ. The Gospel requires us to help the weak, but the Kanaka is fleeced and trodden down.

7. The bed-rock of this Traffic is that the life and liberty of a black man are of less value than those of a white man. And a Traffic that has grown out of "slave-hunting" will certainly remain to the end not unlike its origin.

Chapter VII

Truth is the most valuable thing we have. Let us econo-mize it.

— Pudd'nhead Wilson's New Calendar.

FROM DIARY:—For a day or two we have been plowing among an invisible vast wilderness of islands, catching now and then a shadowy glimpse of a member of it. There does seem to be a prodigious lot of islands this year; the map of this region is freckled and fly-specked all over with them. Their number would seem to be uncountable. We are moving among the Fijis now—two hundred and twenty-four islands and islets in the group. In front of us, to the west, the wilder-ness stretches toward Australia, then curves upward to New Guinea, and still up and up to Japan; behind us, to the east, the wilderness stretches sixty degrees across the wastes of the Pacific; south of us is New Zealand. Somewhere or other among these myriads Samoa is concealed, and not dis-coverable on the map. Still, if you wish to go there, you will have no trouble about finding it if you follow the directions given by Robert Louis Stevenson to Dr. Conan Doyle and to Mr. J. M. Barrie. "You go to America, cross the continent

to San Francisco, and then it's the second turning to the left."
To get the full flavor of the joke one must take a glance at
the map.

Wednesday, Sept. 11. Yesterday we passed close to an
island or so, and recognized the published Fiji characteristics:
a broad belt of clean white coral sand around the island; back
of it a graceful fringe of leaning palms, with native huts
nestling cozily among the shrubbery at their bases; back of
these a stretch of level land clothed in tropic vegetation; back
of that, rugged and picturesque mountains. A detail of the
immediate foreground: a moldering ship perched high upon
a reef-bench.

This completes the composition, and makes the picture
artistically perfect.

In the afternoon we sighted Suva, the capital of the
group, and threaded our way into the secluded little harbor—
a placid basin of brilliant blue and green water tucked snugly
in among the sheltering hills. A few ships rode at anchor in
it—one of them a sailing-vessel flying the American flag; and
they said she came from Duluth! There's a journey! Duluth
is several thousand miles from the sea, and yet she is entitled
to the proud name of Mistress of the Commercial Marine
of the United States of America. There is only one free,
independent, unsubsidized American ship sailing the foreign
seas, and Duluth owns it. All by itself that ship is the American fleet. All by itself it causes the American name and power
to be respected in the far regions of the globe. All by itself it
certifies to the world that the most populous civilized nation
in the earth has a just pride in her stupendous stretch of sea-
front, and is determined to assert and maintain her rightful
place as one of the Great Maritime Powers of the Planet. All
by itself it is making foreign eyes familiar with a Flag which
they have not seen before for forty years, outside of the
museum. For what Duluth has done, in building, equipping,

and maintaining at her sole expense the American Foreign Commercial Fleet, and in thus rescuing the American name from shame and lifting it high for the homage of the nations, we owe her a debt of gratitude which our hearts shall confess with quickened beats whenever her name is named henceforth. Many national toasts will die in the lapse of time, but while the flag flies and the Republic survives, they who live under their shelter will still drink this one, standing and uncovered: Health and prosperity to Thee, O Duluth, American Queen of the Alien Seas!

Rowboats began to flock from the shore; their crews were the first natives we had seen. These men carried no overplus of clothing, and this was wise, for the weather was hot. Handsome, great dusky men they were, muscular, clean-limbed, and with faces full of character and intelligence. It would be hard to find their superiors anywhere among the dark races, I should think.

Everybody went ashore to look around, and spy out the land, and have that luxury of luxuries to sea-voyagers—a land-dinner. And there we saw more natives: wrinkled old women, with their flat mammals flung over their shoulders, or hanging down in front like the cold-weather drip from the molasses faucet; plump and smily young girls, blithe and content, easy and graceful, a pleasure to look at; young matrons, tall, straight, comely, nobly built, sweeping by with chin up, and a gait incomparable for unconscious stateliness and dignity; majestic young men—athletes for build and muscle—clothed in a loose arrangement of dazzling white, with bronze breast and bronze legs naked, and the head a cannon-swab of solid hair combed straight out from the skull and dyed a rich brick-red. Only sixty years ago they were sunk in darkness; now they have the bicycle.

We strolled about the streets of the white folks' little town, and around over the hills by paths and roads among

European dwellings and gardens and plantations, and past clumps of hibiscus that made a body blink, the great blossoms were so intensely red; and by and by we stopped to ask an elderly English colonist a question or two, and to sympathize with him concerning the torrid weather; but he was surprised, and said:

"This? This is not hot. You ought to be here in the summer-time once."

"We supposed that this was summer; it has the earmarks of it. You could take it to almost any country and deceive people with it. But if it isn't summer, what does it lack?"

"It lacks half a year. This is midwinter."

I had been suffering from colds for several months, and a sudden change of season, like this, could hardly fail to do me hurt. It brought on another cold. It is odd, these sudden jumps from season to season. A fortnight ago we left America in midsummer, now it is midwinter; about a week hence we shall arrive in Australia in the spring.

After dinner I found in the billiard-room a resident whom I had known somewhere else in the world, and presently made some new friends and drove with them out into the country to visit his Excellency the head of the State, who was occupying his country residence, to escape the rigors of the winter weather, I suppose, for it was on breezy high ground and much more comfortable than the lower regions, where the town is, and where the winter has full swing, and often sets a person's hair afire when he takes off his hat to bow. There is a noble and beautiful view of ocean and islands and castellated peaks from the governor's high-placed house, and its immediate surroundings lie drowsing in that dreamy repose and serenity which are the charm of life in the Pacific Islands.

One of the new friends who went out there with me was a large man, and I had been admiring his size all the way. I was still admiring it as he stood by the governor on the veranda, talking; then the Fijian butler stepped out there to announce tea, and dwarfed him. Maybe he did not quite dwarf him, but at any rate the contrast was quite striking. Perhaps that dark giant was a king in a condition of political suspension. I think that in the talk there on the veranda it was said that in Fiji, as in the Sandwich Islands, native kings and chiefs are of much grander size and build than the commoners. This man was clothed in flowing white vestments, and they were just the thing for him; they comported well with his great stature and his kingly port and dignity. European clothes would have degraded him and made him commonplace. I know that, because they do that with everybody that wears them.

It was said that the old-time devotion to chiefs and reverence for their persons still survive in the native commoner, and in great force. The educated young gentleman who is chief of the tribe that live in the region about the capital dresses in the fashion of high-class European gentlemen, but even his clothes cannot damn him in the reverence of his people. Their pride in his lofty rank and ancient lineage lives on, in spite of his lost authority and the evil magic of his tailor. He has no need to defile himself with work, or trouble his heart with the sordid cares of life; the tribe will see to it that he shall not want, and that he shall hold up his head and live like a gentleman. I had a glimpse of him down in the town. Perhaps he is a descendant of the last king—the king with the difficult name whose memory is preserved by a notable monument of cut stone which one sees in the inclosure in the middle of the town. Thakombau—I remember, now; that is the name. It is easier to preserve it on a granite block than in your head.

Fiji was ceded to England by this king in 1858. One of the gentlemen present at the governor's quoted a remark made by the king at the time of the cession—a neat retort, and with a touch of pathos in it, too. The English Commissioner had offered a crumb of comfort to Thakombau by saying that the transfer of the kingdom to Great Britain was merely "a sort of hermit-crab formality, you know." "Yes," said poor Thakombau, "but with this difference—the crab moves into an unoccupied shell, but mine isn't."

However, as far as I can make out from the books, the king was between the devil and the deep sea at the time, and hadn't much choice. He owed the United States a large debt—a debt which he could pay if allowed time, but time was denied him. He must pay up right away or the war-ships would be upon him. To protect his people from this disaster he ceded his country to Britain, with a clause in the contract providing for the ultimate payment of the American debt.

In old times the Fijians were fierce fighters; they were very religious, and worshiped idols; the big chiefs were proud and haughty, and they were men of great style in many ways; all chiefs had several wives, the biggest chiefs sometimes had as many as fifty; when a chief was dead and ready for burial, four or five of his wives were strangled and put into the grave with him. In 1804 twenty-seven British convicts escaped from Australia to Fiji, and brought guns and ammunition with them. Consider what a power they were, armed like that, and what an opportunity they had. If they had been energetic men and sober, and had had brains and known how to use them, they could have achieved the sovereignty of the archipelago—twenty-seven kings and each with eight or nine islands under his scepter. But nothing came of this chance. They lived worthless lives of sin and luxury, and died without honor—in most cases by violence. Only one of them had any ambition; he was an Irishman named Connor. He tried to raise a family of fifty children, and scored forty-eight. He died lamenting his failure. It was a foolish sort of avarice. Many a father would have been rich with forty.

It is a fine race, the Fijians, with brains in their heads and an inquiring turn of mind. It appears that their savage ancestors had a doctrine of immortality in their scheme of religion—with limitations. That is to say, their dead friend would go to a happy hereafter if he could be accumulated, but not otherwise. They drew the line; they thought that the missionary's doctrine was too sweeping, too comprehensive. They called his attention to certain facts. For instance, many of their friends had been devoured by sharks; the sharks, in their turn, were caught and eaten by other men; later, these men were captured in war, and eaten by the enemy. The original persons had entered into the composition of the sharks; next, they and the sharks had become part of the flesh and blood and bone of the cannibals. How, then, could the particles of the original men be searched out from the final conglomerate and put together again? The inquirers were full of doubts, and considered that the missionary had not examined the matter with the gravity and attention which so serious a thing deserved.

The missionary taught these exacting savages many valuable things, and got from them one—a very dainty and poetical idea: Those wild and ignorant poor children of Nature believed that the flowers, after they perish, rise on the winds and float away to the fair fields of heaven, and flourish there forever in immortal beauty!

Chapter VIII

It could probably be shown by facts and figures that there is no distinctly native American criminal class except Congress.
—Pudd'nhead Wilson's New Calendar.

WHEN one glances at the map the members of the stupendous island wilderness of the Pacific seem to crowd upon each other; but no, there is no crowding, even in the center of a group; and between groups there are lonely wide deserts of sea. Not everything is known about the islands, their peoples and their languages. A startling reminder of this is furnished by the fact that in Fiji, twenty years ago, were living two strange and solitary beings who came from an unknown country and spoke an unknown language. "They were picked up by a passing vessel *many hundreds of miles from any known land*, floating in the same tiny canoe in which they had been blown out to sea. When found they were but skin and bone. No one could understand what they said, and they have never named their country; or, if they have, the name does not correspond with that of any island on any chart. They are now fat and sleek, and as happy as the day is long. In the ship's log there is an entry of the latitude and longitude in which they were found, and this is probably all the clue they will ever have to their lost homes."[1]

What a strange and romantic episode it is; and how one is tortured with curiosity to know whence those mysterious creatures came, those Men Without a Country, errant waifs who cannot name their lost home, wandering Children of Nowhere.

Indeed, the Island Wilderness is the very home of romance and dreams and mystery. The loneliness, the solemnity, the beauty, and the deep repose of this wilderness have a charm which is all their own for the bruised spirit of men who have fought and failed in the struggle for life in the great world; and for men who have been hunted out of the great world for crime; and for other men who love an easy and indolent existence; and for others who love a roving free life, and stir and change and adventure; and for yet others who love an easy and comfortable career of trading and money-getting, mixed with plenty of loose matrimony by purchase, divorce without trial or expense, and limitless spreeing thrown in to make life ideally perfect.

We sailed again, refreshed.

The most cultivated person in the ship was a young Englishman whose home was in New Zealand. He was a naturalist. His learning in his specialty was deep and thorough, his interest in his subject amounted to a passion, he had an easy gift of speech; and so, when he talked about animals it was a pleasure to listen to him. And profitable, too, though he was sometimes difficult to understand because now and then he used scientific technicalities which were above the reach of some of us. They were pretty sure to be above my reach, but as he was quite willing to explain them I always made it a point to get him to do it. I had a fair

[1] Forbes's *Two Years in Fiji.*

knowledge of his subject—layman's knowledge—to begin with, but it was his teachings which crystallized it into scientific form and clarity—in a word, gave it value.

His special interest was the fauna of Australasia, and his knowledge of the matter was as exhaustive as it was accurate. I already knew a good deal about the rabbits in Australasia and their marvelous fecundity, but in my talks with him I found that my estimate of the great hindrance and obstruction inflicted by the rabbit pest upon traffic and travel was far short of the facts. He told me that the first pair of rabbits imported into Australasia bred so wonderfully that within six months rabbits were so thick in the land that people had to dig trenches through them to get from town to town.

He told me a great deal about worms, and the kangaroo, and other coleoptera, and said he knew the history and ways of all such pachydermata. He said the kangaroo had pockets, and carried its young in them when it couldn't get apples. And he said that the emu was as big as an ostrich, and looked like one, and had an amorphous appetite and would eat bricks. Also, that the dingo was not a dingo at all, but just a wild dog; and that the only difference between a dingo and a dodo was that neither of them barked; otherwise they were just the same.

He said that the only game-bird in Australasia was the wombat, and the only song-bird the larrikin, and that both were protected by government. The most beautiful of the native birds was the bird of paradise. Next came the two kinds of lyres; not spelt the same. He said the one kind was dying out, the other thickening up. He explained that the "Sundowner" was not a bird, it was a man; sundowner was merely the Australian equivalent of our word, tramp. He is a loafer, a hard drinker, and a sponge. He tramps across the country in the sheep-shearing season, pretending to look for work; but he always times himself to arrive at a sheep-run just at sundown, when the day's labor ends; all he wants is whisky and supper and bed and breakfast; he gets them and then disappears. The naturalist spoke of the bell-bird, the creature that at short intervals all day rings out its mellow and exquisite peal from the deeps of the forest. It is the favorite and best friend of the weary and thirsty sundowner; for he knows that wherever the bell-bird is, there is water; and he goes somewhere else. The naturalist said that the oddest bird in Australasia was the Laughing Jackass, and the biggest the now extinct Great Moa.

The Moa stood thirteen feet high, and could step over an ordinary man's head or kick his hat off; and his head, too, for that matter. He said it was wingless, but a swift runner. The natives used to ride it. It could make forty miles an hour, and keep it up for four hundred miles and come out reasonably fresh. It was still in existence when the railway was introduced into New Zealand; still in existence and carrying the mails. The railroad began with the same schedule it has now: two expresses a week—time, twenty miles an hour. The company exterminated the Moa to get the mails.

Speaking of the indigenous coneys and bactrian camels, the naturalist said that the coniferous and bacteriological output of Australasia was remarkable for its many and curious departures from the accepted laws governing these species of tubercles, but that in his opinion Nature's fondness for dabbling in the erratic was most notably exhibited in that curious combination of bird, fish, amphibian, burrower, crawler, quadruped, and Christian called the Ornithorhyncus—grotesquest of animals, king of the animalculæ of the world for versatility of character and make-up. Said he:

> You can call it anything you want to, and be right. It is a fish, for it lives in the river half the time; it is a land-animal, for it resides on the land half the time; it is an amphibian,

since it likes both and does not know which it prefers; it is a hybernian, for when times are dull and nothing much is going on it buries itself under the mud at the bottom of a puddle and hybernates there a couple of weeks at a time; it is a kind of duck, for it has a duck-bill and four webbed paddles; it is a fish and quadruped together, for in the water it swims with the paddles and on shore it paws itself across country with them; it is a kind of seal, for it has a seal's fur; it is carnivorous, herbivorous, insectivorous, and vermifuginous, for it eats fish and grass and butterflies, and in the season digs worms out of the mud and devours them; it is clearly a bird, for it lays eggs and hatches them; it is clearly a mammal, for it nurses its young; and it is manifestly a kind of Christian, for it keeps the Sabbath when there is anybody around, and when there isn't, doesn't. It has all the tastes there are except refined ones, it has all the habits there are except good ones.

It is a survival—a survival of the fittest. Mr. Darwin invented the theory that goes by that name, but the Ornithorhyncus was the first to put it to actual experiment and prove that it could be done. Hence it should have as much of the credit as Mr. Darwin. It was never in the Ark; you will find no mention of it there; it nobly stayed out and worked the theory. Of all creatures in the world it was the only one properly equipped for the test. The Ark was thirteen months afloat, and all the globe submerged; no land visible above the flood, no vegetation, no food for a mammal to eat, nor water for a mammal to drink; for all mammal food was destroyed, and when the pure floods from heaven and the salt oceans of the earth mingled their waters and rose above the mountain-tops, the result was a drink which no bird or beast of ordinary construction could use and live. But this combination was nuts for the Ornithorhyncus, if I may use a term like that without offense. Its river home had always been salted by the flood-tides of the sea. On the face of the Noachian deluge innumerable forest trees were floating. Upon these the Ornithorhyncus voyaged in peace; voyaged from clime to clime, from hemisphere to hemisphere, in contentment and comfort, in virile interest in the constant change of scene, in humble thankfulness for its privileges, in ever-increasing enthusiasm in the development of the great theory upon whose validity it had staked its life, its fortunes, and its sacred honor, if I may use such expressions without impropriety in connection with an episode of this nature.

It lived the tranquil and luxurious life of a creature of independent means. Of things actually necessary to its existence and its happiness not a detail was wanting. When it wished to walk, it scrambled along the tree-trunk; it mused in the shade of the leaves by day, it slept in their shelter by night; when it wanted the refreshment of a swim, it had it; it ate leaves when it wanted a vegetable diet, it dug under the bark for worms and grubs; when it wanted fish it caught them, when it wanted eggs it laid them. If the grubs gave out in one tree it swam to another; and as for fish, the very opulence of the supply was an embarrassment. And finally, when it was thirsty it smacked its chops in gratitude over a blend that would have slain a crocodile.

When at last, after thirteen months of travel and research in all the Zones, it went aground on a mountain-summit, it strode ashore, saying in its heart, "Let them that come after me invent theories and dream dreams about the Survival of the Fittest if they like, but I am the first that has *done* it!"

This wonderful creature dates back, like the kangaroo and many other Australian hydrocephalous invertebrates, to an age long anterior to the advent of man upon the earth; they date back, indeed, to a time when a causeway, hundreds of miles wide and thousands of miles long, joined Australia to Africa, and the animals of the two countries were alike, and all belonged to that remote geological epoch known to science as the Old Red Grindstone Post-Pleosaurian. Later the causeway sank under the sea; subterranean convulsions lifted the African continent a thousand feet higher than it was before, but Australia kept her old level. In Africa's new climate the animals necessarily began to develop and shade off into new forms and families and species, but the animals of Australia as necessarily remained stationary, and have so remained until this day. In the course of some millions of years the African Ornithorhyncus developed and developed and developed, and sloughed off detail after detail of its make-up until at last the creature became wholly disintegrated and scattered. Whenever you see a bird or a beast or a seal or an otter in Africa you know that he is merely a sorry surviving fragment of that sublime original of whom I have been speaking—that creature which was everything in general and nothing in particular— the opulently endowed *e pluribus unum* of the animal world.

Such is the history of the most hoary, the most ancient, the most venerable creature that exists in the earth to-day— *Ornithorhyncus Platypus Extraordinariensis*—whom God preserve!

When he was strongly moved he could rise and soar like that with ease. And not only in the prose form, but in the poetical as well. He had written many pieces of poetry in his time, and these manuscripts he lent around among the passengers, and was willing to let them be copied. It seemed to me that the least technical one in the series, and the one which reached the loftiest note, perhaps, was his

INVOCATION

Come forth from thy oozy couch,
   O Ornithorhyncus dear!
And greet with a cordial claw
   The stranger that longs to hear

From thy own lips the tale
   Of thy origin all unknown:
Thy misplaced bone where flesh should be
   And flesh where should be bone;

> And fishy fin where should be paw,
>   And beaver-trowel tail,
> And snout of beast equip'd with teeth
>   Where gills ought *to* prevail.
>
> Come, Kangaroo, the good and true!
>   Foreshortened as to legs,
> And body tapered like a churn,
>   And sack marsupial, i' fegs,
>
> And tell us why you linger here,
>   Thou relic of a vanished time,
> When all your friends as fossils sleep,
>   Immortalized in lime!

Perhaps no poet is a conscious plagiarist; but there seems to be warrant for suspecting that there is no poet who is not at one time or another an unconscious one. The above verses are indeed beautiful, and, in a way, touching; but there is a haunting something about them which unavoidably suggests the Sweet Singer of Michigan. It can hardly be doubted that the author had read the works of that poet and been impressed by them. It is not apparent that he has borrowed from them any word or yet any phrase, but the style and swing and mastery and melody of the Sweet Singer all are there. Compare this Invocation with "Frank Dutton"—particularly stanzas first and seventeenth—and I think the reader will feel convinced that he who wrote the one had read the other:[1]

I

> Frank Dutton was as fine a lad
>   As ever you wish to see,
> And he was drowned in Pine Island Lake,
>   On earth no more will he be,

---

[1] *The Sentimental Song Book.* By Mrs. Julia Moore, p. 36.

His age was near fifteen years,
    And he was a motherless boy,
He was living with his grandmother
    When he was drowned, poor boy.

XVII

He was drowned on Tuesday afternoon,
    On Sunday he was found,
And the tidings of that drowned boy
    Was heard for miles around.
His form was laid by his mother's side,
    Beneath the cold, cold ground,
His friends for him will drop a tear
    When they view his little mound.

Chapter IX

It is your human environment that makes climate.
—Pudd'nhead Wilson's New Calendar.

*S*EPT. *15—Night.* Close to Australia now. Sydney fifty
miles distant.

That note recalls an experience. The passengers were
sent for, to come up in the bow and see a fine sight. It was
very dark. One could not follow with the eye the surface of
the sea more than fifty yards in any direction—it dimmed
away and became lost to sight at about that distance from us.
But if you patiently gazed into the darkness a little while,
there was a sure reward for you. Presently, a quarter of a
mile away you would see a blinding splash or explosion of
light on the water—a flash so sudden and so astonishingly
brilliant that it would make you catch your breath; then that
blotch of light would instantly extend itself and take the cork-
screw shape and imposing length of the fabled sea-serpent,
with every curve of its body and the "break" spreading away
from its head, and the wake following behind its tail clothed
in a fierce splendor of living fire. And my, but it was coming

at a lightning gait! Almost before you could think, this monster of light, fifty feet long, would go flaming and storming by, and suddenly disappear. And out in the distance whence he came you would see another flash; and another and another and another, and see them turn into sea-serpents on the instant; and once sixteen flashed up at the same time and came tearing toward us, a swarm of wiggling curves, a moving conflagration, a vision of bewildering beauty, a spectacle of fire and energy whose equal the most of those people will not see again until after they are dead.

It was porpoises—porpoises aglow with phosphorescent light. They presently collected in a wild and magnificent jumble under the bows, and there they played for an hour, leaping and frolicking and carrying on, turning somersaults in front of the stem or across it and never getting hit, never making a miscalculation, though the stem missed them only about an inch, as a rule. They were porpoises of the ordinary length—eight or ten feet—but every twist of their bodies sent a long procession of united and glowing curves astern. That fiery jumble was an enchanting thing to look at, and we stayed out the performance; one cannot have such a show as that twice in a lifetime. The porpoise is the kitten of the sea; he never has a serious thought, he cares for nothing but fun and play. But I think I never saw him at his winsomest until that night. It was near a center of civilization, and he could have been drinking.

By and by, when we had approached to somewhere within thirty miles of Sydney Heads the great electric light that is posted on one of those lofty ramparts began to show, and in time the little spark grew to a great sun and pierced the firmament of darkness with a far-reaching sword of light.

Sydney Harbor is shut in behind a precipice that extends some miles like a wall, and exhibits no break to the ignorant stranger. It has a break in the middle, but it makes so little show that even Captain Cook sailed by it without seeing it. Near by that break is a false break which resembles it, and which used to make trouble for the mariner at night, in the early days before the place was lighted. It caused the memorable disaster to the *Duncan Dunbar*, one of the most pathetic tragedies in the history of that pitiless ruffian, the sea. The ship was a sailing-vessel; a fine and favorite passenger-packet, commanded by a popular captain of high reputation. She was due from England, and Sydney was waiting, and counting the hours; counting the hours, and making ready to give her a heart-stirring welcome; for she was bringing back a great company of mothers and daughters, the long-missed light and bloom of life of Sydney homes; daughters that had been years absent at school, and mothers that had been with them all that time watching over them. Of all the world only India and Australasia have by custom freighted ships and fleets with their hearts, and know the tremendous meaning of that phrase; only they know what the waiting is like when this freightage is intrusted to the fickle winds, not steam, and what the joy is like when the ship that is returning this treasure comes safe to port and the long dread is over.

On board the *Duncan Dunbar*, flying toward Sydney Heads in the waning afternoon, the happy home-comers made busy preparation, for it was not doubted that they would be in the arms of their friends before the day was done; they put away their sea-going clothes and put on clothes meeter for the meeting, their richest and their loveliest, these poor brides of the grave. But the wind lost force, or there was a miscalculation, and before the Heads were sighted the darkness came on. It was said that ordinarily the captain would have made a safe offing and waited for the morning; but this was no ordinary occasion; all about him were appealing faces, faces pathetic with disappointment. So his sympathy moved him to try the dangerous passage in the dark. He had entered the Heads seventeen times, and believed he knew the ground. So he steered straight for the false opening, mistaking it for the true one. He did not find out that he was wrong until it was too late. There was no saving the ship. The great seas swept her in and crushed her to splinters and rubbish upon the rock tushes at the base of the precipice. Not one of all that fair and gracious company was ever seen again alive. The tale is told to every stranger that passes the spot, and it will continue to be told to all that come, for generations; but it will never grow old, custom cannot stale it, the heart-break that is in it can never perish out of it.

There were two hundred persons in the ship, and but one survived the disaster. He was a sailor. A huge sea flung him up the face of the precipice and stretched him on a narrow shelf of rock midway between the top and the bottom, and there he lay all night. At any other time he would have lain there for the rest of his life, without chance of discovery; but the next morning the ghastly news swept through Sydney that the *Duncan Dunbar* had gone down in sight of home, and straightway the walls of the Heads were black with mourners; and one of these, stretching himself out over the precipice to spy out what might be seen below, discovered this miraculously preserved relic of the wreck. Ropes were brought, and the nearly impossible feat of rescuing the man was accomplished. He was a person with a practical turn of mind, and he hired a hall in Sydney and exhibited himself at sixpence a head till he exhausted the output of the gold-fields for that year.

We entered and cast anchor, and in the morning went oh-ing and ah-ing in admiration up through the crooks and turns of the spacious and beautiful harbor—a harbor which is the darling of Sydney and the wonder of the world. It is not surprising that the people are proud of it, nor that they put their enthusiasm into eloquent words. A returning citizen asked me what I thought of it, and I testified with a cordiality which I judged would be up to the market rate. I said it was beautiful—superbly beautiful. Then by a natural impulse I gave God the praise. The citizen did not seem altogether satisfied. He said:

"It *is* beautiful, of course it's beautiful—the Harbor; but that isn't all of it, it's only half of it; Sydney's the other half, and it takes both of them together to ring the supremacy-bell. God made the Harbor, and that's all right; but Satan made Sydney."

Of course I made an apology; and asked him to convey it to his friend. He was right about Sydney being half of it. It would be beautiful without Sydney, but not above half as beautiful as it is now, with Sydney added. It is shaped somewhat like an oak-leaf—a roomy sheet of lovely blue water, with narrow off-shoots of water running up into the country on both sides between long fingers of land, high wooden ridges with sides sloped like graves. Handsome villas are perched here and there on these ridges, snuggling amongst the foliage, and one catches alluring glimpses of them as the ship swims by toward the city. The city clothes a cluster of hills and a ruffle of neighboring ridges with its undulating masses of masonry, and out of these masses spring towers and spires and other architectural dignities and grandeurs that break the flowing lines and give picturesqueness to the general effect.

The narrow inlets which I have mentioned go wandering out into the land everywhere and hiding themselves in it, and pleasure launches are always exploring them with picnic parties on board. It is said by trustworthy people that if you explore them all you will find that you have covered seven hundred miles of water passage. But there are liars everywhere this year, and they will double that when their works are in good going order.

October was close at hand, spring was come. It was really spring—everybody said so; but you could have sold it for summer in Canada, and nobody would have suspected. It was the very weather that makes our home summers the perfection of climatic luxury; I mean, when you are out in the wood or by the sea. But these people said it was cool, now—a person ought to see Sydney in the summer-time if he wanted to know what warm weather is; and he ought to go north ten or fifteen hundred miles if he wanted to know what hot weather is. They said that away up there toward the equator the hens laid fried eggs. Sydney is the place to go to get information about other people's climates. It seems to me that the occupation of Unbiased Traveler Seeking Information is the pleasantest and most irresponsible trade there is. The traveler can always find out anything he wants to, merely by asking. He can get at all the facts, and more. Everybody helps him, nobody hinders him. Anybody who has an old fact in stock that is no longer negotiable in the domestic market will let him have it at his own price. An accumulation of such goods is easily and quickly made. They cost almost nothing and they bring par in the foreign market. Travelers who come to America always freight up with the same old nursery tales that their predecessors selected, and they carry them back and always work them off without any trouble in the home market.

If the climates of the world were determined by parallels of latitude, then we could know a place's climate by its position on the map; and so we should know that the climate of Sydney was the counterpart of the climate of Columbia, South Carolina, and of Little Rock, Arkansas, since Sydney is about the same distance south of the equator that those other towns are north of it—thirty-four degrees. But no, climate disregards the parallels of latitude. In Arkansas they have a winter; in Sydney they have the name of it, but not the thing itself. I have seen the ice in the Mississippi floating past the mouth of the Arkansas River; and at Memphis, but a little way above, the Mississippi has been frozen over, from bank to bank. But they have never had a cold spell in Sydney which brought the mercury down to freezing-point. Once in a midwinter day there, in the month of July, the mercury went down to thirty-six degrees, and that remains the memorable "cold day" in the history of the town. No doubt Little Rock has seen it below zero. Once, in Sydney, in midsummer, about New Year's Day, the mercury went up to one hundred and six degrees in the shade, and that is Sydney's memorable hot day. That would about tally with Little Rock's hottest day also, I imagine. My Sydney figures are taken from a government report, and are trustworthy. In the matter of summer weather Arkansas has no advantage over Sydney, perhaps, but when it comes to winter weather, that is another affair. You could cut up an Arkansas winter into a hundred Sydney winters and have enough left for Arkansas and the poor.

The whole narrow, hilly belt of the Pacific side of New South Wales has the climate of its capital—a mean winter temperature of fifty-four degrees and a mean summer one of seventy-one degrees. It is a climate which cannot be improved upon for healthfulness. But the experts say that ninety degrees in New South Wales is harder to bear than one hundred and twelve degrees in the neighboring colony of Victoria, because the atmosphere of the former is humid, and of the latter dry.

The mean temperature of the southernmost point of New South Wales is the same as that of Nice—sixty degrees—yet Nice is further from the equator by four hundred and sixty miles than is the former.

But Nature is always stingy of perfect climates; stingier in the case of Australia than usual. Apparently, this vast continent has a really good climate nowhere but around the edges.

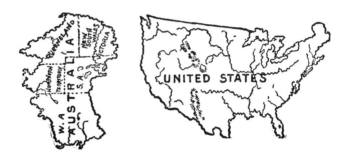

If we look at a map of the world we are surprised to see how big Australia is. It is about two-thirds as large as the United States was before we added Alaska.

But whereas one finds a sufficiently good climate and fertile land almost everywhere in the United States, it seems settled that inside of the Australian border-belt one finds many deserts and in spots a climate which nothing can stand except a few of the hardier kinds of rocks. In effect, Australia is as yet unoccupied. If you take a map of the United States and leave the Atlantic seaboard states in their places; also the fringe of Southern states from Florida west to the mouth of the Mississippi; also a narrow, inhabited streak up the Mississippi half-way to its headwaters; also a narrow, inhabited border along the Pacific coast; then take a brushful of paint and obliterate the whole remaining mighty stretch of country that lies between the Atlantic states and the Pacific-coast strip, your map will look like the latest map of Australia.

This stupendous blank is hot, not to say torrid; a part of it is fertile, the rest is desert; it is not liberally watered; it has no towns. One has only to cross the mountains of New South Wales and descend into the westward-lying regions to find that he has left the choice climate behind him, and found a new one of a quite different character. In fact, he would not know by the thermometer that he was not in the blistering

Plains of India. Captain Sturt, the great explorer, gives us a sample of the heat.

> The wind, which had been blowing all the morning from the N.E., increased to a heavy gale, and I shall never forget its withering effect. I sought shelter behind a large gum tree, but the blasts of heat were so terrific that I wondered *the very grass did not take fire.* This really was nothing ideal: everything both animate and inanimate gave way before it; the horses stood with their backs to the wind and their noses to the ground, without the muscular strength to raise their heads; the birds were mute, and the leaves of the trees under which we were sitting *fell like a snow-shower around us.* At noon I took a thermometer graded to 127°, out of my box, and observed that the mercury was up to 125°. Thinking that it had been unduly influenced, I put it in the fork of a tree close to me, sheltered alike from the wind and the sun. I went to examine it about an hour afterward, when I found the mercury had risen to the top of the instrument and had *burst the bulb*, a circumstance that I believe no traveler has ever before had to record. I cannot find language to convey to the reader's mind an idea of the intense and oppressive nature of the heat that prevailed.

That hot wind sweeps over Sydney sometimes, and brings with it what is called a "dust-storm." It is said that most Australian towns are acquainted with the dust-storm. I think I know what it is like, for the following description by Mr. Gane tallies very well with the alkali dust-storm of Nevada, if you leave out the "shovel" part. Still the shovel part is a pretty important part, and seems to indicate that my Nevada storm is but a poor thing, after all.

> As we proceeded the altitude became less, and the heat proportionately greater until we reached Dubbo, which is only

six hundred feet above sea-level. It is a pretty town, built on an extensive plain. . . . After the effects of a shower of rain have passed away the surface of the ground crumbles into a thick layer of dust, and occasionally, when the wind is in a particular quarter, *it is lifted bodily from the ground in one long opaque cloud.* In the midst of such a storm nothing can be seen a few yards ahead, and the unlucky person who happens to be out at the time is compelled to seek the nearest retreat at hand. When the thrifty housewife sees in the distance the dark column advancing in a steady whirl toward her house, she closes the doors and windows with all expedition. A drawing-room, the window of which has been carelessly left open during a dust-storm, is indeed an extraordinary sight. A lady who has resided in Dubbo for some years says that the dust lies so thick on the carpet that it is necessary to use a shovel to remove it.

And probably a wagon. I was mistaken; I have not seen a proper dust-storm. To my mind the exterior aspects and character of Australia are fascinating things to look at and think about, they are so strange, so weird, so new, so uncommonplace, such a startling and interesting contrast to the other sections of the planet, the sections that are known to us all, familiar to us all. In the matter of particulars—a detail here, a detail there—we have had the choice climate of New South Wales's seacoast; we have had the Australian heat as furnished by Captain Sturt; we have had the wonderful dust-storm; and we have considered the phenomenon of an almost empty hot wilderness half as big as the United States, with a narrow belt of civilization, population, and good climate around it.

Chapter X

Everything human is pathetic. The secret source of Humor itself is not joy but sorrow. There is no humor in heaven.
                    —*Pudd'nhead Wilson's New Calendar.*

CAPTAIN COOK found Australia in 1770, and eighteen years later the British government began to transport convicts to it. Altogether, New South Wales received eighty-three thousand in fifty-three years. The convicts wore heavy chains; they were ill-fed and badly treated by the officers set over them; they were heavily punished for even slight infractions of the rules; "the cruelest discipline ever known" is one historian's description of their life.[1]

English law was hard-hearted in those days. For trifling offenses which in our day would be punished by a small fine or a few days' confinement, men, women, and boys were sent to this other end of the earth to serve terms of seven and fourteen years; and for serious crimes they were transported for life. Children were sent to the penal colonies for seven years for stealing a rabbit!

[1] *The Story of Australasia.* J. S. Laurie.

When I was in London twenty-three years ago there was a new penalty in force for diminishing garroting and wife-beating—twenty-five lashes on the bare back with the cat-o'-nine-tails. It was said that this terrible punishment was able to bring the stubbornest ruffians to terms; and that no man had been found with grit enough to keep his emotions to himself beyond the ninth blow; as a rule the man shrieked earlier. That penalty had a great and wholesome effect upon the garroters and wife-beaters; but humane modern London could not endure it; it got its law rescinded. Many a bruised and battered English wife has since had occasion to deplore that cruel achievement of sentimental "humanity."

Twenty-five lashes! In Australia and Tasmania they gave a convict fifty for almost any little offense; and sometimes a brutal officer would add fifty, and then another fifty, and so on, as long as the sufferer could endure the torture and live. In Tasmania I read the entry, in an old manuscript official record, of a case where a convict was given *three hundred* lashes—for stealing some silver spoons. And men got more than that, sometimes. Who handled the cat? Often it was another convict; sometimes it was the culprit's dearest comrade; and he had to lay on with all his might; otherwise he would get a flogging himself for his mercy—for he was under watch—and yet not do his friend any good: the friend would be attended to by another hand and suffer no lack in the matter of full punishment.

The convict life in Tasmania was so unendurable, and suicide so difficult to accomplish, that once or twice despairing men got together and drew straws to determine which of them should kill another of the group—this murder to secure death to the perpetrator and to the witnesses of it by the hand of the hangman!

The incidents quoted above are mere hints, mere suggestions of what convict life was like—they are but a couple of details tossed into view out of a shoreless sea of such; or, to change the figure, they are but a pair of flaming steeples photographed from a point which hides from sight the burning city which stretches away from their bases on every hand.

Some of the convicts—indeed, a good many of them— were very bad people, even for that day; but the most of them were probably not noticeably worse than the average of the people they left behind them at home. We must believe this; we cannot avoid it. We are obliged to believe that a nation that could look on, unmoved, and see starving or freezing women hanged for stealing twenty-six cents' worth of bacon or rags, and boys snatched from their mothers, and men from their families, and sent to the other side of the world for long terms of years for similar trifling offenses, was a nation to whom the term "civilized" could not in any large way be applied. And we must also believe that a nation that knew, during more than forty years, what was happening to those exiles and was still content with it, was not advancing in any showy way toward a higher grade of civilization.

If we look into the characters and conduct of the officers and gentlemen who had charge of the convicts and attended to their backs and stomachs, we must grant again that as between the convict and his masters, and between both and the nation at home, there was a quite noticeable monotony of sameness.

Four years had gone by, and many convicts had come. Respectable settlers were beginning to arrive. These two classes of colonists had to be protected, in case of trouble among themselves or with the natives. It is proper to mention the natives, though they could hardly count, they were so scarce. At a time when they had not as yet begun to be much disturbed—not as yet being in the way—it was estimated that in New South Wales there was but one native to forty-five thousand acres of territory.

People had to be protected. Officers of the regular army did not want this service—away off there where neither honor nor distinction was to be gained. So England recruited and officered a kind of militia force of one thousand uniformed civilians called the "New South Wales Corps" and shipped it.

This was the worst blow of all. The colony fairly staggered under it. The Corps was an object-lesson of the moral condition of England outside of the jails. The colonists trembled. It was feared that next there would be an importation of the nobility.

In those early days the colony was non-supporting. All the necessaries of life—food, clothing, and all—were sent out from England, and kept in great government storehouses, and given to the convicts and sold to the settlers—sold at a trifling advance upon cost. The Corps saw its opportunity. Its officers went into commerce, and in a most lawless way. They went to importing rum, and also to manufacturing it in private stills, in defiance of the government's commands and protests. They leagued themselves together and ruled the market; they boycotted the government and the other dealers; they established a close monopoly and kept it strictly in their own hands. When a vessel arrived with spirits, they allowed nobody to buy but themselves, and they forced the owner to sell to them at a price named by themselves—and it was always low enough. They bought rum at an average of two dollars a gallon and sold it at an average of ten. They *made rum the currency of the country*—for there was little or no money—and they maintained their devastating hold and kept the colony under their heel for eighteen or twenty years before they were finally conquered and routed by the government.

Meantime, they had spread intemperance everywhere. And they had squeezed farm after farm out of the settlers' hands for rum, and thus had bountifully enriched themselves. When a farmer was caught in the last agonies of thirst they took advantage of him and sweated him for a drink.

In one instance they sold a man a gallon of rum worth two dollars for a piece of property which was sold some years later for one hundred thousand dollars.

When the colony was about eighteen or twenty years old it was discovered that the land was specially fitted for the wool culture. Prosperity followed, commerce with the world began, by and by rich mines of the noble metals were opened, immigrants flowed in, capital likewise. The result is the great and wealthy and enlightened commonwealth of New South Wales.

It is a country that is rich in mines, wool ranches, trams, railways, steamship lines, schools, newspapers, botanical gardens, art-galleries, libraries, museums, hospitals, learned societies; it is the hospitable home of every species of culture and of every species of material enterprise, and there is a church at every man's door, and a race-track over the way.

Chapter XI

> *We should be careful to get out of an experience*
> *only the wisdom that is in it—and stop there; lest we be*
> *like the cat that sits down on a hot stove-lid. She will*
> *never sit down on a hot stove-lid again—and that is well;*
> *but also she will never sit down on a cold one any more.*
> *—Pudd'nhead Wilson's New Calendar.*

ALL English-speaking colonies are made up of lavishly hospitable people, and New South Wales and its capital are like the rest in this. The English-speaking colony of the United States of America is always called lavishly hospitable by the English traveler. As to the other English-speaking colonies throughout the world from Canada all around, I know by experience that the description fits them. I will not go more particularly into this matter, for I find that when writers try to distribute their gratitude here and there and yonder by detail they run across difficulties and do some ungraceful stumbling.

Mr. Gane (*New South Wales and Victoria in 1885*) tried to distribute his gratitude, and was not lucky:

> The inhabitants of Sydney are renowned for their hospi-
> tality. The treatment which we experienced at the hands of
> this generous-hearted people will help more than anything else

to make us recollect with pleasure our stay amongst them. In the character of hosts and hostesses they excel. The "new chum" needs only the acquaintanceship of one of their number, and he becomes at once the happy recipient of numerous complimentary invitations and thoughtful kindnesses. Of the towns it has been our good fortune to visit, none have portrayed home so faithfully as Sydney.

Nobody could say it finer than that. If he had put in his cork then, and stayed away from Dubbo—but no; heedless man, he pulled it again. Pulled it when he was away along in his book, and his memory of what he had said about Sydney had grown dim:

> We cannot quit the promising town of Dubbo without testifying, in warm praise, to the kind-hearted and hospitable usages of its inhabitants. Sydney, though well deserving the character it bears of its kindly treatment of strangers, possesses a little formality and reserve. In Dubbo, on the contrary, though the same congenial manners prevail, there is a pleasing degree of respectful familiarity which gives the town a homely comfort not often met with elsewhere. In laying on one side our pen we feel contented in having been able, though so late in this work, to bestow a panegyric, however unpretentious, on a town which, though possessing no picturesque natural surroundings, nor interesting architectural productions, has yet a body of citizens whose hearts cannot but obtain for their town a reputation for benevolence and kind-heartedness.

I wonder what soured him on Sydney. It seems strange that a pleasing degree of three or four fingers of respectful familiarity should fill a man up and give him the panegyrics so bad. For he *has* them, the worst way—any one can see that. A man who is perfectly at himself does not throw cold detraction at people's architectural productions and picturesque surroundings, and let on that what he prefers is a Dubbonese dust-storm and a pleasing degree of respectful familiarity. No, these are old, old symptoms; and when they appear we know that the man has got the panegyrics.

Sydney has a population of four hundred thousand. When a stranger from America steps ashore there, the first thing that strikes him is that the place is eight or nine times as large as he was expecting it to be; and the next thing that strikes him is that it is an English city with American trimmings. Later on, in Melbourne, he will find the American trimmings still more in evidence; there, even the architecture will often suggest America; a photograph of its stateliest business street might be passed upon him for a picture of the finest street in a large American city. I was told that the most of the fine residences were the city residences of squatters. The name seemed out of focus somehow. When the explanation came, it offered a new instance of the curious changes which words, as well as animals, undergo through change of habitat and climate. With us, when you speak of a squatter you are always supposed to be speaking of a poor man, but in Australia when you speak of a squatter you are supposed to be speaking of a millionaire; in America the word indicates the possessor of a few acres and a doubtful title, in Australia it indicates a man whose land front is as long as a railroad, and whose title has been perfected in one way or another; in America the word indicates a man who owns a dozen head of live stock, in Australia a man who owns anywhere from fifty thousand up to half a million head; in America the word indicates a man who is obscure and not important, in Australia a man who is prominent and of the first importance; in America you take off your hat to no squatter, in Australia you do; in America if your uncle is a squatter you keep it dark, in Australia you advertise it; in America if your friend is a squatter nothing comes of it, but with a squatter for your friend in Australia you may sup with kings if there are any around.

In Australia it takes about two acres and a half of pasture-land (some people say twice as many) to support a sheep; and when the squatter has half a million sheep his private domain is about as large as Rhode Island, to speak in general terms. His annual wool crop may be worth a quarter or a half million dollars.

He will live in a palace in Melbourne or Sydney or some other of the large cities, and make occasional trips to his sheep-kingdom several hundred miles away in the great plains to look after his battalions of riders and shepherds and other hands. He has a commodious dwelling out there, and if he approve of you he will invite you to spend a week in it, and will make you at home and comfortable, and let you see the great industry in all its details, and feed you and slake you and smoke you with the best that money can buy.

On at least one of these vast estates there is a considerable town, with all the various businesses and occupations that go to make an important town; and the town and the land it stands upon are the property of the squatters. I have seen that town, and it is not unlikely that there are other squatter-owned towns in Australia.

Australia supplies the world not only with fine wool, but with mutton also. The modern invention of cold storage and its application in ships has created this great trade. In Sydney I visited a huge establishment where they kill and clean and solidly freeze a thousand sheep a day, for shipment to England.

The Australians did not seem to me to differ noticeably from Americans, either in dress, carriage, ways, pronuncia-tion, inflections, or general appearance. There were fleeting and subtle suggestions of their English origin, but these were not pronounced enough, as a rule, to catch one's attention.

The people have easy and cordial manners from the beginning—from the moment that the introduction is completed.
This is American. To put it in another way, it is English
friendliness with the English shyness and self-consciousness
left out.

Now and then—but this is rare—one hears such words
as *piper* for paper, *lydy* for lady, and *tyble* for table fall from
lips whence one would not expect such pronunciations to
come. There is a superstition prevalent in Sydney that this
pronunciation is an Australianism, but people who have been
"home"—as the native reverently and lovingly calls England—know better. It is "costermonger." All over Australasia this pronunciation is nearly as common among servants
as it is in London among the uneducated and the partially
educated of all sorts and conditions of people. That mislaid *y*
is rather striking when a person gets enough of it into a short
sentence to enable it to show up. In the hotel in Sydney the
chambermaid said one morning:

"The tyble is set, and here is the piper; and if the lydy is
ready I'll tell the wyter to bring up the breakfast."

I have made passing mention, a moment ago, of the
native Australasian's custom of speaking of England as
"home." It was always pretty to hear it, and often it was said
in an unconsciously caressing way that made it touching; in
a way which transmuted a sentiment into an embodiment,
and made one seem to see Australasia as a young girl stroking
mother England's old gray head.

In the Australasian home the table-talk is vivacious and
unembarrassed; it is without stiffness or restraint. This does
not remind one of England so much as it does of America.
But Australasia is strictly democratic, and reserves and re-
straints are things that are bred by differences of rank.

English and colonial audiences are phenomenally alert
and responsive. Where masses of people are gathered together

in England, caste is submerged, and with it the English re-serve; equality exists for the moment, and every individual is free; so free from any consciousness of fetters, indeed, that the Englishman's habit of watching himself and guarding himself against any injudicious exposure of his feelings is forgotten, and falls into abeyance—and to such a degree, indeed, that he will bravely applaud all by himself if he wants to—an exhibition of daring which is unusual elsewhere in the world.

But it is hard to move a new English acquaintance when he is by himself, or when the company present is small, and new to him. He is on his guard then, and his natural reserve is to the fore. This has given him the false reputation of being without humor and without the appreciation of humor. Americans are not Englishmen, and American humor is not English humor; but both the American and his humor had their origin in England, and have merely undergone changes brought about by changed conditions and a new environ-ment. About the best humorous speeches I have yet heard were a couple that were made in Australia at club suppers—one of them by an Englishman, the other by an Australian.

Chapter XII

*There are those who scoff at the school-boy, calling
him frivolous and shallow. Yet it was the school-boy
who said, "Faith is believing what you know ain't so."
—Pudd'nhead Wilson's New Calendar.*

IN Sydney I had a large dream, and in the course of talk I
told it to a missionary from India who was on his way to
visit some relatives in New Zealand. I dreamed that the visible
universe is the physical person of God; that the vast worlds
that we see twinkling millions of miles apart in the fields of
space are the blood-corpuscles in His veins; and that we and
the other creatures are the microbes that charge with multitudinous life the corpuscles.

Mr. X., the missionary, considered the dream awhile,
then said:

> It is not surpassable for magnitude, since its metes and
> bounds are the metes and bounds of the universe itself; and it
> seems to me that it almost accounts for a thing which is other-
> wise nearly unaccountable—the origin of the sacred legends
> of the Hindus. Perhaps they dream them, and then honestly
> believe them to be divine revelations of fact. It looks like that,

for the legends are built on so vast a scale that it does not seem reasonable that plodding priests would happen upon such colossal fancies when awake.

He told some of the legends, and said that they were implicitly believed by all classes of Hindus, including those of high social position and intelligence; and he said that this universal credulity was a great hindrance to the missionary in his work. Then he said something like this:

At home, people wonder why Christianity does not make faster progress in India. They hear that the Indians believe easily, and that they have a natural trust in miracles and give them a hospitable reception. Then they argue like this: since the Indian believes easily, place Christianity before them and they must believe; confirm its truths by the Biblical miracles, and they will no longer doubt. The natural deduction is, that as Christianity makes but indifferent progress in India, the fault is with us: we are not fortunate in presenting the doctrines and the miracles.

But the truth is, we are not by any means so well equipped as they think. We have *not* the easy task that they imagine. To use a military figure, we are sent against the enemy with good powder in our guns, but only wads for bullets; that is to say, our miracles are not effective; the Hindus do not care for them; they have more extraordinary ones of their own. All the details of their own religion are proven and established by miracles; the details of ours must be proven in the same way. When I first began my work in India I greatly underestimated the difficulties thus put upon my task. A correction was not long in coming. I thought as our friends think at home—that to prepare my childlike wonder-lovers to listen with favor to my grave message I only needed to charm the way to it with wonders, marvels, miracles. With full confidence I told the wonders performed by Samson, the strongest man that had ever lived—for so I called him.

At first I saw lively anticipation and strong interest in the faces of my people, but as I moved along from incident to incident of the great story, I was distressed to see that I was steadily losing the sympathy of my audience. I could not understand it. It was a surprise to me, and a disappointment. Before I was through, the fading sympathy had paled to indifference. Thence to the end the indifference remained; I was not able to make any impression upon it.

A good old Hindu gentleman told me where my trouble lay. He said: "We Hindus recognize a god by the work of his hands—we accept no other testimony. Apparently, this is also the rule with you Christians. And we know when a man has his power from a god by the fact that he does things which he could not do, as a man, with the mere powers of a man. Plainly, this is the Christian's way also, of knowing when a man is working by a god's power and not by his own. You saw that there was a supernatural property in the hair of Samson; for you perceived that when his hair was gone he was as other men. It is our way, as I have said. There are many nations in the world, and each group of nations has its own gods, and will pay no worship to the gods of the others. Each group believes its own gods to be strongest, and it will not exchange them except for gods that shall be proven to be their superiors in power. Man is but a weak creature, and needs the help of gods—he cannot do without it. Shall he place his fate in the hands of weak gods when there may be stronger ones to be found? That would be foolish. No, if he hear of gods that are stronger than his own, he should not turn a deaf ear, for it is not a light matter that is at stake. How then shall he determine which gods are the stronger, his own or those that preside over the concerns of other nations? By comparing the known works of his own gods with the works of those others; there is no other way. Now, when we make this comparison, we are not drawn toward the gods of any other nation. Our gods are shown by their works to be the strongest, the most powerful. The Christians have but few gods, and they are

new—new, and not strong, as it seems to us. They will in-
crease in number, it is true, for this has happened with all
gods, but that time is far away, many ages and decades of ages
away, for gods multiply slowly, as is meet for beings to whom
a thousand years is but a single moment. Our own gods have
been born millions of years apart. The process is slow, the
gathering of strength and power is similarly slow. In the slow
lapse of the ages the steadily accumulating power of our gods
has at last become prodigious. We have a thousand proofs of
this in the colossal character of their personal acts and the
acts of ordinary men to whom they have given supernatural
qualities. To your Samson was given supernatural power, and
when he broke the withes, and slew the thousands with the
jawbone of an ass, and carried away the gates of the city
upon his shoulders, you were amazed—and also awed, for you
recognized the divine source of his strength. But it could not
profit to place these things before your Hindu congregation
and invite their wonder; for they would compare them with
the deed done by Hanuman, when our gods infused their
divine strength into his muscles; and they would be indifferent
to them—as you saw. In the old, old times, ages and ages
gone by, when our god Rama was warring with the demon
god of Ceylon, Rama bethought him to bridge the sea and
connect Ceylon with India, so that his armies might pass easily
over; and he sent his general, Hanuman, inspired like your
own Samson with divine strength, to bring the materials for
the bridge. In two days Hanuman strode fifteen hundred miles,
to the Himalayas, and took upon his shoulder a range of those
lofty mountains two hundred miles long, and started with it
toward Ceylon. It was in the night; and, as he passed along
the plain, the people of Govardhun heard the thunder of his
tread and felt the earth rocking under it, and they ran out, and
there, with their snowy summits piled to heaven, they saw
the Himalayas passing by. And as this huge continent swept
along overshadowing the earth, upon its slopes they discerned
the twinkling lights of a thousand sleeping villages, and it was

as if the constellations were filing in procession through the sky. While they were looking, Hanuman stumbled, and a small ridge of red sandstone twenty miles long was jolted loose and fell. Half of its length has wasted away in the course of the ages, but the other ten miles of it remain in the plain by Govardhun to this day as proof of the might of the inspiration of our gods. You must know, yourself, that Hanuman could not have carried those mountains to Ceylon except by the strength of the gods. You know that it was not done by his own strength, therefore you know that it *was* done by the strength of the gods, just as you know that Samson carried the gates by the divine strength and not by his own. I think you must concede two things: First, That in carrying the gates of the city upon his shoulders, Samson did not establish the superiority of his gods over ours; secondly, That his feat is not supported by any but verbal evidence, while Hanuman's is not only supported by verbal evidence, but this evidence is confirmed, established, proven, by visible, tangible evidence, which is the strongest of all testimony. We have the sandstone ridge, and while it remains we cannot doubt, and shall not. Have you the gates?"

Chapter XIII

The timid man yearns for full value and demands a tenth. The bold man strikes for double value and compromises on par.
— *Pudd'nhead Wilson's New Calendar.*

ONE is sure to be struck by the liberal way in which Australasia spends money upon public works—such as legislative buildings, town-halls, hospitals, asylums, parks, and botanical gardens. I should say that where minor towns in America spend a hundred dollars on the town-hall and on public parks and gardens the like towns in Australasia spend a thousand. And I think that this ratio will hold good in the matter of hospitals, also. I have seen a costly and well-equipped and architecturally handsome hospital in an Australian village of fifteen hundred inhabitants. It was built by private funds furnished by the villagers and the neighboring planters, and its running expenses were drawn from the same sources. I suppose it would be hard to match this in any country. This village was about to close a contract for lighting the streets with the electric light, when I was there. That is ahead of London. London is still obscured by gas—gas pretty widely scattered, too, in some of the districts; so widely indeed, that except on moonlight nights it is difficult to find the gas-lamps.

The botanical garden of Sydney covers thirty-eight acres, beautifully laid out and rich with the spoil of all the lands and all the climes of the world. The garden is on high ground in the middle of the town, overlooking the great harbor, and it adjoins the spacious grounds of Government House—fifty-six acres; and at hand, also, is a recreation-ground containing eighty-two acres. In addition, there are the zoological gardens, the race-course, and the great cricket-grounds where the international matches are played. Therefore there is plenty of room for reposeful lazying and lounging, and for exercise too, for such as like that kind of work.

There are four specialties attainable in the way of social pleasure. If you enter your name on the Visitors' Book at Government House you will receive an invitation to the next ball that takes place there, if nothing can be proven against you. And it will be very pleasant; for you will see everybody except the Governor, and add a number of acquaintances and several friends to your list. The Governor will be in England. He always is. The continent has four or five governors, and I do not know how many it takes to govern the outlying archipelago; but anyway you will not see them. When they are appointed they come out from England and get inaugurated, and give a ball, and help pray for rain, and get aboard ship and go back home. And so the Lieutenant-Governor has to do all the work. I was in Australasia three months and a half, and saw only one Governor. The others were at home.

The Australasian Governor would not be so restless, perhaps, if he had a war, or a veto, or something like that to call for his reserve energies, but he hasn't. There isn't any war, and there isn't any veto in his hands. And so there is really little or nothing doing in his line. The country governs itself, and prefers to do it; and is so strenuous about it and so jealous of its independence that it grows restive if even the Imperial Government at home proposes to help; and so the Imperial veto, while a fact, is yet mainly a name.

Thus the Governor's functions are much more limited than are a Governor's functions with us. And therefore more fatiguing. He is the apparent head of the State, he is the real head of Society. He represents culture, refinement, elevated sentiment, polite life, religion; and by his example he propagates these, and they spread and flourish and bear fruit. He creates the fashion, and leads it. His ball is the ball of balls, and his countenance makes the horse-race thrive.

He is usually a lord, and this is well; for his position compels him to lead an expensive life, and an English lord is generally well equipped for that.

Another of Sydney's social pleasures is the visit to the Admiralty House; which is nobly situated on high ground overlooking the water. The trim boats of the service convey the guests thither; and there, or on board the flagship, they have the duplicate of the hospitalities of Government House. The Admiral commanding a station in British waters is a magnate of the first degree, and he is sumptuously housed, as becomes the dignity of his office.

Third in the list of special pleasures is the tour of the harbor in a fine steam pleasure launch. Your richer friends own boats of this kind, and they will invite you, and the joys of the trip will make a long day seem short.

And finally comes the shark-fishing. Sydney harbor is populous with the finest breeds of man-eating sharks in the world. Some people make their living catching them; for the Government pays a cash bounty on them. The larger the shark the larger the bounty, and some of the sharks are twenty feet long. You not only get the bounty, but everything that is in the shark belongs to you. Sometimes the contents are quite valuable.

MARK TWAIN

The shark is the swiftest fish that swims. The speed of the fastest steamer afloat is poor compared to his. And he is a great gad-about, and roams far and wide in the oceans, and visits the shores of all of them, ultimately, in the course of his restless excursions. I have a tale to tell now, which has not as yet been in print. In 1870 a young stranger arrived in Sydney, and set about finding something to do; but he knew no one, and brought no recommendations, and the result was that he got no employment. He had aimed high, at first, but as time and his money wasted away he grew less and less exacting, until at last he was willing to serve in the humblest capacities if so he might get bread and shelter. But luck was still against him; he could find no opening of any sort. Finally his money was all gone. He walked the streets all day, thinking; he walked them all night, thinking, thinking, and growing hungrier and hungrier. At dawn he found himself well away from the town and drifting aimlessly along the harbor shore. As he was passing by a nodding shark-fisher the man looked up and said:

"Say, young fellow, take my line a spell, and change my luck for me."

"How do you know I won't make it worse?"

"Because you can't. It has been at its worst all night. If you can't change it, no harm's done; if you do change it, it's for the better, of course. Come."

"All right, what will you give?"

"I'll give you the shark, if you catch one."

"And I will eat it, bones and all. Give me the line."

"Here you are. I will get away, now, for a while, so that my luck won't spoil yours; for many and many a time I've noticed that if—there, pull in, pull in, man, you've got a bite! *I* knew how it would be. Why, I knew you for a born son of luck the minute I saw you. All right—he's landed."

It was an unusually large shark—"a full nineteen-footer," the fisherman said, as he laid the creature open with his knife.

"Now you rob him, young man, while I step to my hamper for a fresh bait. There's generally something in them worth going for. You've changed my luck, you see. But, my goodness, I hope you haven't changed your own."

"Oh, it wouldn't matter; don't worry about that. Get your bait. I'll rob him."

When the fisherman got back the young man had just finished washing his hands in the bay and was starting away.

"What! you are not going?"

"Yes. Good-by."

"But what about your shark?"

"The shark? Why, what use is he to me?"

"What *use* is he? I like that. Don't you know that we can go and report him to Government, and you'll get a clean solid eighty shillings bounty? Hard cash, you know. What do you think about it *now*?"

"Oh, well, you can collect it."

"And *keep* it? Is that what you mean?"

"Yes."

"Well, this is odd. You're one of those sort they call eccentrics, I judge. The saying is, you mustn't judge a man by his clothes, and I'm believing it now. Why yours are looking just ratty, don't you know; and yet you must be rich."

"I am."

The young man walked slowly back to the town, deeply musing as he went. He halted a moment in front of the best restaurant, then glanced at his clothes and passed on, and got his breakfast at a "stand-up." There was a good deal of it, and it cost five shillings. He tendered a sovereign, got his change, glanced at his silver, muttered to himself, "There isn't enough to buy clothes with," and went his way.

At half past nine the richest wool-broker in Sydney was sitting in his morning-room at home, settling his breakfast with the morning paper. A servant put his head in and said:

"There's a sundowner at the door wants to see you, sir."

"What do you bring that kind of a message here for? Send him about his business."

"He won't go, sir. I've tried."

"He won't go? That's—why, that's unusual. He's one of two things, then: he's a remarkable person, or he's crazy. Is he crazy?"

"No, sir. He don't look it."

"Then he's remarkable. What does he say he wants?"

"He won't tell, sir; only says it's very important."

"And won't go. Does he *say* he won't go?"

"Says he'll stand there till he sees you, sir, if it's all day."

"And yet isn't crazy. Show him up."

The sundowner was shown in. The broker said to himself, "No, he's not crazy; that is easy to see; so he must be the other thing."

Then aloud, "Well, my good fellow, be quick about it; don't waste any words; what is it you want?"

"I want to borrow a hundred thousand pounds."

"Scott! (It's a mistake; he *is* crazy. . . . No—he *can't* be—not with that eye.) Why, you take my breath away. Come, who *are* you?"

"Nobody that you know."

"What is your name?"

"Cecil Rhodes."

"No, I don't remember hearing the name before. Now then—just for curiosity's sake—what has sent you to me on this extraordinary errand?"

"The intention to make a hundred thousand pounds for you and as much for myself within the next sixty days."

"Well, well, well. It is the most extraordinary idea that I—sit *down*—you interest me. And somehow you—well, you fascinate me, I think that that is about the word. And it isn't your proposition—no, that doesn't fascinate me; it's something else, I don't quite know what; something that's born in you and oozes out of you, I suppose. Now then—just for curiosity's sake again, nothing more: as I understand it, it is your desire to bor—"

"I said *intention.*"

"Pardon, so you did. I thought it was an unheedful use of the word—an unheedful valuing of its strength, you know."

"I knew its strength."

"Well, I must say—but look here, let me walk the floor a little, my mind is getting into a sort of whirl, though *you* don't seem disturbed any. (Plainly this young fellow isn't crazy; but as to his being remarkable—well, really he amounts to that, and something over.) Now then, I believe I am beyond the reach of further astonishment. Strike, and spare not. What is your scheme?"

"To buy the wool crop—deliverable in sixty days."

"What, the *whole* of it?"

"The whole of it."

"No, I was not quite out of the reach of surprises, after all. Why, how you talk. Do you know what our crop is going to foot up?"

"Two and a half million sterling—maybe a little more."

"Well, you've got your statistics right, anyway. Now then, do you know what the margins would foot up, to buy it at sixty days?"

"The hundred thousand pounds I came here to get."

"Right, once more. Well, dear me, just to see what would happen, I wish you had the money. And if you had it, what would you do with it?"

"I shall make two hundred thousand pounds out of it in sixty days."

"You mean, of course, that you *might* make it if—"

"I said, 'shall.'"

"Yes, by George, you *did* say 'shall'! You are the most definite devil I ever saw, in the matter of language. Dear, dear, dear, look here! Definite speech means clarity of mind. Upon my word I believe you've got what you believe to be a rational *reason* for venturing into this house, an entire stranger, on this wild scheme of buying the wool crop of an entire colony on speculation. Bring it out—I am prepared—acclimatized, if I may use the word. *Why* would you buy the crop, and *why* would you make that sum out of it? That is to say, what makes you think you—"

"I don't think—I know."

"Definite again. *How* do you know?"

"Because France has declared war against Germany, and wool has gone up fourteen per cent. in London and is still rising."

"Oh, in-deed? *Now* then, I've *got* you! Such a thunderbolt as you have just let fly ought to have made me jump out of my chair, but it didn't stir me the least little bit, you see. And for a very simple reason: I have read the morning paper. You can look at it if you want to. The fastest ship in the service arrived at eleven o'clock last night, fifty days out from London. All her news is printed here. There are no war-clouds anywhere; and as for wool, why, it is the low-spiritedest commodity in the English market. It is your turn to jump, now. . . . Well, why don't you jump? Why do you sit there in that placid fashion, when—"

"Because I have later news."

"Later news? Oh, come—later news than fifty days, brought steaming hot from London by the—"

"My news is only ten days old."

"Oh, Mun-*chausen*, hear the maniac talk! Where did you get it?"

"Got it out of a shark."

"Oh, oh, oh, this is *too* much! Front! call the police—bring the gun—raise the town! All the asylums in Christendom have broken loose in the single person of—"

"Sit down! And collect yourself. Where is the use in getting excited? Am I excited? There is nothing to get excited *about*. When I make a statement which I cannot prove, it will be time enough for you to begin to offer hospitality to damaging fancies about me and my sanity."

"Oh, a thousand thousand pardons! I ought to be ashamed of myself, and I *am* ashamed of myself for thinking that a little bit of a circumstance like sending a shark to England to fetch back a market report—"

"What does your middle initial stand for, sir?"

"Andrew. What are you writing?"

"Wait a moment. Proof about the shark—and another matter. Only ten lines. There—now it is done. Sign it."

"Many thanks—many. Let me see; it says—it says—oh, come, this is *interesting*! Why—why—look here! prove what you say here, and I'll put up the money, and double as much, if necessary, and divide the winnings with you, half and half. There, now—I've signed; make your promise good if you can. Show me a copy of the London *Times* only ten days old."

"Here it is—and with it these buttons and a memorandum-book that belonged to the man the shark swallowed. Swallowed him in the Thames, without a doubt; for you will notice that the last entry in the book is dated 'London,' and is of the same date as the *Times*, and says '*Der consequens der Kriegeserflärung, reise ich heute nach Deutschland ab, auf daß ich mein Leben auf dem Ultar meines Landes Legen mag*'—as clean native German as anybody can put upon paper, and means that in consequence of the declaration of war, this loyal soul is leaving for home *to-day*, to fight. And he did leave, too, but the shark had him before the day was done, poor fellow."

"And a pity, too. But there are times for mourning, and we will attend to this case further on; other matters are pressing, now. I will go down and set the machinery in motion in a quiet way and buy the crop. It will cheer the drooping spirits of the boys, in a transitory way. Everything is transitory in this world. Sixty days hence, when they are called to deliver the goods, they will think they've been struck by lightning. But there is a time for mourning, and we will attend to that case along with the other one. Come along, I'll take you to my tailor. What did you say your name is?"

"Cecil Rhodes."

"It is hard to remember. However, I think you will make it easier by and by, if you live. There are three kinds of people—Commonplace Men, Remarkable Men, and Lunatics. I'll classify you with the Remarkables, and take the chances."

The deal went through, and secured to the young stranger the first fortune he ever pocketed.

The people of Sydney ought to be afraid of the sharks, but for some reason they do not seem to be. On Saturdays the young men go out in their boats, and sometimes the water is fairly covered with the little sails. A boat upsets now and then, by accident, a result of tumultuous skylarking; sometimes the boys upset their boat for fun—such as it is—with sharks visibly waiting around for just such an occurrence. The young fellows scramble aboard whole—sometimes—not always. Tragedies have happened more than once. While I was in Sydney it was reported that a boy fell out of a boat in the mouth of the Paramatta River and screamed for help and a boy jumped overboard from another boat to save him

from the assembling sharks; but the sharks made swift work
with the lives of both.

The government pays a bounty for the shark; to get the
bounty the fishermen bait the hook or the seine with agreeable
mutton; the news spreads and the sharks come from all over
the Pacific Ocean to get the free board. In time the shark
culture will be one of the most successful things in the colony.

Chapter XIV

*We can secure other people's approval, if we do
right and try hard; but our own is worth a hundred of it,
and no way has been found out of securing that.*
—Pudd'nhead Wilson's New Calendar.

MY health had broken down in New York in May; it
had remained in a doubtful but fairish condition during
a succeeding period of eighty-two days; it broke again on the
Pacific. It broke again in Sydney, but not until after I had had
a good outing, and had also filled my lecture engagements.
This latest break lost me the chance of seeing Queensland. In
the circumstances, to go north toward hotter weather was
not advisable.

So we moved south with a westward slant, seventeen
hours by rail to the capital of the colony of Victoria, Melbourne—that juvenile city of sixty years, and half a million
inhabitants. On the map the distance looked small; but that
is a trouble with all divisions of distance in such a vast country
as Australia. The colony of Victoria itself looks small on the
map—looks like a county, in fact—yet it is about as large as
England, Scotland, and Wales combined. Or, to get another

focus upon it, it is just eighty times as large as the state of Rhode Island, and one third as large as the state of Texas.

Outside of Melbourne, Victoria seems to be owned by a handful of squatters, each with a Rhode Island for a sheep-farm. That is the impression which one gathers from common talk, yet the wool industry of Victoria is by no means so great as that of New South Wales. The climate of Victoria is favorable to other great industries—among others, wheat-growing and the making of wine.

We took the train at Sydney at about four in the afternoon. It was American in one way, for we had a most rational sleeping-car; also the car was clean and fine and new—nothing about it to suggest the rolling-stock of the continent of Europe. But our baggage was weighed, and extra weight charged for. That was continental. Continental and troublesome. Any detail of railroading that is not troublesome cannot honorably be described as continental.

The tickets were round-trip ones—to Melbourne, and clear to Adelaide in South Australia, and then all the way back to Sydney. Twelve hundred more miles than we really expected to make; but then as the round trip wouldn't cost much more than the single trip, it seemed well enough to buy as many miles as one could afford, even if one was not likely to need them. A human being has a natural desire to have more of a good thing than he needs.

Now comes a singular thing: the oddest thing, the strangest thing, the most baffling and unaccountable marvel that Australasia can show. At the frontier between New South Wales and Victoria our multitude of passengers were routed out of their snug beds by lantern-light in the morning in the biting cold of a high altitude to change cars on a road that has no break in it from Sydney to Melbourne! Think of the paralysis of intellect that gave that idea birth; imagine the boulder it emerged from on some petrified legislator's shoulders.

It is a narrow-gage road to the frontier, and a broader gage thence to Melbourne. The two governments were the builders of the road and are the owners of it. One or two reasons are given for this curious state of things. One is, that it represents the jealousy existing between the colonies—the two most important colonies of Australasia. What the other one is, I have forgotten. But it is of no consequence. It could be but another effort to explain the inexplicable.

All passengers fret at the double-gage; all shippers of freight must of course fret at it; unnecessary expense, delay, and annoyance are imposed upon everybody concerned, and no one is benefited.

Each Australian colony fences itself off from its neighbor with a custom-house. Personally, I have no objection, but it must be a good deal of inconvenience to the people. We have something resembling it here and there in America, but it goes by another name. The large empire of the Pacific coast requires a world of iron machinery, and could manufacture it economically on the spot if the imposts on foreign iron were removed. But they are not. Protection to Pennsylvania and Alabama forbids it. The result to the Pacific coast is the same as if there were several rows of custom-fences between the coast and the East. Iron carted across the American continent at luxurious railway rates would be valuable enough to be coined when it arrived.

We changed cars. This was at Albury. And it was there, I think, that the growing day and the early sun exposed the distant range called the Blue Mountains. Accurately named. "My word!" as the Australians say, but it was a stunning color, that blue. Deep, strong, rich, exquisite; towering and majestic masses of blue—a softly luminous blue, a smoldering blue, as if vaguely lit by fires within. It extinguished the blue of the sky—made it pallid and unwholesome, whitey and washed out. A wonderful color—just divine.

A resident told me that those were not mountains; he said they were rabbit-piles. And explained that long exposure and the over-ripe condition of the rabbits was what made them look so blue. This man may have been right, but much reading of books of travel has made me distrustful of gratis information furnished by unofficial residents of a country. The facts which such people give to travelers are usually erroneous, and often intemperately so. The rabbit-plague has indeed been very bad in Australia, and it could account for one mountain, but not for a mountain range, it seems to me. It is too large an order.

We breakfasted at the station. A good breakfast, except the coffee; and cheap. The government establishes the prices and placards them. The waiters were men, I think; but that is not usual in Australasia. The usual thing is to have girls. No, not girls, young ladies—generally duchesses. Dress? They would attract attention at any royal levée in Europe. Even empresses and queens do not dress as they do. Not that they could not afford it, perhaps, but they would not know how.

All the pleasant morning we slid smoothly along over the plains, through thin—not thick—forests of great melancholy gum trees, with trunks rugged with curled sheets of flaking bark—erysipelas convalescents, so to speak, shedding their dead skins. And all along were tiny cabins, built sometimes of wood, sometimes of gray-blue corrugated iron; and the doorsteps and fences were clogged with children—rugged little simply clad chaps that looked as if they had been imported from the banks of the Mississippi without breaking bulk.

And there were little villages, with neat stations well placarded with showy advertisements—mainly of almost *too*

self-righteous brands of "sheep-dip," if that is the name—
and I think it is. It is a stuff like tar, and is dabbed onto places
where the shearer clips a piece out of the sheep. It bars out
the flies, and has healing properties, and a nip to it which
makes the sheep skip like the cattle on a thousand hills. It is
not good to eat. That is, it is not good to eat except when
mixed with railroad coffee. It improves railroad coffee. Without it railroad coffee is too vague. But with it, it is quite
assertive and enthusiastic. By itself, railroad coffee is too
passive; but sheep-dip makes it wake up and get down to
business. I wonder where they get railroad coffee?

We saw birds, but not a kangaroo, not an emu, not an
ornithorhyncus, not a lecturer, not a native. Indeed, the land
seemed quite destitute of game. But I have misused the word
native. In Australia it is applied to Australian-born whites
only. I should have said that we saw no Aboriginals—no
"blackfellows." And to this day I have never seen one. In the
great museums you will find all the other curiosities, but in
the curio of chiefest interest to the stranger all of them are
lacking. We have at home an abundance of museums, and
not an American Indian in them. It is clearly an absurdity,
but it never struck me before.

Chapter XV

*Truth is stranger than fiction—to some people, but
I am measurably familiar with it.*
            —Pudd'nhead Wilson's New Calendar.

*Truth is stranger than fiction, but it is because Fic-
tion is obliged to stick to possibilities; Truth isn't.*
            —Pudd'nhead Wilson's New Calendar.

THE air was balmy and delicious, the sunshine radiant; it
was a charming excursion. In the course of it we came
to a town whose odd name was famous all over the world a
quarter of a century ago—Wagga-Wagga. This was because
the Tichborne Claimant had kept a butcher-shop there. It was
out of the midst of his humble collection of sausages and tripe
that he soared up into the zenith of notoriety and hung there
in the wastes of space a time, with the telescopes of all nations
leveled at him in unappeasable curiosity—curiosity as to
which of the two long-missing persons he was: Arthur Orton, the mislaid roustabout of Wapping, or Sir Roger Tichborne, the lost heir of a name and estates as old as English
history. We all know now, but not a dozen people knew then;
and the dozen kept the mystery to themselves and allowed the
most intricate and fascinating and marvelous real-life romance that has ever been played upon the world's stage to

unfold itself serenely, act by act, in a British court, by the long and laborious processes of judicial development.

When we recall the details of that great romance we marvel to see what daring chances truth may freely take in constructing a tale, as compared with the poor little conservative risks permitted to fiction. The fiction-artist could achieve no success with the materials of this splendid Tichborne romance. He would have to drop out the chief characters; the public would say such people are impossible. He would have to drop out a number of the most picturesque incidents; the public would say such things could never happen. And yet the chief characters did exist, and the incidents did happen.

It cost the Tichborne estates four hundred thousand dollars to unmask the Claimant and drive him out; and even after the exposure multitudes of Englishmen still believed in him. It cost the British Government another four hundred thousand dollars to convict him of perjury; and after the conviction the same old multitudes still believed in him; and among these believers were many educated and intelligent men; and some of them had personally known the real Sir Roger. The Claimant was sentenced to fourteen years' imprisonment. When he got out of prison he went to New York and kept a whisky saloon in the Bowery for a time, then disappeared from view.

He always claimed to be Sir Roger Tichborne until death called for him. This was but a few months ago—not very much short of a generation since he left Wagga-Wagga to go and possess himself of his estates. On his deathbed he yielded up his secret, and confessed in writing that he was only Arthur Orton, of Wapping, able seaman and butcher—that and nothing more. But it is scarcely to be doubted that there are people whom even his dying confession will not convince. The old habit of assimilating incredibilities must have made strong food a necessity in their case; a weaker article would probably disagree with them.

I was in London when the Claimant stood his trial for perjury. I attended one of his showy evenings in the sumptuous quarters provided for him from the purses of his adherents and well-wishers. He was in evening dress, and I thought him a rather fine and stately creature. There were about twenty-five gentlemen present; educated men, men moving in good society, none of them commonplace; some of them were men of distinction, none of them were obscurities. They were his cordial friends and admirers. It was "S'r Roger," always "S'r Roger," on all hands; no one withheld the title, all turned it from the tongue with unction, and as if it tasted good.

For many years I had had a mystery in stock. Melbourne, and only Melbourne, could unriddle it for me. In 1873 I arrived in London with my wife and young child, and presently received a note from Naples signed by a name not familiar to me. It was not Bascom, and it was not Henry; but I will call it Henry Bascom for convenience' sake. This note, of about six lines, was written on a strip of white paper whose end-edges were ragged. I came to be familiar with those strips in later years. Their size and pattern were always the same. Their contents were usually to the same effect: would I and mine come to the writer's country-place in England on such and such a date, by such and such a train, and stay twelve days and depart by such and such a train at the end of the specified time? A carriage would meet us at the station.

These invitations were always for a long time ahead; if we were in Europe, three months ahead; if we were in America, six to twelve months ahead. They always named the exact date and train for the beginning and also for the end of the visit.

This first note invited us for a date three months in the future. It asked us to arrive by the 4.10 P.M. train from London, August 6th. The carriage would be waiting. The carriage would take us away seven days later—train specified. And there were these words: "Speak to Tom Hughes."

I showed the note to the author of *Tom Brown at Rugby*, and he said:

"Accept, and be thankful."

He described Mr. Bascom as being a man of genius, a man of fine attainments, a choice man in every way, a rare and beautiful character. He said that Bascom Hall was a particularly fine example of the stately manorial mansion of Elizabeth's days, and that it was a house worth going a long way to see—like Knowle; that Mr. B. was of a social disposition, liked the company of agreeable people, and always had samples of the sort coming and going.

We paid the visit. We paid others, in later years—the last one in 1879. Soon after that Mr. Bascom started on a voyage around the world in a steam-yacht—a long and leisurely trip, for he was making collections, in all lands, of birds, butterflies, and such things.

The day that President Garfield was shot by the assassin Guiteau, we were at a little watering-place on Long Island Sound; and in the mail-matter of that day came a letter with the Melbourne postmark on it. It was for my wife, but I recognized Mr. Bascom's handwriting on the envelope, and opened it. It was the usual note—as to paucity of lines—and was written on the customary strip of paper; but there was nothing usual about the contents. The note informed my wife that if it would be any assuagement of her grief to know that her husband's lecture-tour in Australia was a satisfactory venture from the beginning to the end, he, the writer, could testify that such was the case; also, that her husband's untimely death had been mourned by all classes, as she would already know by the press telegrams, long before the reception of this note; that the funeral was attended by the officials of the colonial and city governments; and that while he, the writer, her friend and mine, had not reached Melbourne in time to see the body, he had at least had the sad privilege of acting as one of the pallbearers. Signed, "Henry Bascom."

My first thought was, why didn't he have the coffin opened? He would have seen that the corpse was an impostor, and he could have gone right ahead and dried up the most of those tears, and comforted those sorrowing governments, and sold the remains and sent me the money.

I did nothing about the matter. I had set the law after living lecture-doubles of mine a couple of times in America, and the law had not been able to catch them; others in my trade had tried to catch *their* impostor-doubles and had failed. Then where was the use in harrying a ghost? None—and so I did not disturb it. I had a curiosity to know about that man's lecture-tour and last moments, but that could wait. When I should see Mr. Bascom he would tell me all about it. But he passed from life, and I never saw him again. My curiosity faded away.

However, when I found that I was going to Australia it revived. And naturally: for if the people should say that I was a dull, poor thing compared to what I was before I died, it would have a bad effect on business. Well, to my surprise the Sydney journalists had *never heard of that impostor!* I pressed them, but they were firm—they had never heard of him, and didn't believe in him.

I could not understand it; still, I thought it would all come right in Melbourne. The government would remember; and the other mourners. At the supper of the Institute of Journalists I should find out all about the matter. But no—it turned out that *they* had never heard of it.

So my mystery was a mystery still. It was a great

disappointment. I believed it would never be cleared up—in this life—so I dropped it out of my mind.

But at last! just when I was least expecting it—

However, this is not the place for the rest of it; I shall come to the matter again, in a far-distant chapter.

Chapter XVI

There is a Moral Sense, and there is an Immoral Sense. History shows us that the Moral Sense enables us to perceive morality and how to avoid it, and that the Immoral Sense enables us to perceive immorality and how to enjoy it.
  —Pudd'nhead Wilson's New Calendar.

MELBOURNE spreads around over an immense area of ground. It is a stately city architecturally as well as in magnitude. It has an elaborate system of cable-car service; it has museums, and colleges, and schools, and public gardens, and electricity, and gas, and libraries, and theaters, and mining centers, and wool centers, and centers of the arts and sciences, and boards of trade, and ships, and railroads, and a harbor, and social clubs, and journalistic clubs, and racing clubs, and a squatter club sumptuously housed and appointed, and as many churches and banks as can make a living. In a word, it is equipped with everything that goes to make the modern great city. It is the largest city of Australasia, and fills the post with honor and credit. It has one specialty; this must not be jumbled in with those other things. It is the mitered Metropolitan of the Horse-Racing Cult. Its race-ground is the Mecca of Australasia. On the great annual day of sacrifice—the 5th of November, Guy Fawkes's Day—

business is suspended over a stretch of land and sea as wide as from New York to San Francisco, and deeper than from the northern lakes to the Gulf of Mexico; and every man and woman, of high degree or low, who can afford the expense, put away their other duties and come. They begin to swarm in by ship and rail a fortnight before the day, and they swarm thicker and thicker day after day, until all the vehicles of transportation are taxed to their uttermost to meet the demands of the occasion, and all hotels and lodgings are bulging outward because of the pressure from within. They come a hundred thousand strong, as all the best authorities say, and they pack the spacious grounds and grandstands and make a spectacle such as is never to be seen in Australasia elsewhere.

It is the "Melbourne Cup" that brings this multitude together. Their clothes have been ordered long ago, at unlimited cost, and without bounds as to beauty and magnificence, and have been kept in concealment until now, for unto this day are they consecrate. I am speaking of the *ladies'* clothes; but one might know that.

And so the grand-stands make a brilliant and wonderful spectacle, a delirium of color, a vision of beauty. The champagne flows, everybody is vivacious, excited, happy; everybody bets, and gloves and fortunes change hands right along, all the time. Day after day the races go on, and the fun and the excitement are kept at white heat; and when each day is done, the people dance all night so as to be fresh for the race in the morning. And at the end of the great week the swarms secure lodgings and transportation for next year, then flock away to their remote homes and count their gains and losses, and order next year's Cup clothes, and then lie down and sleep two weeks, and get up sorry to reflect that a whole year must be put in somehow or other before they can be wholly happy again.

The Melbourne Cup is the Australasian National Day.

It would be difficult to overstate its importance. It overshadows all other holidays and specialized days of whatever sort in that congeries of colonies. Overshadows them? I might almost say it blots them out. Each of them gets attention, but not everybody's; each of them evokes interest, but not everybody's; each of them rouses enthusiasm, but not everybody's; in each case a part of the attention, interest, and enthusiasm is a matter of habit and custom, and another part of it is official and perfunctory. Cup Day, and Cup Day only, commands an attention, an interest, and an enthusiasm which are universal—and spontaneous, not perfunctory. Cup Day is supreme—it has no rival. I can call to mind no specialized annual day, in any country, which can be named by that large name—Supreme. I can call to mind no specialized annual day, in any country, whose approach fires the whole land with a conflagration of conversation and preparation and anticipation and jubilation. No day save this one; but this one does it.

In America we have no annual supreme day; no day whose approach makes the whole nation glad. We have the Fourth of July, and Christmas, and Thanksgiving. Neither of them can claim the primacy; neither of them can arouse an enthusiasm which comes near to being universal. Eight grown Americans out of ten dread the coming of the Fourth, with its pandemonium and its perils, and they rejoice when it is gone—if still alive. The approach of Christmas brings harassment and dread to many excellent people. They have to buy a cart-load of presents, and they never know what to buy to hit the various tastes; they put in three weeks of hard and anxious work, and when Christmas morning comes they are so dissatisfied with the result, and so disappointed that they want to sit down and cry. Then they give thanks that Christmas comes but once a year. The observance of Thanksgiving Day—as a function—has become general of late years.

The Thankfulness is not so general. This is natural. Two-thirds of the nation have always had hard luck and a hard time during the year, and this has a calming effect upon their enthusiasm.

We *have* a supreme day—a sweeping and tremendous and tumultuous day, a day which commands an absolute universality of interest and excitement; but it is not annual. It comes but once in four years; therefore it cannot count as a rival of the Melbourne Cup.

In Great Britain and Ireland they have two great days—Christmas and the Queen's birthday. But they are equally popular; there is no supremacy.

I think it must be conceded that the position of the Australasian Day is unique, solitary, unfellowed; and likely to hold that high place a long time.

The things which interest us when we travel are, first, the people; next, the novelties; and finally the history of the places and countries visited. Novelties are rare in cities which represent the most advanced civilization of the modern day. When one is familiar with such cities in the other parts of the world he is in effect familiar with the cities of Australasia. The outside aspects will furnish little that is new. There will be new names, but the things which they represent will sometimes be found to be less new than their names. There may be shades of difference, but these can easily be too fine for detection by the incompetent eye of the passing stranger. In the larrikin he will not be able to discover a new species, but only an old one met elsewhere, and variously called loafer, rough, tough, bummer, or blatherskite, according to his geographical distribution. The larrikin differs by a shade from those others, in that he is more sociable toward the stranger than they, more kindly disposed, more hospitable, more hearty, more friendly. At least it seemed so to me, and I had opportunity to observe. In Sydney, at least. In Melbourne I had to drive to and from the lecture-theater, but in Sydney I was able to walk both ways, and did it. Every night, on my way home at ten, or a quarter past, I found the larrikin grouped in considerable force at several of the street-corners, and he always gave me this pleasant salutation:

"Hello, Mark!"

"Here's to you, old chap!"

"Say—Mark!—is he dead?"—a reference to a passage in some book of mine, though I did not detect, at that time, that that was its source. And I didn't detect it afterward in Melbourne, when I came on the stage for the first time, and the same question was dropped down upon me from the dizzy height of the gallery. It is always difficult to answer a sudden inquiry like that, when you have come unprepared and don't know what it means. I will remark here—if it is not an indecorum—that the welcome which an American lecturer gets from a British colonial audience is a thing which will move him to his deepest deeps, and veil his sight and break his voice. And from Winnipeg to Africa, experience will teach him nothing; he will never learn to expect it, it will catch him as a surprise each time. The war-cloud hanging black over England and America made no trouble for me. I was a prospective prisoner of war, but at dinners, suppers, on the platform, and elsewhere, there was never anything to remind me of it. This was hospitality of the right metal, and would have been prominently lacking in some countries, in the circumstances.

And speaking of the war-flurry, it seemed to me to bring to light the unexpected, in a detail or two. It seemed to relegate the war-talk to the politicians on both sides of the water; whereas whenever a prospective war between two nations had been in the air theretofore, the public had done most of the talking and the bitterest. The attitude of the newspapers was new also. I speak of those of Australasia and

India, for I had access to those only. They treated the subject argumentatively and with dignity, not with spite and anger. That was a new spirit, too, and not learned of the French and German press, either before Sedan or since. I heard many public speeches, and they reflected the moderation of the journals. The outlook is that the English-speaking race will dominate the earth a hundred years from now, if its sections do not get to fighting each other. It would be a pity to spoil that prospect by baffling and retarding wars when arbitration would settle their differences so much better and also so much more definitely.

No, as I have suggested, novelties are rare in the great capitals of modern times. Even the wool exchange in Melbourne could not be told from the familiar stock exchange of other countries. Wool-brokers are just like stock-brokers; they all bounce from their seats and put up their hands and yell in unison—no stranger can tell what—and the president calmly says—"Sold to Smith & Co., threppence farthing—next!"—when probably nothing of the kind happened; for how should he know?

In the museums you will find acres of the most strange and fascinating things; but all museums are fascinating, and they do so tire your eyes, and break your back, and burn out your vitalities with their consuming interest. You always say you will never go again, but you do go. The palaces of the rich, in Melbourne, are much like the palaces of the rich in America, and the life in them is the same; but there the resemblance ends. The grounds surrounding the American palace are not often large, and not often beautiful, but in the Melbourne case the grounds are often ducally spacious, and the climate and the gardeners together make them as beautiful as a dream. It is said that some of the country-seats have grounds—domains—about them which rival in charm and magnitude those which surround the country mansion of an

English lord; but I was not out in the country; I had my hands full in town.

And what was the origin of this majestic city and its efflorescence of palatial town houses and country-seats? Its first brick was laid and its first house built by a passing convict. Australian history is almost always picturesque; indeed, it is so curious and strange, that it is itself the chiefest novelty the country has to offer, and so it pushes the other novelties into second and third place. It does not read like history, but like the most beautiful lies. And all of a fresh new sort, no moldy old stale ones. It is full of surprises, and adventures, and incongruities, and contradictions, and incredibilities; but they are all true, they all happened.

Chapter XVII

*The English are mentioned in the Bible: Blessed
are the meek, for they shall inherit the earth.
—Pudd'nhead Wilson's New Calendar.*

WHEN we consider the immensity of the British Empire
in territory, population, and trade, it requires a stern
exercise of faith to believe in the figures which represent
Australasia's contribution to the Empire's commercial gran-
deur. As compared with the landed estate of the British Empire, the landed estate dominated by any other Power except
one—Russia—is not very impressive for size. My authorities
make the British Empire not much short of a fourth larger
than the Russian Empire. Roughly proportioned, if you will
allow your entire hand to represent the British Empire, you
may then cut off the fingers a trifle above the middle joint of
the middle finger, and what is left of the hand will represent
Russia. The populations ruled by Great Britain and China are
about the same—400,000,000 each. No other Power approaches these figures. Even Russia is left far behind.

The population of Australasia—4,000,000—sinks into
nothingness, and is lost from sight in that British ocean of

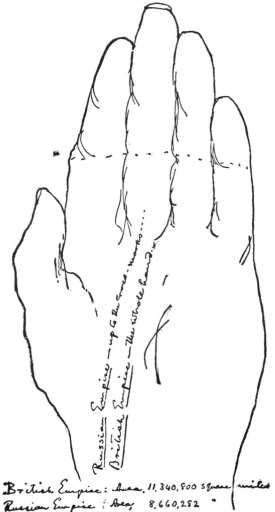

Russian Empire — up to the same marks...
British Empire — The whole hand

British Empire: Area, 11,340,800 square miles
Russian Empire: Area, 8,660,282 "

400,000,000. Yet the statistics indicate that it rises again and shows up very conspicuously when its share of the Empire's commerce is the matter under consideration. The value of England's annual exports and imports is stated at three billions of dollars,[1] and it is claimed that more than one-tenth of this great aggregate is represented by Australasia's exports to England and imports from England.[2] In addition to this, Australasia does a trade with countries other than England, amounting to $100,000,000 a year, and a domestic intercolonial trade amounting to $150,000,000.[2]

In round numbers the 4,000,000 buy and sell about $600,000,000 worth of goods a year. It is claimed that about half of this represents commodities of Australasian production. The products exported annually by India are worth a trifle over $500,000,000.[1] Now, here are some faith-straining figures:

Indian production (300,000,000 population), $500,000,000.

Australasian production (4,000,000 population), $300,000,000.

That is to say, the product of the individual Indian, annually (for export some whither), is worth $1.75; that of the individual Australasian (for export some whither), $75! Or, to put it in another way, the Indian family of man and wife and three children sends away an annual result worth $8.75, while the Australasian family sends away $375 worth.

There are trustworthy statistics furnished by Sir Richard Temple and others, which show that the individual Indian's whole annual product, both for export and home use, is worth in gold only $7.50; or, $37.50 for the family-aggregate. Ciphered out on a like ratio of multiplication, the Australasian family's aggregate production would be nearly $1,600.

[1] New South Wales Blue Book.
[2] D. M. Luckie.

Truly, nothing is so astonishing as figures, if they once get started.

We left Melbourne by rail for Adelaide, the capital of the vast province of South Australia—a seventeen-hour excursion. On the train we found several Sydney friends; among them a Judge who was going out on circuit, and was going to hold court at Broken Hill, where the celebrated silver-mine is. It seemed a curious road to take to get to that region. Broken Hill is close to the western border of New South Wales, and Sydney is on the eastern border. A fairly straight line, seven hundred miles long, drawn westward from Sydney, would strike Broken Hill, just as a somewhat shorter one drawn west from Boston would strike Buffalo. The way the Judge was traveling would carry him over two thousand miles by rail, he said; southwest from Sydney down to Melbourne, then northward up to Adelaide, then a cant back northeastward and over the border into New South Wales once more—to Broken Hill. It was like going from Boston southwest to Richmond, Virginia, then northwest up to Erie, Pennsylvania, then a cant back northeast and over the border—to Buffalo, New York.

But the explanation was simple. Years ago the fabulously rich silver discovery at Broken Hill burst suddenly upon an unexpectant world. Its stocks started at shillings, and went by leaps and bounds to the most fanciful figures. It was one of those cases where the cook puts a month's wages into shares, and comes next month and buys your house at your own price, and moves into it herself; where the coachman takes a few shares, and next month sets up a bank; and where the common sailor invests the price of a spree, and the next month buys out the steamship company and goes into business on his own hook. In a word, it was one of those excitements which bring multitudes of people to a common center with a rush, and whose needs must be supplied, and at once.

MARK TWAIN

Adelaide was close by, Sydney was far away. Adelaide threw a short railway across the border before Sydney had time to arrange for a long one; it was not worth while for Sydney to arrange at all. The whole vast trade-profit of Broken Hill fell into Adelaide's hands, irrevocably. New South Wales furnishes law for Broken Hill and sends her Judges two thousand miles—mainly through alien countries—to administer it, but Adelaide takes the dividends and makes no moan.

We started at four-twenty in the afternoon, and moved across level plains until night. In the morning we had a stretch of "scrub" country—the kind of thing which is so useful to the Australian novelist. In the scrub the hostile aboriginal lurks, and flits mysteriously about, slipping out from time to time to surprise and slaughter the settler; then slipping back again, and leaving no track that the white man can follow. In the scrub the novelist's heroine gets lost, search fails of result; she wanders here and there, and finally sinks down exhausted and unconscious, and the searchers pass within a yard or two of her, not suspecting that she is near, and by and by some rambler finds her bones and the pathetic diary which she had scribbled with her failing hand and left behind. Nobody can find a lost heroine in the scrub but the aboriginal "tracker," and he will not lend himself to the scheme if it will interfere with the novelist's plot. The scrub stretches miles and miles in all directions, and looks like a level roof of bush-tops without a break or a crack in it—as seamless as a blanket, to all appearance. One might as well walk under water and hope to guess out a route and stick to it, I should think. Yet it is claimed that the aboriginal "tracker" was able to hunt out people lost in the scrub. Also in the "bush"; also in the desert; and even follow them over patches of bare rocks and over alluvial ground which had to all appearance been washed clear of footprints.

From reading Australian books and talking with the people, I became convinced that the aboriginal tracker's performances evince a craft, a penetration, a luminous sagacity, and a minuteness and accuracy of observation in the matter of detective work not found in nearly so remarkable a degree in any other people, white or colored. In an official account of the blacks of Australia published by the government of Victoria, one reads that the aboriginal not only notices the faint marks left on the bark of a tree by the claws of a climbing opossum, but knows in some way or other whether the marks were made to-day or yesterday.

And there is the case, on record, where A, a settler, makes a bet with B, that B may lose a cow as effectually as he can, and A will produce an aboriginal who will find her. B selects a cow and lets the tracker see the cow's footprint, then be put under guard. B then drives the cow a few miles over the course which drifts in all directions, and frequently doubles back upon itself; and he selects difficult ground all the time, and once or twice even drives the cow through herds of other cows, and mingles her tracks in the wide confusion of theirs. He finally brings his cow home; the aboriginal is set at liberty, and at once moves around in a great circle, examining all cow-tracks until he finds the one he is after; then sets off and follows it throughout its erratic course, and ultimately tracks it to the stable where B has hidden the cow. Now wherein does one cow-track differ from another? There must be a difference, or the tracker could not have performed the feat; a difference minute, shadowy, and not detectible by you or me, or by the late Sherlock Holmes, and yet discernible by a member of a race charged by some people with occupying the bottom place in the gradations of human intelligence.

Chapter XVIII

It is easier to stay out than get out.
—Pudd'nhead Wilson's New Calendar.

THE train was now exploring a beautiful hill country, and went twisting in and out through lovely little green valleys. There were several varieties of gum trees; among them many giants. Some of them were bodied and barked like the sycamore; some were of fantastic aspect, and reminded one of the quaint apple trees in Japanese pictures. And there was one peculiarly beautiful tree whose name and breed I did not know. The foliage seemed to consist of big bunches of pine spines, the lower half of each bunch a rich brown or old-gold color, the upper half a most vivid and strenuous and shouting green. The effect was altogether bewitching. The tree was apparently rare. I should say that the first and last samples of it seen by us were not more than half an hour apart. There was another tree of striking aspect, a kind of pine, we were told. Its foliage was as fine as hair, apparently, and its mass sphered itself above the naked straight stem like an explosion of misty smoke. It was not a sociable sort; it did not gather in groups or couples, but each individual stood far away from its nearest neighbor. It scattered itself in this spacious and exclusive fashion about the slopes of swelling grassy great knolls, and stood in the full flood of the wonderful sunshine; and as far as you could see the tree itself you could also see the ink-black blot of its shadow on the shining green carpet at its feet.

On some part of this railway journey we saw gorse and broom—importations from England—and a gentleman who came into our compartment on a visit tried to tell me which was which; but as he didn't know, he had difficulty. He said he was ashamed of his ignorance, but that he had never been confronted with the question before during the fifty years and more that he had spent in Australia, and so he had never happened to get interested in the matter. But there was no need to be ashamed. The most of us have his defect. We take a natural interest in novelties, but it is against nature to take an interest in familiar things. The gorse and the broom were a fine accent in the landscape. Here and there they burst out in sudden conflagrations of vivid yellow against a background of sober or somber color, with a so startling effect as to make a body catch his breath with the happy surprise of it. And then there was the wattle, a native bush or tree, an inspiring cloud of sumptuous yellow bloom. It is a favorite with the Australians, and has a fine fragrance, a quality usually wanting in Australian blossoms.

The gentleman who enriched me with the poverty of his information about the gorse and the broom told me that he came out from England a youth of twenty and entered the province of South Australia with thirty-six shillings in his pocket—an adventurer without trade, profession, or friends, but with a clearly defined purpose in his head: he would stay until he was worth £200, then go back home. He would allow himself five years for the accumulation of this fortune.

"That was more than fifty years ago," said he. "And here I am, yet."

As he went out at the door he met a friend, and turned and introduced him to me, and the friend and I had a talk and a smoke. I spoke of the previous conversation and said there was something very pathetic about this half-century of exile, and that I wished the £200 scheme had succeeded.

"With *him*? Oh, it did. It's not so sad a case. He is modest, and he left out some of the particulars. The lad reached South Australia just in time to help discover the Burra-Burra copper-mines. They turned out £700,000 in the first three years. Up to now they have yielded £20,000,000. He has had his share. Before that boy had been in the country two years he could have gone home and bought a village; he could go now and buy a city, I think. No, there is nothing very pathetic about his case. He and his copper arrived at just a handy time to save South Australia. It had got mashed pretty flat under the collapse of a land boom a while before."

There it is again; picturesque history—Australia's specialty. In 1829 South Australia hadn't a white man in it. In 1836 the British Parliament erected it—still a solitude—into a province, and gave it a governor and other governmental machinery. Speculators took hold, now, and inaugurated a vast land scheme, and invited immigration, encouraging it with lurid promises of sudden wealth. It was well worked in London; and bishops, statesmen, and all sorts of people made a rush for the land company's shares. Immigrants soon began to pour into the region of Adelaide and select town lots and farms in the sand and the mangrove swamps by the sea. The crowds continued to come, prices of land rose high, then higher and still higher, everybody was prosperous and happy, the boom swelled into gigantic proportions. A village of sheet-iron huts and clapboard sheds sprang up in the sand, and in these wigwams fashion made display; richly dressed ladies played on costly pianos, London swells in evening dress and patent-leather boots were abundant, and this fine society drank champagne, and in other ways conducted itself in this capital of humble sheds as it had been accustomed to do in the aristocratic quarters of the metropolis of the world. The provincial government put up expensive buildings for its own use, and a palace with gardens for the use of its governor. The governor had a guard, and maintained a court. Roads, wharves, and hospitals were built. All this on credit, on paper, on wind, on inflated and fictitious values—on the boom's moonshine, in fact.

This went on handsomely during four or five years. Then all of a sudden came a smash. Bills for a huge amount drawn by the governor upon the Treasury were dishonored, the land company's credit went up in smoke, a panic followed, values fell with a rush, the frightened immigrants seized their grip-sacks and fled to other lands, leaving behind them a good imitation of a solitude, where lately had been a buzzing and populous hive of men.

Adelaide was indeed almost empty; its population had fallen to three thousand. During two years or more the death-trance continued. Prospect of revival there was none; hope of it ceased. Then, as suddenly as the paralysis had come, came the resurrection from it. Those astonishingly rich copper-mines were discovered, and the corpse got up and danced.

The wool production began to grow; grain-raising followed—followed so vigorously, too, that four or five years after the copper discovery, this little colony, which had had to import its breadstuffs formerly, and pay hard prices for them—once fifty dollars a barrel for flour—had become an exporter of grain. The prosperities continued. After many years, Providence, desiring to show especial regard for New South Wales and exhibit a loving interest in its welfare which should certify to all nations the recognition of that colony's conspicuous righteousness and distinguished well-deserving, conferred upon it that treasury of inconceivable riches, Broken Hill; and South Australia went over the border and took it, giving thanks.

Among our passengers was an American with a unique vocation. Unique is a strong word, but I use it justifiably if I did not misconceive what the American told me; for I understood him to say that in the world there was not another man engaged in the business which he was following. He was buying the kangaroo-skin crop; buying all of it, both the Australian crop and the Tasmanian; and buying it for an American house in New York. The prices were not high, as there was no competition, but the year's aggregate of skins would cost him thirty thousand pounds. I had had the idea that the kangaroo was about extinct in Tasmania and well thinned out on the continent. In America the skins are tanned and made into shoes. After the tanning, the leather takes a new name—which I have forgotten—I only remember that the new name does not indicate that the kangaroo furnishes the leather. There was a German competition for a while, some years ago, but that has ceased. The Germans failed to arrive at the secret of tanning the skins successfully, and they withdrew from the business. Now then, I suppose that I have seen a man whose occupation is really entitled to bear that high epithet—unique. And I suppose that there is not another occupation in the world that is restricted to the hands of a sole person. I can think of no instance of it. There is more than one Pope, there is more than one Emperor, there is even more than one living god, walking upon the earth and worshiped in all sincerity by large populations of men. I have seen and talked with two of these Beings myself in India, and I have the autograph of one of them. It can come good, by and by, I reckon, if I attach it to a "permit."

Approaching Adelaide we dismounted from the train, as

the French say, and were driven in an open carriage over the hills and along their slopes to the city. It was an excursion of an hour or two, and the charm of it could not be overstated, I think. The road wound around gaps and gorges, and offered all varieties of scenery and prospect—mountains, crags, country homes, gardens, forests—color, color, color every-where, and the air fine and fresh, the skies blue, and not a shred of cloud to mar the downpour of the brilliant sunshine. And finally the mountain gateway opened, and the immense plain lay spread out below and stretching away into dim distances on every hand, soft and delicate and dainty and beautiful. On its near edge reposed the city.

We descended and entered. There was nothing to remind one of the humble capital of huts and sheds of the long-vanished day of the land-boom. No, this was a modern city, with wide streets, compactly built; with fine homes everywhere, em-bowered in foliage and flowers, and with imposing masses of public buildings nobly grouped and architecturally beautiful.

There was prosperity in the air; for another boom was on. Providence, desiring to show especial regard for the neighboring colony on the west—called Western Australia—and exhibit a loving interest in its welfare which should certify to all nations the recognition of that colony's conspicuous righteousness and distinguished well-deserving, had recently conferred upon it that majestic treasury of golden riches, Coolgardie; and now South Australia had gone around the corner and taken it, giving thanks. Everything comes to him who is patient and good, and waits.

But South Australia deserves much, for apparently she is a hospitable home for every alien who chooses to come; and for his religion, too. She has a population, as per the latest census, of only three hundred and twenty thousand odd, and yet her varieties of religion indicate the presence within her borders of samples of people from pretty nearly every part of the globe you can think of. Tabulated, these varieties of religion make a remarkable show. One would have to go far to find its match. I copy here this cosmopolitan curiosity, and it comes from the published census:

Church of England	89,271
Roman Catholic	47,179
Wesleyan	49,159
Lutheran	23,328
Presbyterian	18,206
Congregationalist	11,882
Bible Christian	15,762
Primitive Methodist	11,654
Baptist	17,547
Christian Brethren	465
Methodist New Connexion	39
Unitarian	688
Church of Christ	3,367
Society of Friends	100
Salvation Army	4,356
New Jerusalem Church	168
Jews	840
Protestants (undefined)	5,532
Mohammedans	299
Confucians, etc.	3,884
Other religions	1,719
Object	6,940
Not stated	8,046
Total	320,431

The item in the above list "Other religions" includes the following as returned:

Agnostics	50
Atheists	22

Believers in Christ 4
Buddhists 52
Calvinists 46
Christadelphians 134
Christians 308
Christ's Chapel 9
Christian Israelites 2
Christian Socialists 6
Church of God 6
Cosmopolitans 3
Deists 14
Evangelists 60
Exclusive Brethren 8
Free Church 21
Free Methodists 5
Free-thinkers 258
Followers of Christ 8
Gospel Meetings 11
Greek Church 44
Infidels 9
Maronites 2
Mennonists 1
Moravians 139
Mormons 4
Naturalists 2
Orthodox 4
Others (indefinite) 17
Pagans 20
Pantheists 3
Plymouth Brethren 111
Rationalists 4
Reformers 7
Secularists 12
Seventh-day Adventists 203
Shaker 1
Shintoists 24

About sixty-four roads to the other world. You see how healthy the religious atmosphere is. Anything can live in it. Agnostics, Atheists, Free-thinkers, Infidels, Mormons, Pagans, Indefinites: they are all there. And all the big sects of the world can do more than merely live in it: they can spread, flourish, prosper. All except the Spiritualists and the Theosophists. That is the most curious feature of this curious table. What is the matter with the specter? Why do they puff him away? He is a welcome toy everywhere else in the world.

Chapter XIX

Pity is for the living, envy is for the dead.
             —Pudd'nhead Wilson's New Calender.

THE successor of the sheet-iron hamlet of the mangrove marshes has that other Australian specialty, the Botanical Gardens. We cannot have these paradises. The best we could do would be to cover a vast acreage under glass and apply steam heat. But it would be inadequate, the lacks would still be so great: the confined sense, the sense of suffocation, the atmospheric dimness, the sweaty heat—these would all be there, in place of the Australian openness to the sky, the sunshine, and the breeze. Whatever will grow under glass with us will flourish rampantly out-of-doors in Australia.[1] When the white man came the continent was nearly as poor, in variety of vegetation, as the desert of Sahara; now it has everything that grows on the earth. In fact, not Australia only, but all Australasia has levied tribute upon the flora of

---

[1] The greatest heat in Victoria, that there is an authoritative record of, was at Sandhurst, in January, 1862. The thermometer then registered 117 degrees in the shade. In January, 1880, the heat at Adelaide, South Australia, was 172 degrees in the sun.

the rest of the world; and wherever one goes the results appear, in gardens private and public, in the woodsy walls of the highways, and in even the forests. If you see a curious or beautiful tree or bush or flower, and ask about it, the people, answering, usually name a foreign country as the place of its origin—India, Africa, Japan, China, England, America, Java, Sumatra, New Guinea, Polynesia, and so on.

In the Zoological Gardens of Adelaide I saw the only laughing jackass that ever showed any disposition to be courteous to me. This one opened his head wide and laughed like a demon; or like a maniac who was consumed with humorous scorn over a cheap and degraded pun. It was a very human laugh. If he had been out of sight I could have believed that the laughter came from a man. It is an odd-looking bird, with a head and beak that are much too large for its body. In time man will exterminate the rest of the wild creatures of Australia, but this one will probably survive, for man is his friend and lets him alone. Man always has a good reason for his charities toward wild things, human or animal—when he has any. In this case the bird is spared because he kills snakes. If L. J. will take my advice he will not kill all of them.

In that garden I also saw the wild Australian dog—the dingo. He was a beautiful creature—shapely, graceful, a little wolfish in some of his aspects, but with a most friendly eye and sociable disposition. The dingo is not an importation; he was present in great force when the whites first came to the continent. It may be that he is the oldest dog in the universe; his origin, his descent, the place where his ancestors first appeared, are as unknown and as untraceable as are the camel's. He is the most precious dog in the world, for he does not bark. But in an evil hour he got to raiding the sheep-runs to appease his hunger, and that sealed his doom. He is hunted, now, just as if he were a wolf. He has been sentenced to extermination, and the sentence will be carried out. This is all right, and not objectionable. The world was made for man—the white man.

South Australia is confusingly named. All of the colonies have a southern exposure except one—Queensland. Properly speaking, South Australia is *middle* Australia. It extends straight up through the center of the continent like the middle board in a center-table. It is two thousand miles high, from south to north, and about a third as wide. A wee little spot down in its southeastern corner contains eight or nine tenths of its population; the other one or two tenths are elsewhere— as elsewhere as they could be in the United States with all the country between Denver and Chicago, and Canada and the Gulf of Mexico to scatter over. There is plenty of room.

A telegraph line stretches straight up north through that two thousand miles of wilderness and desert from Adelaide to Port Darwin on the edge of the upper ocean. South Australia built the line; and did it in 1871–72 when her population numbered only one hundred and eighty-five thousand. It was a great work; for there were no roads, no paths; thirteen hundred miles of the route had been traversed but once before by white men; provisions, wire, and poles had to be carried over immense stretches of desert; wells had to be dug along the route to supply the men and cattle with water.

A cable had been previously laid from Port Darwin to Java and thence to India, and there was telegraphic communication with England from India. And so, if Adelaide could make connection with Port Darwin it meant connection with the whole world. The enterprise succeeded. One could watch the London markets daily, now; the profit to the wool-growers of Australia was instant and enormous.

A telegram from Melbourne to San Francisco covers .approximately twenty thousand miles—the equivalent of five-sixths of the way around the globe. It has to halt along the way a good many times and be repeated; still, but little time is lost. These halts, and the distances between them, are here tabulated.[1]

	Miles
Melbourne—Mount Gambier.	300
Mount Gambier—Adelaide	270
Adelaide—Port Augusta	200
Port Augusta—Alice Springs	1,036
Alice Springs—Port Darwin	898
Port Darwin—Banjoewangie	1,150
Banjoewangie—Batavia	480
Batavia—Singapore	553
Singapore—Penang	399
Penang—Madras	1,280
Madras—Bombay	650
Bombay—Aden	1,662
Aden—Suez	1,346
Suez—Alexandria	224
Alexandria—Malta	828
Malta—Gibraltar	1,008
Gibraltar—Falmouth	1,061
Falmouth—London	350
London—New York	2,500
New York—San Francisco	3,500

I was in Adelaide again, some months later, and saw the multitudes gather in the neighboring city of Glenelg to commemorate the Reading of the Proclamation—in 1836— which founded the Province. If I have at any time called it a Colony, I withdraw the discourtesy. It is not a Colony, it is a Province; and officially so. Moreover, it is the only one so named in Australasia. There was great enthusiasm; it was the Province's national holiday, its Fourth of July, so to speak.

[1]From *Round the Empire* (George R. Parkin), all but the last two.

It is the pre-eminent holiday; and that is saying much, in a country where they seem to have a most un-English mania for holidays. Mainly they are working-men's holidays; for in South Australia the working-man is sovereign; his vote is the desire of the politician—indeed, it is the very breath of the politician's being; the parliament exists to deliver the will of the working-man, and the Government exists to execute it. The working-man is a great power everywhere in Australia, but South Australia is his paradise. He has had a hard time in this world, and has earned a paradise. I am glad he has found it. The holidays there are frequent enough to be bewildering to the stranger. I tried to get the hang of the system, but was not able to do it.

You have seen that the Province is tolerant, religious-wise. It is so politically, also. One of the speakers at the Commemoration banquet—the Minister of Public Works—was an American, born and reared in New England. There is nothing narrow about the Province, politically, or in any other way that I know of. Sixty-four religions and a Yankee cabinet minister. No amount of horse-racing can damn this community.

The mean temperature of the Province is sixty-two degrees. The death-rate is thirteen in the one thousand—about half what it is in the city of New York, I should think, and New York is a healthy city. Thirteen is the death-rate for the average citizen of the Province, but there seems to be no death-rate for the old people. There were people at the Commemoration banquet who could remember Cromwell. There were six of them. These Old Settlers had all been present at the original Reading of the Proclamation, in 1836. They showed signs of the blightings and blastings of time, in their outward aspect, but they were young within; young and cheerful, and ready to talk; ready to talk, and talk all you wanted; in their turn, and out of it. They were down for six

THE OLD SETTLERS

speeches, and they made forty-two. The governor and the cabinet and the mayor were down for forty-two speeches, and they made six. They have splendid grit, the Old Settlers, splendid staying power. But they do not hear well, and when they see the mayor going through motions which they recognize as the introducing of a speaker, they think they are the one, and they all get up together, and begin to respond, in the most animated way; and the more the mayor gesticulates, and shouts "Sit down! Sit down!" the more they take it for applause, and the more excited and reminiscent and enthusiastic they get; and next, when they see the whole house laughing and crying, three of them think it is about the bitter old-time hardships they are describing, and the other three think the laughter is caused by the jokes they have been uncorking—jokes of the vintage of 1836—and then the way they *do* go on! And finally when ushers come and plead, and beg, and gently and reverently crowd them down into their seats, they say, "Oh, I'm not tired—I could bang along a week!" and they sit there looking simple and childlike, and gentle, and proud of their oratory, and wholly unconscious of what is going on at the other end of the room. And so one of the great dignitaries gets a chance, and begins his carefully prepared speech, impressively and with solemnity:

> When we, now great and prosperous and powerful, bow our heads in reverent wonder in the contemplation of those sublimities of energy, of wisdom, of forethought, of—

Up come the immortal six again, in a body, with a joyous "Hey, I've thought of another one!" and at it they go, with might and main, hearing not a whisper of the pandemonium that salutes them, but taking all the visible violences for applause, as before, and hammering joyously away till the imploring ushers pray them into their seats again. And a pity, too; for those lovely old boys did so enjoy living their heroic youth over, in these days of their honored antiquity; and certainly the things they had to tell were usually worth the telling and the hearing.

It was a stirring spectacle; stirring in more ways than one, for it was amazingly funny, and at the same time deeply pathetic; for they had seen so much, these time-worn veterans, and had suffered so much; and had built so strongly and well, and laid the foundations of their commonwealth so deep, in liberty and tolerance; and had lived to see the structure rise to such state and dignity and hear themselves so praised for their honorable work.

One of these old gentlemen told me some things of interest afterward; things about the aboriginals, mainly. He thought them intelligent—remarkably so in some directions—and he said that along with their unpleasant qualities they had some exceedingly good ones; and he considered it a great pity that the race had died out. He instanced their invention of the boomerang and the "weet-weet" as evidences of their brightness; and as another evidence of it he said he had never seen a white man who had cleverness enough to learn to do the miracles with those two toys that the aboriginals achieved. He said that even the smartest whites had been obliged to confess that they could not learn the trick of the boomerang in perfection; that it had possibilities which they could not master. The white man could not control its motions, could not make it obey him; but the aboriginal could. He told me some wonderful things—some almost incredible things—which he had seen the blacks do with the boomerang and the weet-weet. They have been confirmed to me since by other early settlers and by trustworthy books.

It is contended—and may be said to be conceded—that the boomerang was known to certain savage tribes in Europe in Roman times. In support of this, Virgil and two other

Roman poets are quoted. It is also contended that it was known to the ancient Egyptians.

One of two things is then apparent; either some one with a boomerang arrived in Australia in the days of antiquity before European knowledge of the thing had been lost, or the Australian aboriginal re-invented it. It will take some time to find out which of these two propositions is the fact. But there is no hurry.

Chapter XX

FROM DIARY:
        Mr. G. called. I had not seen him since Nauheim, Germany—several years ago; the time that the cholera broke out at Hamburg. We talked of the people we had known there, or had casually met; and G. said:

"Do you remember my introducing you to an earl—the Earl of C.?"

"Yes. That was the last time I saw you. You and he were in a carriage, just starting—belated—for the train. I remember it."

"I remember it too, because of a thing which happened then which I was not looking for. He had told me awhile before about a remarkable and interesting Californian whom he had met and who was a friend of yours, and said that if he should ever meet you he would ask you for some particulars about that Californian. The subject was not mentioned that day at Nauheim, for we were hurrying away, and there was not time; but the thing that surprised me was this: when I introduced you, you said, 'I am glad to meet your lordship—again.' The 'again' was the surprise. He is a little hard of hearing, and didn't catch that word, and I thought you hadn't intended that he should. As we drove off I had only time to say, 'Why, what do you know about him?' and I understood you to say, 'Oh, nothing, except that he is the quickest judge of—' Then we were gone, and I didn't get the rest. I wondered what it was that he was such a quick judge of. I have thought of it many times since, and still wondered what it could be. He and I talked it over, but could not guess it out. He thought it must be fox-hounds or horses, for he is a good judge of those—no one is a better. But *you* couldn't know that, because you didn't know *him*; you had mistaken him for some one else; it must be that, he said, because he knew you had never met him before. And of course you hadn't—had you?"

"Yes, I had."

"Is that so? Where?"

"At a fox-hunt, in England."

"How curious that is. Why, he hadn't the least recollection of it. Had you any conversation with him?"

"Some—yes."

"Well, it left not the least impression upon him. What did you talk about?"

"About the fox. I think that was all."

"Why, *that* would interest him; that ought to have left an impression. What did *he* talk about?"

"The fox."

"It's very curious. I don't understand it. Did what he said leave an impression upon you?"

"Yes. It showed me that he was a quick judge of—however, I will tell you all about it, then you will understand. It was a quarter of a century ago—1873 or '74. I had an

American friend in London named F., who was fond of hunting, and his friends the Blanks invited him and me to come out to a hunt and be their guests at their country place. In the morning the mounts were provided, but when I saw the horses I changed my mind and asked permission to walk. I had never seen an English hunter before, and it seemed to me that I could hunt a fox safer on the ground. I had always been diffident about horses, anyway, even those of the common altitudes, and I did not feel competent to hunt on a horse that went on stilts. So then Mrs. Blank came to my help and said I could go with her in the dog-cart and we would drive to a place she knew of, and there we should have a good glimpse of the hunt as it went by.

"When we got to that place I got out and went and leaned my elbows on a low stone wall which inclosed a turfy and beautiful great field with heavy wood on all its sides except ours. Mrs. Blank sat in the dog-cart fifty yards away, which was as near as she could get with the vehicle. I was full of interest, for I had never seen a fox-hunt. I waited, dreaming and imagining, in the deep stillness and impressive tranquility which reigned in that retired spot. Presently, from away off in the forest on the left, a mellow bugle-note came floating; then all of a sudden a multitude of dogs burst out of that forest and went tearing by and disappeared in the forest on the right; there was a pause, and then a cloud of horsemen in black caps and crimson coats plunged out of the left-hand forest and went flaming across the field like a prairie-fire, a stirring sight to see. There was one man ahead of the rest, and he came spurring straight at me. He was fiercely excited. It was fine to see him ride; he was a master horseman. He came like a storm till he was within seven feet of me, where I was leaning on the wall, then he stood his horse straight up in the air on his hind toe-nails, and shouted like a demon:

" 'Which way'd the fox go?'

"I didn't much like the tone, but I did not let on; for he was excited, you know. But I was calm; so I said softly, and without acrimony:

" '*Which* fox?'

"It seemed to anger him. I don't know why; and he thundered out:

" '*Which* fox? Why, *the* fox! Which way did the *fox* go?'

"I said, with great gentleness—even argumentatively:

" 'If you could be a little more definite—a little less vague—because I am a stranger, and there are many foxes, as you will know even better than I, and unless I know which one it is that you desire to identify, and—'

" 'You're certainly the damnedest idiot that has escaped in a thousand years!' and he snatched his great horse around as easily as I would snatch a cat, and was away like a hurricane. A very excitable man.

"I went back to Mrs. Blank, and *she* was excited, too— oh, all alive. She said:

" 'He *spoke* to you!—*didn't* he?'

" 'Yes, it is what happened.'

" 'I *knew* it! I couldn't hear what he said, but I *knew* he spoke to you! Do you know who it was? It was Lord C.,— and he is Master of the Buckhounds! Tell me—what do you think of him?'

" 'Him? Well, for sizing up a stranger, he's got the most sudden and accurate judgment of any man I ever saw.'

"It pleased her. I thought it would."

G. got away from Nauheim just in time to escape being shut in by the quarantine-bars on the frontiers; and so did we, for we left the next day. But G. had a great deal of trouble in getting by the Italian custom-house, and we should have fared likewise but for the thoughtfulness of our consul-general in Frankfort. He introduced me to the Italian consul-general, and I brought away from that consulate a letter which made our way smooth. It was a dozen lines merely commending me in a general way to the courtesies of servants in his Italian Majesty's service, but it was more powerful than it looked. In addition to a raft of ordinary baggage, we had six or eight trunks which were filled exclusively with dutiable stuff—household goods purchased in Frankfort for use in Florence, where we had taken a house. I was going to ship these through by express; but at the last moment an order went throughout Germany forbidding the moving of any parcels by train unless the owner went with them. This was a bad outlook. We must take these things along, and the delay sure to be caused by the examination of them in the custom-house might lose us our train. I imagined all sorts of terrors, and enlarged them steadily as we approached the Italian frontier. We were six in number, clogged with all that baggage, and I was courier for the party—the most incapable one they ever employed.

We arrived, and pressed with the crowd into the immense custom-house, and the usual worries began; everybody crowding to the center and begging to have his baggage examined first, and all hands clattering and chattering at once. It seemed to me that I could do nothing; it would be better to give it all up and go away and leave the baggage. I couldn't speak the language; I should never accomplish anything. Just then a tall, handsome man in a fine uniform was passing by, and I knew he must be the station-master—and that reminded me of my letter. I ran to him and put it into his hands. He took it out of the envelope, and the moment his eye caught the royal coat of arms printed at its top, he took off his cap and made a beautiful bow to me, and said in English:

"Which is your baggage? Please show it to me."

I showed him the mountain. Nobody was disturbing it; nobody was interested in it; all the family's attempts to get attention to it had failed—except in the case of one of the trunks containing the dutiable goods. It was just being opened. My officer said:

"There, let that alone! Lock it. Now chalk it. Chalk all of the lot. Now please come and show me the hand-baggage."

He plowed through the waiting crowd, I following to the counter, and he gave orders again, in his emphatic military way:

"Chalk these. Chalk *all* of them."

Then he took off his cap and made that beautiful bow again, and went his way. By this time these attentions had attracted the wonder of that acre of passengers, and the whisper had gone around that the royal family were present getting their baggage chalked; and as we passed down in review on our way to the door, I was conscious of a pervading atmosphere of envy which gave me deep satisfaction.

But soon there was an accident. My overcoat pockets were stuffed with German cigars and linen packages of American smoking-tobacco, and a porter was following us around with this overcoat on his arm, and gradually getting it upside down. Just as I, in the rear of my family, moved by the sentinels at the door, about three hatfuls of the tobacco tumbled out on the floor. One of the soldiers pounced upon it, gathered it up in his arms, pointed back whence I had come, and marched me ahead of him past that long wall of passengers again—he chattering and exulting like a devil, they smiling in peaceful joy, and I trying to look as if my pride was not hurt, and as if I did not mind being brought to shame before these pleased people who had so lately envied me. But at heart I was cruelly humbled.

When I had been marched two-thirds of the long distance and the misery of it was at the worst, the stately station-master stepped out from somewhere, and the soldier left me and darted after him and overtook him; and I could see by the soldier's excited gestures that he was betraying to him the whole shabby business. The station-master was plainly very angry. He came striding down toward me, and when he was come near he began to pour out a stream of indignant Italian; then suddenly took off his hat and made that beautiful bow and said:

"Oh, it is *you*! I beg a thousand pardons! This idiot here—" He turned to the exulting soldier and burst out with a flood of white-hot Italian lava, and the next moment he was bowing, and the soldier and I were moving in procession again—*he* in the lead and ashamed, this time, I with my chin up. And so we marched by the crowd of fascinated passengers, and I went forth to the train with the honors of war. Tobacco and all.

Chapter XXI

Man will do many things to get himself loved, he will do all things to get himself envied.
—Pudd'nhead Wilson's New Calendar.

BEFORE I saw Australia I had never heard of the "weet-weet" at all. I met but few men who had seen it thrown— at least I met but few who mentioned having seen it thrown. Roughly described, it is a fat wooden cigar with its butt-end fastened to a flexible twig. The whole thing is only a couple of feet long, and weighs less than two ounces. This feather— so to call it—is not thrown through the air, but is flung with an underhanded throw and made to strike the ground a little way in front of the thrower; then it glances and makes a long skip; glances again, skips again, and again and again, like the flat stone which a boy sends skating over the water. The water is smooth, and the stone has a good chance; so a strong man may make it travel fifty or seventy-five yards; but the weet-weet has no such good chance, for it strikes sand, grass, and earth in its course. Yet an expert aboriginal has sent it a measured distance of *two hundred and twenty yards*. It would have gone even further, but it encountered rank ferns and underwood on its passage and they damaged its speed. Two hundred and twenty yards; and so weightless a toy—a mouse on the end of a bit of wire, in effect; and not sailing through the accommodating air, but encountering grass and sand and stuff at every jump. It looks wholly impossible; but Mr. Brough Smyth saw the feat and did the measuring, and set down the facts in his book about aboriginal life, which he wrote by command of the Victorian Government.

What is the secret of the feat? No one explains. It cannot be physical strength, for that could not drive such a feather-weight any distance. It must be art. But no one explains what the art of it is; nor how it gets around that law of nature which says you shall not throw any two-ounce thing two hundred and twenty yards, either through the air or bumping along the ground. Rev. J. G. Wood says:

> The distance to which the weet-weet or kangaroo-rat can be thrown is truly astonishing. I have seen an Australian stand at one side of Kennington Oval and throw the kangaroo-rat completely across it. [Width of Kennington Oval not stated.] It darts through the air with the sharp and menacing hiss of a rifle-ball, its greatest height from the ground being some seven or eight feet. . . . When properly thrown it looks just like a living animal leaping along. . . . Its movements have a wonderful resemblance to the long leaps of a kangaroo-rat fleeing in alarm, with its long tail trailing behind it.

The Old Settler said that he had seen distances made by the weet-weet, in the early days, which almost convinced him that it was as extraordinary an instrument as the boomerang.

There must have been a large distribution of acuteness among those naked, skinny aboriginals, or they couldn't have been such unapproachable trackers and boomerangers and weet-weeters. It must have been race-aversion that put upon them a good deal of the low-rate intellectual reputation which they bear and have borne this long time in the world's estimate of them.

They were lazy—always lazy. Perhaps that was their trouble. It is a killing defect. Surely they could have invented and built a competent house, but they didn't. And they could have invented and developed the agricultural arts, but they didn't. They went naked and houseless, and lived on fish and grubs and worms and wild fruits, and were just plain savages, for all their smartness.

With a country as big as the United States to live and multiply in, and with no epidemic diseases among them till the white man came with those and his other appliances of civilization, it is quite probable that there was never a day in his history when he could muster one hundred thousand of his race in all Australia. He diligently and deliberately kept population down by infanticide—largely; but mainly by certain other methods. He did not need to practise these artificialities any more after the white man came. The white man knew ways of keeping down population which were worth several of his. The white man knew ways of reducing a native population eighty per cent. in twenty years. The native had never seen anything as fine as that before.

For example, there is the case of the country now called Victoria—a country eighty times as large as Rhode Island, as I have already said. By the best official guess there were forty-five hundred aboriginals in it when the whites came along in the middle of the thirties. Of these one thousand lived in Gippsland, a patch of territory the size of fifteen or sixteen Rhode Islands: they did not diminish as fast as some of the other communities; indeed, at the end of forty years there were still two hundred of them left. The Geelong tribe diminished more satisfactorily: from one hundred and seventy-three persons it faded to thirty-four in twenty years; at the end of another twenty the tribe numbered one person altogether. The two Melbourne tribes could muster almost three hundred when the white man came; they could muster but twenty thirty-seven years later, in 1875. In that year there were still odds and ends of tribes scattered about the colony of Victoria, but I was told that natives of full blood are very scarce now. It is said that the aboriginals continue in some force in the huge territory called Queensland.

The early whites were not used to savages. They could not understand the primary law of savage life: that if a man do you a wrong, his whole tribe is responsible—each individual of it—and you may take your change out of any individual of it, without bothering to seek out the guilty one. When a white killed an aboriginal, the tribe applied the ancient law, and killed the first white they came across. To the whites this was a monstrous thing. Extermination seemed to be the proper medicine for such creatures as this. They did not kill all the blacks, but they promptly killed enough of them to make their own persons safe. From the dawn of civilization down to this day the white man has always used that very precaution. Mrs. Campbell Praed lived in Queensland, as a child, in the early days, and in her *Sketches of Australian Life* we get informing pictures of the early struggles of the white and the black to reform each other.

Speaking of pioneer days in the mighty wilderness of Queensland, Mrs. Praed says:

> At first the natives retreated before the whites; and, except that they every now and then speared a beast in one of the herds, gave little cause for uneasiness. But, as the number of squatters increased, each one taking up miles of country and bringing two or three men in his train, so that shepherds' huts and stockmen's camps lay far apart, and defenseless in the

midst of hostile tribes, the Blacks' depredations became more frequent and murder was no unusual event.

The loneliness of the Australian bush can hardly be painted in words. Here extends mile after mile of primeval forest where perhaps foot of white man has never trod— interminable vistas where the eucalyptus trees rear their lofty trunks and spread forth their lanky limbs, from which the red gum oozes and hangs in fantastic pendants like crimson stalactites; ravines along the sides of which the long-bladed grass grows rankly; level untimbered plains alternating with undulating tracts of pasture, here and there broken by a stony ridge, steep gully, or dried-up creek. All wild, vast, and desolate; all the same monotonous gray coloring, except where the wattle, when in blossom, shows patches of feathery gold, or a belt of scrub lies green, glossy, and impenetrable as Indian jungle.

The solitude seems intensified by the strange sounds of reptiles, birds, and insects, and by the absence of larger creatures; of which in the daytime the only audible signs are the stampede of a herd of kangaroo, or the rustle of a wallabi, or a dingo stirring the grass as it creeps to its lair. But there are the whirring of locusts, the demoniac chuckle of the laughing jackass, the screeching of cockatoos and parrots, the hissing of the frilled lizard, and the buzzing of innumerable insects hidden under the dense undergrowth. And then at night, the melancholy wailing of the curlews, the dismal howling of dingoes, the discordant croaking of tree-frogs, might well shake the nerves of the solitary watcher.

That is the theater for the drama. When you comprehend one or two other details, you will perceive how well suited for trouble it was, and how loudly it invited it. The cattlemen's stations were scattered over that profound wilderness miles and miles apart—at each station half a dozen persons. There was a plenty of cattle, the black natives were always ill-nourished and hungry. The land belonged to *them*. The whites had not bought it, and couldn't buy it; for the tribes had no chiefs, nobody in authority, nobody competent to sell and convey; and the tribes themselves had no comprehension of the idea of transferable ownership of land. The ousted owners. were despised by the white interlopers, and this opinion was not hidden under a bushel. More promising materials for a tragedy could not have been collated. Let Mrs. Praed speak:

> At Nie Nie station, one dark night, the unsuspecting hut-keeper, having, as he believed, secured himself against assault, was lying wrapped in his blankets sleeping profoundly. The Blacks crept stealthily down the chimney and battered in his skull while he slept.

One could guess the whole drama from that little text. The curtain was up. It would not fall until the mastership of one party or the other was determined—and permanently:

> There was treachery on both sides. The Blacks killed the Whites when they found them defenseless, and the Whites slew the Blacks in a wholesale and promiscuous fashion which offended against my childish sense of justice. . . . They were regarded as little above the level of brutes, and in some cases *were destroyed like vermin.*
>
> Here is an instance. A squatter, whose station was sur-rounded by Blacks, whom he suspected to be hostile and from whom he feared an attack, parleyed with them from his house-door. He told them it was Christmas-time—a time at which all men, black or white, feasted; that there were flour, sugar-plums, good things in plenty in the store, and that he would make for them such a pudding as they had never dreamed of—a great pudding of which all might eat and be filled. The Blacks listened and were lost. The pudding was made and distributed. Next morning there was howling in the camp, for it had been sweetened with sugar and arsenic!

The white man's spirit was right, but his method was wrong. His spirit was the spirit which the civilized white has always exhibited toward the savage, but the use of poison was a departure from custom. True, it was merely a technical departure, not a real one; still, it was a departure, and therefore a mistake, in my opinion. It was better, kinder, swifter, and much more humane than a number of the methods which have been sanctified by custom, but that does not justify its employment. That is, it does not wholly justify it. Its unusual nature makes it stand out and attract an amount of attention which it is not entitled to. It takes hold upon morbid imaginations and they work it up into a sort of exhibition of cruelty, and this smirches the good name of our civilization, whereas one of the old harsher methods would have had no such effect because usage has made those methods familiar to us and innocent. In many countries we have chained the savage and starved him to death; and this we do not care for, because custom has inured us to it; yet a quick death by poison is loving-kindness to it. In many countries we have burned the savage at the stake; and this we do not care for, because custom has inured us to it; yet a quick death is loving-kindness to it. In more than one country we have hunted the savage and his little children and their mother with dogs and guns through the woods and swamps for an afternoon's sport, and filled the region with happy laughter over their sprawling and stumbling flight, and their wild supplications for mercy; but this method we do not mind, because custom has inured us to it; yet a quick death by poison is loving-kindness to it. In many countries we have taken the savage's land from him, and made him our slave, and lashed him every day, and broken his pride, and made death his only friend, and overworked him till he dropped in his tracks; and this we do not care for, because custom has inured us to it; yet a quick death by poison is loving-kindness to it. In the Matabeleland today—why, there we are confining ourselves to sanctified custom, we Rhodes-Beit millionaires in South Africa and Dukes in London; and nobody cares, because we are used to the old holy customs, and all we ask is that no notice-inviting new ones shall be intruded upon the attention of our comfortable consciences. Mrs. Praed says of the poisoner, "That squatter deserves to have his name handed down to the contempt of posterity."

I am sorry to hear her say that. I myself blame him for one thing, and severely, but I stop there. I blame him for the indiscretion of introducing a novelty which was calculated to attract attention to our civilization. There was no occasion to do that. It was his duty, and it is every loyal man's duty, to protect that heritage in every way he can; and the best way to do that is to attract attention elsewhere. The squatter's judgment was bad—that is plain; but his heart was right. He is almost the only pioneering representative of civilization in history who has risen above the prejudices of his caste and his heredity and tried to introduce the element of mercy into the superior race's dealings with the savage. His name is lost, and it is a pity; for it deserves to be handed down to posterity with homage and reverence.

This paragraph is from a London journal:

To learn what France is doing to spread the blessings of civilization in her distant dependencies we may turn with advantage to New Caledonia. With a view to attracting free settlers to that penal colony, M. Feillet, the Governor, forcibly expropriated the Kanaka cultivators from the best of their plantations, with a derisory compensation, in spite of the protests of the Council General of the island. Such immigrants as could be induced to cross the seas thus found themselves in possession of thousands of coffee, cocoa, banana, and breadfruit trees, the raising of which had cost the wretched natives years of toil, whilst the latter had a few five-franc pieces to spend in the liquor stores of Noumea.

You observe the combination? It is robbery, humiliation, and slow, slow murder, through poverty and the white man's whisky. The savage's gentle friend, the savage's noble friend, the only magnanimous and unselfish friend the savage has ever had, was not there with the merciful swift release of his poisoned pudding.

There are many humorous things in the world; among them the white man's notion that he is less savage than the other savages.[1]

[1]See Chapter on Tasmania, *post*.

Chapter XXII

Nothing is so ignorant as a man's left hand, except a lady's watch.
  —Pudd'nhead Wilson's New Calendar.

YOU notice that Mrs. Praed knows her art. She can place a thing before you so that you can see it. She is not alone in that. Australia is fertile in writers whose books are faithful mirrors of the life of the country and of its history. The materials were surprisingly rich, both in quality and in mass, and Marcus Clarke, Rolf Boldrewood, Gordon, Kendall, and the others, have built out of them a brilliant and vigorous literature, and one which must endure. Materials—there is no end to them! Why, a literature might be made out of the aboriginal all by himself, his character and ways are so freckled with varieties—varieties not staled by familiarity, but new to us. You do not need to invent any picturesquenesses; whatever you want in that line he can furnish you; and they will not be fancies and doubtful, but realities and authentic. In his history, as preserved by the white man's official records, he is everything—everything that a human creature can be. He covers the entire ground. He is a coward—there are a thousand facts to prove it. He is brave—there are a thousand facts to prove it. He is treacherous—oh, beyond imagination! He is faithful, loyal, true—the white man's records supply you with a harvest of instances of it that are noble, worshipful, and pathetically beautiful. He kills the starving stranger who comes begging for food and shelter— there is proof of it. He succors, and feeds, and guides to safety, to-day, the lost stranger who fired on him only yesterday—there is proof of it. He takes his reluctant bride by force, he courts her with a club, then loves her faithfully through a long life—it is of record. He gathers to himself another wife by the same processes, beats and bangs her as a daily diversion, and by and by lays down his life in defending her from some outside harm—it is of record. He will face a hundred hostiles to rescue one of his children, and will kill another of his children because the family is large enough without it. His delicate stomach turns, at certain details of the white man's food; but he likes over-ripe fish, and braised dog, and cat, and rat, and will eat his own uncle with relish. He is a sociable animal, yet he turns aside and hides behind his shield when his mother-in-law goes by. He is childishly afraid of ghosts and other trivialities that menace his soul, but dread of physical pain is a weakness which he is not acquainted with. He knows all the great and many of the little constellations, and has names for them; he has a symbol-writing by means of which he can convey messages far and wide among the tribes; he has a correct eye for form and expression, and draws a good picture; he can track a fugitive by delicate traces which the white man's eye cannot discern, and by methods which the finest white intelligence cannot master; he makes a missile which science itself cannot duplicate without the model—if with it; a missile whose secret baffled and defeated the searchings and theorizings of the white mathematicians for seventy years; and by an art all his own he performs miracles with it which the white man cannot approach untaught, nor parallel after teaching. Within certain limits this savage's intellect is the alertest and the brightest known to history or tradition; and yet the poor creature was never able to invent a counting system that would reach above five, nor a vessel that he could boil water in. He is the prize-curiosity of all the races. To all intents and purposes he is dead—in the body; but he has features that will live in literature.

Mr. Philip Chauncy, an officer of the Victorian Government, contributed to its archives a report of his personal observations of the aboriginals which has in it some things which I wish to condense slightly and insert here. He speaks of the quickness of their eyes and the accuracy of their judgment of the direction of approaching missiles as being quite extraordinary, and of the answering suppleness and accuracy of limb and muscle in avoiding the missile as being extraordinary also. He has seen an aboriginal stand as a target for cricket-balls thrown with great force ten or fifteen yards, by professional bowlers, and successfully dodge them or parry them with his shield during about half an hour. One of those balls, properly placed, could have killed him; "Yet he depended, with the utmost self-possession, on the quickness of his eye and his agility."

The shield was the customary war-shield of his race, and would not be a protection to you or to me. It is no broader than a stovepipe, and is about as long as a man's arm. The opposing surface is not flat, but slopes away from the center-line like a boat's bow. The difficulty about a cricket-ball that has been thrown with a scientific "twist" is, that it suddenly changes its course when it is close to its target and comes straight for the mark when apparently it was going overhead or to one side. I should not be able to protect myself from such balls for half an hour, or less.

Mr. Chauncy once saw "a little native man" throw a cricket-ball one hundred and nineteen yards. This is said to beat the English professional record by thirteen yards.

We have all seen the circus-man bound into the air from a spring-board and make a somersault over eight horses standing side by side. Mr. Chauncy saw an aboriginal do it over eleven; and was assured that he had sometimes done it over fourteen. But what is that to this:

> I saw the same man leap from the *ground*, and in going over he dipped his head, unaided by his hands, into a hat placed in an inverted position on the top of the head of another man sitting upright on horseback—both man and horse being of the average size. The native landed on the other side of the horse with the hat fairly on his head. The prodigious height of the leap, and the precision with which it was taken so as to enable him to dip his head into the hat, exceeded any feat of the kind I have ever beheld.

I should think so! On board a ship lately I saw a young Oxford athlete *run four steps* and spring into the air and squirm his hips by a side-twist over a bar that was five and one-half feet high; but he could not have stood still and cleared a bar that was *four* feet high. I know this, because I tried it myself.

One can see now where the kangaroo learned its art.

Sir George Grey and Mr. Eyre testify that the native dug wells fourteen or fifteen feet deep and two feet in diameter at the bore—dug them in the *sand*—wells that were "quite circular, carried straight down, and the work beautifully executed."

Their tools were their hands and feet. How did they throw sand out from such a depth? How could they stoop down and get it, with only two feet of space to stoop in? How did they keep that sand-pipe from caving in on them?

I do not know. Still, they did manage those seeming impossibilities. Swallowed the sand, maybe.

Mr. Chauncy speaks highly of the patience and skill and alert intelligence of the native huntsman when he is stalking the emu, the kangaroo, and other game:

> As he walks through the bush his step is light, elastic, and noiseless; every track on the earth catches his keen eye; a leaf, or fragment of a stick turned, or a blade of grass recently bent by the tread of one of the lower animals, instantly arrests his attention; in fact, nothing escapes his quick and powerful sight on the ground, in the trees, or in the distance, which may supply him with a meal or warn him of danger. A little examination of the trunk of a tree which may be nearly covered with the scratches of opossums ascending and descending is sufficient to inform him whether one *went up the night before without coming down again or not.*

Fenimore Cooper lost his chance. He would have known how to value these people. He wouldn't have traded the dullest of them for the brightest Mohawk he ever invented.

All savages draw outline pictures upon bark; but the resemblances are not close, and expression is usually lacking. But the Australian aboriginal's pictures of animals were nicely accurate in form, attitude, carriage; and he put spirit into them, and expression. And his pictures of white people and natives were pretty nearly as good as his pictures of the other animals. He dressed his whites in the fashion of their day, both the ladies and the gentlemen. As an untaught wielder of the pencil it is not likely that he has his equal among savage people.

His place in art—as to drawing, not color-work—is well up, all things considered. His art is not to be classified with savage art at all, but on a plane two degrees above it and one degree above the lowest plane of civilized art. To be exact, his place in art is between Botticelli and Du Maurier. That is to say, he could not draw as well as Du Maurier, but better than Botticelli. In feeling, he resembles both; also in grouping and in his preferences in the matter of subjects. His "corrobboree" of the Australian wilds reappears in Du Maurier's Belgravian ballrooms, with clothes and the smirk of civilization added; Botticelli's "Spring" is the corrobboree further idealized, but with fewer clothes and more smirk. And well enough as to intention, *but*—my word!

The aboriginal can make a fire by friction. I have tried that.

All savages are able to stand a good deal of physical pain. The Australian aboriginal has this quality in a well-developed degree. Do not read the following instances if horrors are not pleasant to you. They were recorded by the Rev. Henry N. Wolloston, of Melbourne, who had been a surgeon before he became a clergyman:

(1) In the summer of 1852 I started on horseback from Albany, King George's Sound, to visit at Cape Riche, accompanied by a native on foot. We traveled about forty miles the first day, then camped by a water-hole for the night. After cooking and eating our supper, I observed the native, who had said nothing to me on the subject, collect the hot embers of the fire together, and deliberately place his right foot in the glowing mass for a moment, then suddenly withdraw it, stamping on the ground and uttering a long-drawn guttural sound of mingled pain and satisfaction. This operation he repeated several times. On my inquiring the meaning of his strange conduct, he only said, "Me carpenter-make 'em" ("I am mending my foot"), and then showed me his charred great toe, the nail of which had been torn off by a tea-tree stump, in which it had been caught during the journey, and the pain of which he had borne with stoical composure until the evening,

when he had an opportunity of cauterizing the wound in the primitive manner above described.

And he proceeded on the journey the next day, "as if nothing had happened"—and walked thirty miles. It was a strange idea, to keep a surgeon and then do his own surgery.

(2) A native about twenty-five years of age once applied to me, as a doctor, to extract the wooden barb of a spear, which, during a fight in the bush some four months previously, had entered his chest, just missing the heart, and penetrated the viscera to a considerable depth. The spear had been cut off, leaving the barb behind, which continued to force its way by muscular action gradually toward the back; and when I examined him I could feel a hard substance between the ribs below the left-blade bone. I made a deep incision, and with a pair of forceps extracted the barb, which was made, as usual, of hard wood, about four inches long and from half an inch to an inch thick. It was very smooth, and partly digested, so to speak, by the maceration to which it had been exposed during its four months' journey through the body. The wound made by the spear had long since healed, leaving only a small cicatrix; and after the operation, which the native bore without flinching, he appeared to suffer no pain. Indeed, judging from his good state of health, the presence of the foreign matter did not materially annoy him. He was perfectly well in a few days.

But No. 3 is my favorite. Whenever I read it I seem to enjoy all that the patient enjoyed—whatever it was:

(3) Once at King George's Sound a native presented himself to me with one leg only, and requested me to supply him with a wooden leg. He had traveled in this maimed state about ninety-six miles, for this purpose. I examined the limb, which had been severed just below the knee, and found that it had

been charred by fire, while about two inches of the partially calcined bone protruded through the flesh. I at once removed this with the saw; and having made as presentable a stump of it as I could, covered the amputated end of the bone with a surrounding of muscle, and kept the patient a few days under my care to allow the wound to heal. On inquiring, the native told me that in a fight with other black fellows a spear had struck his leg and penetrated the bone below the knee. Finding it was serious, he had recourse to the following crude and barbarous operation, which it appears is not uncommon among these people in their native state. He made a fire, and dug a hole in the earth only sufficiently large to admit his leg, and deep enough to allow the wounded part to be on a level with the surface of the ground. He then *surrounded the limb with the live coals* or charcoal, which was replenished until the leg was literally burnt off. The cauterization thus applied completely checked the hemorrhage, and he was able in a day or two to hobble down to the Sound, with the aid of a long stout stick, although he was more than a week on the road.

But he was a fastidious native. He soon discarded the wooden leg made for him by the doctor, because "it had no feeling in it." It must have had as much as the one he burnt off, I should think.

So much for the Aboriginals. It is difficult for me to let them alone. They are marvelously interesting creatures. For a quarter of a century, now, the several colonial governments have housed their remnants in comfortable stations, and fed them well and taken good care of them in every way. If I had found this out while I was in Australia I could have seen some of those people—but I didn't. I would walk thirty miles to see a stuffed one.

Australia has a slang of its own. This is a matter of course. The vast cattle and sheep industries, the strange aspects of the country, and the strange native animals, brute

MARK TWAIN

and human, are matters which would naturally breed a local slang. I have notes of this slang somewhere, but at the moment I can call to mind only a few of the words and phrases. They are expressive ones. The wide, sterile, unpeopled deserts have created eloquent phrases like "No Man's Land" and the "Never-never Country"—also this felicitous form: "She lives in the Never-never Country"—that is, she is an old maid. And this one is not without merit: "heifer-paddock"— young ladies' seminary. "Bail up" and "stick up"—equivalent of our highwayman-term to "hold up" a stage-coach or a train. "New-chum" is the equivalent of our "tenderfoot"— new arrival.

And then there is the immortal "My word!" We must import it. "M-y *word!*" In cold print it is the equivalent of our "Ger-*reat Cæsar!*" but spoken with the proper Australian unction and fervency, it is worth six of it for grace and charm and expressiveness. Our form is rude and explosive; it is not suited to the drawing-room or the heifer-paddock; but "M-y *word!*" is, and is music to the ear, too, when the utterer knows how to say it. I saw it in print several times on the Pacific Ocean, but it struck me coldly, it aroused no sympathy. That was because it was the dead corpse of the thing, the soul was not there—the tones were lacking—the informing spirit—the deep feeling—the eloquence. But the first time I heard an Australian say it, it was positively thrilling.

Chapter XXIII

Be careless in your dress if you must, but keep a tidy soul.
        —Pudd'nhead Wilson's New Calendar.

WE left Adelaide in due course, and went to Horsham, in the colony of Victoria; a good deal of a journey, if I remember rightly, but pleasant. Horsham sits in a plain which is as level as a floor—one of those famous dead levels which Australian books describe so often; gray, bare, somber, melancholy, baked, cracked, in the tedious long droughts, but a horizonless ocean of vivid green grass the day after a rain. A country-town, peaceful, reposeful, inviting, full of snug homes, with garden-plots, and plenty of shrubbery and flowers.

"*Horsham, October 17.* At the hotel. The weather divine. Across the way, in front of the London Bank of Australia, is a very handsome cottonwood. It is in opulent leaf, and every leaf perfect. The full power of the on-rushing spring is upon it, and I imagine I can see it grow. Alongside the bank and a little way back in the garden there is a row of soaring fountain-sprays of delicate feathery foliage quivering in the breeze, and mottled with flashes of light that shift and play through the mass like flashlights through an opal—a most beautiful tree, and a striking contrast to the cottonwood. Every leaf of the cottonwood is distinctly defined—it is a kodak for faithful, hard, unsentimental detail; the other an impressionist picture, delicious to look upon, full of a subtle and exquisite charm, but all details fused in a swoon of vague and soft loveliness."

It turned out, upon inquiry, to be a pepper tree—an importation from China. It has a silky sheen, soft and rich. I saw some that had long red bunches of currantlike berries ambushed among the foliage. At a distance, in certain lights, they give the tree a pinkish tint and a new charm.

There is an agricultural college eight miles from Horsham. We were driven out to it by its chief. The conveyance was an open wagon; the time, noonday; no wind; the sky without a cloud, the sunshine brilliant—and the mercury at ninety-two degrees in the shade. In some countries an indolent unsheltered drive of an hour and a half under such conditions would have been a sweltering and prostrating experience; but there was nothing of that in this case. It is a climate that is perfect. There was no sense of heat; indeed, there was no heat; the air was fine and pure and exhilarating; if the drive had lasted half a day I think we should not have felt any discomfort, or grown silent or droopy or tired. Of course, the secret of it was the exceeding dryness of the atmosphere. In that plain one hundred and twelve degrees in the shade is without doubt no harder upon a man than is eighty-eight degrees or ninety degrees in New York.

The road lay through the middle of an empty space which seemed to me to be a hundred yards wide between the fences. I was not given the width in yards, but only in chains and perches—and furlongs, I think. I would have given a good deal to know what the width was, but I did not pursue the matter. I think it is best to put up with information the way you get it; and seem satisfied with it, and surprised at it, and grateful for it, and say, "My word!" and never let on. It was a wide space; I could tell you how wide, in chains and perches and furlongs and things, but that would not help you any. Those things sound well, but they are shadowy and indefinite, like troy weight and avoirdupois; nobody knows what they mean. When you buy a pound of a drug and the man asks you which you want, troy or avoirdupois, it is best to say "Yes," and shift the subject.

They said that the wide space dates from the earliest sheep and cattle raising days. People had to drive their stock long distances—immense journeys—from worn-out places to new ones where were water and fresh pasturage; and this wide space had to be left in grass and unfenced, or the stock would have starved to death in the transit.

On the way we saw the usual birds—the beautiful little green parrots, the magpie, and some others; and also the slender native bird of modest plumage and the eternally for-gettable name—the bird that is the smartest among birds, and can give a parrot thirty to one in the game and then talk him to death. I cannot recall that bird's name. I think it begins with M. I wish it began with G, or something that a person can remember.

The magpie was out in great force, in the fields and on the fences. He is a handsome large creature, with snowy white decorations, and is a singer; he has a murmurous rich note that is lovely. He was once modest, even diffident; but he lost all that when he found out that he was Australia's sole musical bird. He has talent, and cuteness, and impudence; and in his tame state he is a most satisfactory pet—never coming when he is called, always coming when he isn't, and studying disobedience as an accomplishment. He is not confined, but loafs all over the house and grounds, like the

laughing jackass. I think he learns to talk, I know he learns
to sing tunes, and his friends say that he knows how to steal
without learning. I was acquainted with a tame magpie in
Melbourne. He had lived in a lady's house several years, and
believed he owned it. The lady had tamed him, and in return
he had tamed the lady. He was always on deck when not
wanted, always having his own way, always tyrannizing over
the dog, and always making the cat's life a slow sorrow and
a martyrdom. He knew a number of tunes and could sing
them in perfect time and tune; and would do it, too, at any
time that silence was wanted; and then encore himself and do
it again; but if he was asked to sing he would go out and take
a walk.

It was long believed that fruit trees would not grow
in that baked and waterless plain around Horsham, but the
agricultural college has dissipated that idea. Its ample nurseries were producing oranges, apricots, lemons, almonds,
peaches, cherries, forty-eight varieties of apples—in fact, all
manner of fruits, and in abundance. The trees did not seem
to miss the water; they were in vigorous and flourishing
condition.

Experiments are made with different soils, to see what
things thrive best in them and what climates are best for
them. A man who is ignorantly trying to produce upon his
farm things not suited to its soil and its other conditions can
make a journey to the college from anywhere in Australia,
and go back with a change of scheme which will make his
farm productive and profitable.

There were forty pupils there—a few of them farmers,
relearning their trade, the rest young men mainly from the
cities—novices. It seemed a strange thing that an agricultural
college should have an attraction for city-bred youths, but
such is the fact. They are good stuff, too; they are above the

agricultural average of intelligence, and they come without any inherited prejudices in favor of hoary ignorances made sacred by long descent.

The students work all day in the fields, the nurseries, and the shearing-sheds, learning and doing all the practical work of the business—three days in a week. On the other three they study and hear lectures. They are taught the beginnings of such sciences as bear upon agriculture—like chemistry, for instance. We saw the sophomore class in sheep-shearing shear a dozen sheep. They did it by hand, not with a machine. The sheep was seized and flung down on his side and held there; and the students took off his coat with great celerity and adroitness. Sometimes they clipped off a sample of the sheep, but that is customary with shearers, and they don't mind it; they don't even mind it as much as the sheep. They dab a splotch of sheep-dip on the place and go right ahead.

The coat of wool was unbelievably thick. Before the shearing the sheep looked like the fat woman in the circus; after it he looked like a bench. He was clipped to the skin; and smoothly and uniformly. The fleece comes from him all in one piece and has the spread of a blanket.

The college was flying the Australian flag—the gridiron of England smuggled up in the northwest corner of a big red field that had the random stars of the Southern Cross wandering around over it.

From Horsham we went to Stawell. By rail. Still in the colony of Victoria. Stawell is in the gold-mining country. In the bank-safe was half a peck of surface gold—gold dust, grain gold; rich; pure in fact, and pleasant to sift through one's fingers; and would be pleasanter if it would stick. And there were a couple of gold bricks, very heavy to handle, and worth seventy-five hundred dollars apiece. They were from a very valuable quartz-mine; a lady owns two-thirds of it; she has an income of seventy-five thousand dollars a month from it, and is able to keep house.

The Stawell region is not productive of gold only; it has great vineyards, and produces exceptionally fine wines. One of these vineyards—the Great Western, owned by Mr. Irving—is regarded as a model. Its product has reputation abroad. It yields a choice champagne and a fine claret, and its hock took a prize in France two or three years ago. The champagne is kept in a maze of passages underground, cut in the rock, to secure it an even temperature during the three-year term required to perfect it. In those vaults I saw 120,000 bottles of champagne. The colony of Victoria has a population of 1,000,000, and those people are said to drink 25,000,000 bottles of champagne per year. The driest community on the earth. The government has lately reduced the duty upon foreign wines. That is one of the unkindnesses of Protection. A man invests years of work and a vast sum of money in a worthy enterprise, upon the faith of existing laws; then the law is changed, and the man is robbed by his own government.

On the way back to Stawell we had a chance to see a group of boulders called the Three Sisters—a curiosity oddly located; for it was upon high ground, with the land sloping away from it, and no height above it from whence the boulders could have rolled down. Relics of an early ice-drift, perhaps. They are noble boulders. One of them has the size and smoothness and plump sphericity of a balloon of the biggest pattern. The road led through a forest of great gum trees, lean and scraggy and sorrowful. The road was cream-white—a clayey kind of earth, apparently.

Along it toiled occasional freight-wagons, drawn by long double files of oxen. Those wagons were going a journey of two hundred miles, I was told, and were running a successful opposition to the railway! The railways are owned and run by the government.

Those sad gums stood up out of the dry white clay, pictures of patience and resignation. It is a tree that can get along without water; still it is fond of it—ravenously so. It is a very intelligent tree and will detect the presence of hidden water at a distance of fifty feet, and send out slender long root-fibers to prospect it. They will find it; and will also get at it—even through a cement wall six inches thick. Once a cement water-pipe underground at Stawell began to gradually reduce its output, and finally ceased altogether to deliver water. Upon examining into the matter it was found stopped up, wadded compactly with a mass of root fibers, delicate and hairlike. How this stuff had gotten into the pipe was a puzzle for some little time; finally it was found that it had crept in through a crack that was almost invisible to the eye. A gum tree forty feet away had tapped the pipe and was drinking the water.

Chapter XXIV

There is no such thing as "the Queen's English."
The property has gone into the hands of a joint stock
company and we own the bulk of the shares!
          —Pudd'nhead Wilson's New Calendar.

FREQUENTLY, in Australia, one has cloud-effects of an unfamiliar sort. We had this kind of scenery, finely staged, all the way to Ballarat. Consequently we saw more sky than country on that journey. At one time a great stretch of the vault was densely flecked with wee ragged-edged flakes of painfully white cloud-stuff, all of one shape and size, and equidistant apart, with narrow cracks of adorable blue showing between. The whole was suggestive of a hurricane of snowflakes drifting across the skies. By and by these flakes fused themselves together in interminable lines, with shady faint hollows between the lines, the long satin-surfaced rollers following each other in simulated movement, and enchantingly counterfeiting the majestic march of a flowing sea. Later, the sea solidified itself; then gradually broke up its mass into innumerable lofty white pillars of about one size, and ranged these across the firmament, in receding and fading perspective, in the similitude of a stupendous colonnade—

a mirage without a doubt flung from the far Gates of the Hereafter.

The approaches to Ballarat were beautiful. The features, great green expanses of rolling pastureland, bisected by eye-contenting hedges of commingled new-gold and old-gold gorse—and a lovely lake. One must put in the pause, there, to fetch the reader up with a slight jolt, and keep him from gliding by without noticing the lake. One *must* notice it; for a lovely lake is not as common a thing along the railways of Australia as are the dry places. Ninety-two in the shade again, but balmy and comfortable, fresh and bracing. A perfect climate.

Forty-five years ago the site now occupied by the city of Ballarat was a sylvan solitude as quiet as Eden and as lovely. Nobody had ever heard of it. On the 25th of August, 1851, the first *great* gold strike made in Australia was made here. The wandering prospectors who made it scraped up two pounds and a half of gold the first day—worth six hundred dollars. A few days later the place was a hive—a town. The news of the strike spread everywhere in a sort of instantaneous way—spread like a flash to the very ends of the earth. A celebrity so prompt and so universal has hardly been paralleled in history, perhaps. It was as if the name BALLARAT had suddenly been written on the sky, where all the world could read it at once.

The smaller discoveries made in the colony of New South Wales three months before had already started emigrants toward Australia; they had been coming as a stream, but they came as a flood, now. A hundred thousand people poured into Melbourne from England and other countries in a single month, and flocked away to the mines. The crews of the ships that brought them flocked with them; the clerks in the government offices followed; so did the cooks, the maids, the coachmen, the butlers, and the other domestic servants;

so did the carpenters, the smiths, the plumbers, the painters, the reporters, the editors, the lawyers, the clients, the bar-keepers, the bummers, the blacklegs, the thieves, the loose women, the grocers, the butchers, the bakers, the doctors, the druggists, the nurses; so did the police; even officials of high and hitherto envied place threw up their positions and joined the procession. This roaring avalanche swept out of Melbourne and left it desolate, Sunday-like, paralyzed, every-thing at a standstill, the ships lying idle at anchor, all signs of life departed, all sounds stilled save the rasping of the cloud-shadows as they scraped across the vacant streets.

That grassy and leafy paradise at Ballarat was soon ripped open, and lacerated and scarified and gutted, in the feverish search for its hidden riches. There is nothing like surface-mining to snatch the graces and beauties and benign-ities out of a paradise, and make an odious and repulsive spectacle of it.

What fortunes were made! Immigrants got rich while the ship unloaded and reloaded—and went back home for good in the same cabin they had come out in! Not all of them. Only some. I saw the others in Ballarat myself, forty-five years later—what were left of them by time and death and the disposition to rove. They were young and gay, then; they are patriarchal and grave, now; and they do not get excited any more. They talk of the Past. They live in it. Their life is a dream, a retrospection.

Ballarat was a great region for "nuggets." No such nug-gets were found in California as Ballarat produced. In fact, the Ballarat region has yielded the largest ones known to history. Two of them weighed about one hundred and eighty pounds each, and together were worth ninety thousand dol-lars. They were offered to any poor person who would shoul-der them and carry them away. Gold was so plentiful that it made people liberal like that.

Ballarat was a swarming city of tents in the early days. Everybody was happy, for a time, and apparently prosperous. Then came trouble. The government swooped down with a mining tax. And in its worst form, too; for it was not a tax upon what the miner had taken out, but upon what he was *going* to take out—if he could find it. It was a license tax—license to work his claim—and it had to be paid before he could begin digging.

Consider the situation. No business is so uncertain as surface-mining. Your claim may be good, and it may be worthless. It may make you well off in a month; and then again you may have to dig and slave for half a year, at heavy expense, only to find out at last that the gold is not there in cost-paying quantity, and that your time and your hard work have been thrown away. It might be wise policy to advance the miner a monthly sum to encourage him to develop the country's riches; but to tax him monthly in advance instead— why, such a thing was never dreamed of in America. There, neither the claim itself nor its products, howsoever rich or poor, were taxed.

The Ballarat miners protested, petitioned, complained— it was of no use; the government held its ground, and went on collecting the tax. And not by pleasant methods, but by ways which must have been very galling to free people. The rumblings of a coming storm began to be audible.

By and by there was a result; and I think it may be called the finest thing in Australasian history. It was a revolution— small in size, but great politically; it was a strike for liberty, a struggle for a principle, a stand against injustice and oppression. It was the Barons and John, over again; it was Hampden and Ship-Money; it was Concord and Lexington; small beginnings, all of them, but all of them great in political results, all of them epoch-making. It is another instance of a victory won by a lost battle. It adds an honorable page to history; the people know it and are proud of it. They keep green the memory of the men who fell at the Eureka Stockade, and Peter Lalor has his monument.

The surface-soil of Ballarat was full of gold. This soil the miners ripped and tore and trenched and harried and disemboweled, and made it yield up its immense treasure. Then they went down into the earth with deep shafts, seeking the gravelly beds of ancient rivers and brooks—and found them. They followed the courses of these streams, and gutted them, sending the gravel up in buckets to the upper world, and washing out of it its enormous deposits of gold. The next biggest of the two monster nuggets mentioned above came from an old river-channel one hundred and eighty feet under ground.

Finally the quartz lodes were attacked. That is not poor man's mining. Quartz mining and milling require capital, and staying-power, and patience. Big companies were formed, and for several decades, now, the lodes have been successfully worked, and have yielded great wealth. Since the gold discovery in 1851 the Ballarat mines—taking the three kinds of mining together—have contributed to the world's pocket something over *three hundred millions of dollars*, which is to say that this nearly invisible little spot on the earth's surface has yielded about one-fourth as much gold in forty-four years as all California has yielded in forty-seven. The Californian aggregate, from 1848 to 1895, inclusive, as reported by the Statistician of the United States Mint, is $1,265,217,217.

A citizen told me a curious thing about those mines. With all my experience of mining I had never heard of anything of the sort before. The main gold reef runs about north and south—of course—for that is the custom of a rich gold reef. At Ballarat its course is between walls of slate. Now the citizen told me that throughout a stretch of twelve miles along the reef, the reef is crossed at intervals by a straight black streak of a carbonaceous nature—a streak in the slate; a streak no thicker than a pencil—and that wherever it crosses the reef you will certainly find gold at the junction. It is called the Indicator. Thirty feet on each side of the Indicator (and down in the slate, of course) is a still finer streak—a streak as fine as a pencil-mark; and indeed, that is its name—Pencil Mark. When ever you find the Pencil Mark you know that thirty feet from it is the Indicator; you measure the distance, excavate, find the Indicator, trace it straight to the reef, and sink your shaft; your fortune is made, for certain. If that is true, it is curious. And it is curious anyway.

Ballarat is a town of only forty thousand population; and yet, since it is in Australia, it has every essential of an advanced and enlightened big city. This is pure matter of course. I must stop dwelling upon these things. It is hard to keep from dwelling upon them, though; for it is difficult to get away from the surprise of it. I will let the other details go, this time, but I must allow myself to mention that this little town has a park of three hundred and twenty-six acres; a flower-garden of eighty-three acres, with an elaborate and expensive fernery in it and some costly and unusually fine statuary; and an artificial lake covering six hundred acres, equipped with a fleet of two hundred shells, small sailboats, and little steam-yachts.

At this point I strike out some other praiseful things which I was tempted to add. I do not strike them out because they were not true or not well said, but because I find them better said by another man—and a man more competent to testify, too, because he belongs on the ground, and knows. I clip them from a chatty speech delivered some years ago by Mr. William Little, who was at that time mayor of Ballarat:

The language of our citizens, in this as in other parts of Australasia, is mostly healthy Anglo-Saxon, free from Americanisms, vulgarisms, and the conflicting dialects of our Fatherland, and is pure enough to suit a Trench or a Latham. Our youth, aided by climatic influence, are in point of physique and comeliness unsurpassed in the Sunny South. Our young men are well ordered; and our maidens, "not stepping over the bounds of modesty," are as fair as Psyches, dispensing smiles as charming as November flowers.

The closing clause has the seeming of a rather frosty compliment, but that is apparent only, not real. November is summer-time there. His compliment to the local purity of the language is warranted. It is quite free from impurities; this is acknowledged far and wide. As in the German Empire all cultivated people claim to speak Hanoverian German, so in Australasia all cultivated people claim to speak Ballarat English. Even in England this cult has made considerable progress, and now that it is favored by the two great Universities, the time is not far away when Ballarat English will come into general use among the educated classes of Great Britain at large. Its great merit is, that it is shorter than ordinary English—that is, it is more compressed. At first you have some difficulty in understanding it when it is spoken as rapidly as the orator whom I have quoted speaks it. An illustration will show what I mean. When he called and I handed him a chair, he bowed and said:

"Q."

Presently, when we were lighting our cigars, he held a match to mine and I said:

"Thank you," and he said:

"Km."

Then I saw. Q is the end of the phrase "I thank you." Km is the end of the phrase "You are welcome." Mr. Little puts no emphasis upon either of them, but delivers them so reduced that they hardly have a sound. All Ballarat English is like that, and the effect is very soft and pleasant; it takes all the hardness and harshness out of our tongue and gives to it a delicate whispery and vanishing cadence which charms the ear like the faint rustling of the forest leaves.

Chapter XXV

"Classic." A book which people praise and don't read.
—Pudd'nhead Wilson's New Calendar.

ON the rail again—bound for Bendigo. From diary:
October 23. Got up at six, left at seven-thirty; soon
reached Castlemaine, one of the rich gold-fields of the early
days; waited several hours for a train; left at three-forty and
reached Bendigo in an hour. For comrade, a Catholic priest
who was better than I was, but didn't seem to know it—a
man full of graces of the heart, the mind, and the spirit; a
lovable man. He will rise. He will be a Bishop some day.
Later an Archbishop. Later a Cardinal. Finally an Archangel,
I hope. And then he will recall me when I say, "Do you
remember that trip we made from Ballarat to Bendigo, when
you were nothing but Father C., and I was nothing to what
I am now?" It has actually taken nine hours to come from
Ballarat to Bendigo. We could have saved seven by walking.
However, there was no hurry.

Bendigo was another of the rich strikes of the early days.
It does a great quartz-mining business, now—that business

which, more than any other that I know of, teaches patience, and requires grit and a steady nerve. The town is full of towering chimney-stacks and hoisting-works, and looks like a petroleum-city. Speaking of patience; for example, one of the local companies went steadily on with its deep borings and searchings without show of gold or a penny of reward for *eleven years*—then struck it, and became suddenly rich. The eleven years' work had cost fifty-five thousand dollars, and the first gold found was a grain the size of a pin's head. It is kept under locks and bars, as a precious thing, and is reverently shown to the visitor, "hats off." When I saw it I had not heard its history.

"It is gold. Examine it—take the glass. Now how much should you say it is worth?"

I said:

"I should say about two cents; or in your English dialect, four farthings."

"Well, it cost eleven thousand pounds."

"Oh, come!"

"Yes, it did. Ballarat and Bendigo have produced the three monumental nuggets of the world, and this one is the monumentalest one of the three. The other two represent nine thousand pounds apiece; this one a couple of thousand more. It is small, and not much to look at, but it is entitled to its name—Adam. It is the Adam-nugget of this mine, and its children run up into the millions."

Speaking of patience again, another of the mines was worked, under heavy expenses, during seventeen years before pay was struck, and still another one compelled a wait of twenty-one years before pay was struck; then, in both instances, the outlay was all back in a year or two, with compound interest.

Bendigo has turned out even more gold than Ballarat. The two together have produced six hundred and fifty million dollars' worth—which is half as much as California produced.

It was through Mr. Blank—not to go into particulars about his name—it was mainly through Mr. Blank that my stay in Bendigo was made memorably pleasant and interesting. He explained this to me himself. He told me that it was through his influence that the city government invited me to the town-hall to hear complimentary speeches and respond to them; that it was through his influence that I had been taken on a long pleasure drive through the city and shown its notable features; that it was through his influence that I was invited to visit the great mines; that it was through his influence that I was taken to the hospital and allowed to see the convalescent Chinaman who had been attacked at midnight in his lonely hut eight weeks before by robbers, and stabbed forty-six times and scalped besides; that it was through his influence that when I arrived this awful spectacle of piecings and patchings and bandagings was sitting up in his cot letting on to read one of my books; that it was through his influence that efforts had been made to get the Catholic Archbishop of Bendigo to invite me to dinner; that it was through his influence that efforts had been made to get the Anglican Bishop of Bendigo to ask me to supper; that it was through his influence that the dean of the editorial fraternity had driven me through the woodsy outlying country and shown me, from the summit of Lone Tree Hill, the mightiest and loveliest expanse of forest-clad mountain and valley that I had seen in all Australia. And when he asked me what had most impressed me in Bendigo and I answered and said it was the taste and the public spirit which had adorned the streets with one hundred and five miles of shade trees, he said that it was through his influence that it had been done.

But I am not representing him quite correctly. He did not *say* it was through his influence that all these things had happened—for that would have been coarse; he merely *conveyed* that idea; conveyed it so subtly that I only caught it fleetingly, as one catches vagrant faint breaths of perfume when one traverses the meadows in summer; conveyed it without offense and without any suggestion of egoism or ostentation—but *conveyed* it, nevertheless.

He was an Irishman; an educated gentleman; grave, and kindly, and courteous; a bachelor, and about forty-five or possibly fifty years old, apparently. He called upon me at the hotel, and it was there that we had this talk. He made me like him, and did it without trouble. This was partly through his winning and gentle ways, but mainly through the amazing familiarity with my books which his conversation showed. He was down to date with them, too; and if he had made them the study of his life he could hardly have been better posted as to their contents than he was. He made me better satisfied with myself than I had ever been before. It was plain that he had a deep fondness for humor, yet he never laughed; he never even chuckled; in fact, humor could not win to outward expression on his face at all. No, he was always grave—tenderly, pensively grave; but he made *me* laugh, all along; and this was very trying—and very pleasant at the same time—for it was at quotations from my own books.

When he was going, he turned and said:

"You don't remember me?"

"I? Why, no. Have we met before?"

"No, it was a matter of correspondence."

"Correspondence?"

"Yes, many years ago. Twelve or fifteen. Oh, longer than that. But of course you—" A musing pause. Then he said:

"Do you remember Corrigan Castle?"

"N—no, I believe I don't. I don't seem to recall the name."

He waited a moment, pondering, with the door-knob in his hand, then started out; but turned back and said that I had once been interested in Corrigan Castle, and asked me if I would go with him to his quarters in the evening and take a hot Scotch and talk it over. I was a teetotaler and liked relaxation, so I said I would.

We drove from the lecture-hall together about half past ten. He had a most comfortably and tastefully furnished parlor, with good pictures on the walls, Indian and Japanese ornaments on the mantel, and here and there, and books everywhere—largely mine; which made me proud. The light was brilliant, the easy-chairs were deep-cushioned, the arrangements for brewing and smoking were all there. We brewed and lit up; then he passed a sheet of note-paper to me and said:

"Do you remember that?"

"Oh, yes, indeed!"

The paper was of a sumptuous quality. At the top was a twisted and interlaced monogram printed from steel dies in gold and blue and red, in the ornate English fashion of long years ago; and under it, in neat gothic capitals, was this— printed in blue:

THE MARK TWAIN CLUB
CORRIGAN CASTLE

. . . . 187

"My!" said I, "how did you come by this?"

"I was President of it."

"No!—you don't mean it."

"It is true. I was its first President. I was reelected annually as long as its meetings were held in my castle—Corrigan—which was five years."

Then he showed me an album with twenty-three photographs of me in it. Five of them were of old dates, the others of various later crops; the list closed with a picture taken by Falk in Sydney a month before.

"You sent us the first five; the rest were bought."

This was paradise! We ran late, and talked, talked, talked—subject, the Mark Twain Club of Corrigan Castle, Ireland.

My first knowledge of that Club dates away back; all of twenty years, I should say. It came to me in the form of a courteous letter, written on the note-paper which I have described, and signed "By order of the President; C. PEM-BROKE, Secretary." It conveyed the fact that the Club had been created in my honor, and added the hope that this token of appreciation of my work would meet with my approval.

I answered, with thanks; and did what I could to keep my gratification from over-exposure.

It was then that the long correspondence began. A letter came back, by order of the President, furnishing me the names of the members—thirty-two in number. With it came a copy of the Constitution and By-Laws, in pamphlet form, and artistically printed. The initiation fee and dues were in their proper place; also, schedule of meetings—monthly— for essays upon works of mine, followed by discussions; quarterly for business and a supper, without essays, but with after-supper speeches; also there was a list of the officers: President, Vice-President, Secretary, Treasurer, etc. The let-ter was brief, but it was pleasant reading, for it told me about the strong interest which the membership took in their new venture, etc., etc. It also asked me for a photograph—a special one. I went down and sat for it and sent it—with a letter, of course.

Presently came the badge of the Club, and very dainty and pretty it was; and very artistic. It was a frog peeping out from a graceful tangle of grass-sprays and rushes, and was done in enamels on a gold basis, and had a gold pin back of it. After I had petted it, and played with it, and caressed it, and enjoyed it a couple of hours, the light happened to fall upon it at a new angle, and revealed to me a cunning new detail; with the light just right, certain delicate shadings of the grass-blades and rush-stems wove themselves into a monogram—mine! You can see that that jewel was a work of art. And when you come to consider the intrinsic value of it, you must concede that it is not every literary club that could afford a badge like that. It was easily worth seventy-five dollars, in the opinion of Messrs. Marcus and Ward of New York. They said they could not duplicate it for that and make a profit.

By this time the Club was well under way; and from that time forth its secretary kept my off-hours well supplied with business. He reported the Club's discussions of my books with laborious fullness, and did his work with great spirit and ability. As a rule, he synopsized; but when a speech was especially brilliant, he short-handed it and gave me the best passages from it, written out. There were five speakers whom he particularly favored in that way: Palmer, Forbes, Naylor, Norris, and Calder. Palmer and Forbes could never get through a speech without attacking each other, and each in his own way was formidably effective—Palmer in virile and eloquent abuse, Forbes in courtly and elegant but scalding satire. I could always tell which of them was talking without looking for his name. Naylor had a polished style and a happy knack at felicitous metaphor; Norris's style was wholly without ornament, but enviably compact, lucid, and strong. But after all, Calder was the gem. He never spoke when sober, he spoke continuously when he wasn't. And certainly they were the drunkest speeches that a man ever uttered. They were full of good things, but so incredibly mixed up and wandering that it made one's head swim to follow him. They were not intended to be funny, but they were—funny for the very gravity which the speaker put into his flowing miracles of incongruity. In the course of five years I came to know the styles of the five orators as well as I knew the style of any speaker in my own club at home.

These reports came every month. They were written on foolscap, six hundred words to the page, and usually about twenty-five pages in a report—a good fifteen thousand words, I should say—a solid week's work. The reports were absorbingly entertaining, long as they were; but, unfortunately for me, they did not come alone. They were always accompanied by a lot of questions about passages and purposes in my books, which the Club wanted answered; and additionally accompanied every quarter by the Treasurer's report, and the Auditor's report, and the Committee's report, and the President's review, and my opinion of these was always desired; also suggestions for the good of the Club if any occurred to me.

By and by I came to dread those things; and this dread grew and grew and grew; grew until I got to anticipating them with a cold horror. For I was an indolent man, and not fond of letter-writing, and whenever these things came I had to put everything by and sit down—for my own peace of mind—and dig and dig until I got something out of my head which would answer for a reply. I got along fairly well the first year; but for the succeeding four years the Mark Twain Club of Corrigan Castle was my curse, my nightmare, the grief and misery of my life. And I got so, *so* sick of sitting for photographs. I sat every year for five years, trying to satisfy that insatiable organization. Then at last I rose in revolt. I could endure my oppressions no longer. I pulled my fortitude together and tore off my chains, and was a free man

again, and happy. From that day I burned the Secretary's fat
envelopes the moment they arrived, and by and by they
ceased to come.

Well, in the sociable frankness of that night in Bendigo
I brought this all out in full confession. Then Mr. Blank came
out in the same frank way, and with a preliminary word of
gentle apology said that *he* was the Mark Twain Club, and
the only member it had ever had!

Why, it was matter for anger, but I didn't feel any. He
said he never had to work for a living, and that by the time
he was thirty life had become a bore and a weariness to him.
He had no interests left; they had paled and perished, one by
one, and left him desolate. He had begun to think of suicide.
Then all of a sudden he thought of that happy idea of starting
an imaginary club, and went straightway to work at it, with
enthusiasm and love. He was charmed with it; it gave him
something to do. It elaborated itself on his hands; it became
twenty times more complex and formidable than was his first
rude draft of it. Every new addition to his original plan which
cropped up in his mind gave him a fresh interest and a new
pleasure. He designed the Club badge himself, and worked
over it, altering and improving it, a number of days and
nights; then sent to London and had it made. It was the only
one that was made. It was made for me; the "rest of the
Club" went without.

He invented the thirty-two members and their names.
He invented the five favorite speakers and their five separate
styles. He invented their speeches, and reported them himself.
He would have kept that Club going until now, if I hadn't
deserted, he said. He said he worked like a slave over those
reports; each of them cost him from a week to a fortnight's
work, and the work gave him pleasure and kept him alive
and willing to be alive. It was a bitter blow to him when the
Club died.

Finally, there wasn't any Corrigan Castle. He had invented that, too.

It was wonderful—the whole thing; and altogether the most ingenious and laborious and cheerful and painstaking practical joke I have ever heard of. And I liked it; liked to hear him tell about it; yet I have been a hater of practical jokes from as long back as I can remember. Finally he said:

"Do you remember a note from Melbourne fourteen or fifteen years ago, telling about your lecture tour in Australia, and your death and burial in Melbourne?—a note from Henry Bascom, of Bascom Hall, Upper Holywell, Hants."

"Yes."

"I wrote it."

"M-y—word!"

"Yes, I did it. I don't know why. I just took the notion, and carried it out without stopping to think. It was wrong. It could have done harm. I was always sorry about it afterward. You must forgive me. I was Mr. Bascom's guest on his yacht, on his voyage around the world. He often spoke of you, and of the pleasant times you had had together in his home; and the notion took me, there in Melbourne, and I imitated his hand, and wrote the letter."

So the mystery was cleared up, after so many, many years.

Chapter XXVI

There are people who can do all fine and heroic things but one: keep from telling their happinesses to the unhappy.

—Pudd'nhead Wilson's New Calendar.

A FTER visits to Maryborough and some other Australian towns, we presently took passage for New Zealand. If it would not look too much like showing off, I would tell the reader where New Zealand is; for he is as I was: he thinks he knows. And he thinks he knows where Herzegovina is; and how to pronounce *pariah*; and how to use the word *unique* without exposing himself to the derision of the dictionary. But in truth, he knows none of these things. There are but four or five people in the world who possess this knowledge, and these make their living out of it. They travel from place to place, visiting literary assemblages, geographical societies, and seats of learning, and springing sudden bets that these people do not know these things. Since all people think they know them, they are an easy prey to these adventurers. Or rather they were an easy prey until the law interfered three months ago, and a New York court decided that this kind of gambling is illegal, "because it traverses Article IV, Section

9, of the Constitution of the United States, which forbids betting on a sure thing." This decision was rendered by the full Bench of the New York Supreme Court, after a test sprung upon the court by counsel for the prosecution, which showed that none of the nine Judges was able to answer any of the four questions.

All people think that New Zealand is close to Australia or Asia, or somewhere, and that you cross to it on a bridge. But that is not so. It is not close to anything, but lies by itself, out in the water. It is nearest to Australia, but still not near. The gap between is very wide. It will be a surprise to the reader, as it was to me, to learn that the distance from Australia to New Zealand is really twelve or thirteen hundred miles, and that there is no bridge. I learned this from Professor X., of Yale University, whom I met in the steamer on the great lakes when I was crossing the continent to sail across the Pacific. I asked him about New Zealand, in order to make conversation. I supposed he would generalize a little without compromising himself, and then turn the subject to something he was acquainted with, and my object would then be attained: the ice would be broken, and we could go smoothly on, and get acquainted, and have a pleasant time. But, to my surprise, he was not only not embarrassed by my question, but seemed to welcome it, and to take a distinct interest in it. He began to talk—fluently, confidently, comfortably: and as he talked, my admiration grew and grew; for as the subject developed under his hands, I saw that he not only knew where New Zealand was, but that he was minutely familiar with every detail of its history, politics, religions, and commerce, its fauna, flora, geology, products, and climatic peculiarities. When he was done, I was lost in wonder and admiration, and said to myself, he knows everything; in the domain of human knowledge he is king.

I wanted to see him do more miracles; and so, just for

the pleasure of hearing him answer, I asked him about Herzegovina, and pariah, and unique. But he began to generalize then, and show distress. I saw that with New Zealand gone, he was a Samson shorn of his locks; he was as other men. This was a curious and interesting mystery, and I was frank with him, and asked him to explain it.

He tried to avoid it at first; but then laughed and said that, after all, the matter was not worth concealment, so he would let me into the secret. In substance, this is his story:

Last autumn I was at work one morning at home, when a card came up—the card of a stranger. Under the name was printed a line which showed that this visitor was Professor of Theological Engineering in Wellington University, New Zealand. I was troubled—troubled, I mean, by the shortness of the notice. College etiquette required that he be at once invited to dinner by some member of the Faculty—invited to dine on *that* day—not put off till a subsequent day. I did not quite know what to do. College etiquette requires, in the case of a foreign guest, that the dinner-talk shall begin with complimentary references to his country, its great men, its services to civilization, its seats of learning, and things like that; and of course the host is responsible, and must either begin this talk himself or see that it is done by some one else. I was in great difficulty; and the more I searched my memory, the more my trouble grew. I found that I knew nothing about New Zealand. I thought I knew where it was, and that was all. I had an impression that it was close to Australia, or Asia, or somewhere, and that one went over to it on a bridge. This might turn out to be incorrect; and even if correct, it would not furnish matter enough for the purpose at the dinner, and I should expose my College to shame before my guest; he would see that I, a member of the Faculty of the first University in America, was wholly ignorant of his country, and he would go away and tell this, and laugh at it. The thought of it made my face burn.

I sent for my wife and told her how I was situated, and asked for her help, and she thought of a thing which I might have thought of myself, if I had not been excited and worried. She said she would go and tell the visitor that I was out, but would be in in a few minutes; and she would talk and keep him busy while I got out the back way and hurried over and made Professor Lawson give the dinner. For Lawson knew everything and could meet the guest in a creditable way, and save the reputation of the University. I ran to Lawson, but was disappointed. He did not know anything about New Zealand. He said that as far as his recollection went it was close to Australia, or Asia, or somewhere, and you go over to it on a bridge; but that was all he knew. It was too bad. Lawson was a perfect encyclopedia of abstruse learning; but now in this hour of our need, it turned out that he did not know any useful thing.

We consulted. He saw that the reputation of the University was in very real peril, and he walked the floor in anxiety, talking, and trying to think out some way to meet the difficulty. Presently, he decided that we must try the rest of the Faculty—some of them might know about New Zealand. So we went to the telephone and called up the professor of astronomy and asked him, and he said that all he knew was, that it was close to Australia, or Asia, or somewhere, and you went over to it on—

We shut him off and called up the professor of biology, and he said that all he knew was that it was close to Aus—

We shut him off, and sat down, worried and disheartened, to see if we could think up some other scheme. We shortly hit upon one which promised well, and this one we adopted, and set its machinery going at once. It was this. Lawson must give the dinner. The Faculty must be notified by telephone to prepare. We must all get to work diligently, and at the end of eight hours and a half we must come to dinner acquainted with New Zealand; at least well enough informed to appear without discredit before this native. To seem properly intelligent we should have to know about New Zealand's population, and politics, and form of government, and commerce, and taxes, and products, and ancient history, and modern history, and varieties of religion, and nature of the laws, and their codification, and amount of revenue, and whence drawn, and methods of collection, and percentage of loss, and character of climate, and—well, a lot of things like that; we must suck the maps and cyclopedias dry. And while we posted up in this way, the Faculty's wives must flock over, one after the other, in a studiedly casual way, and help my wife keep the New-Zealander quiet, and not let him get out and come interfering with our studies. The scheme worked admirably; but it stopped business, stopped it entirely.

It is in the official log-book of Yale, to be read and wondered at by future generations—the account of the Great Blank Day—the memorable Blank Day—the day wherein the wheels of culture were stopped, a Sunday silence prevailed all about, and the whole University stood still while the Faculty read up and qualified itself to sit at meat, without shame, in the presence of the Professor of Theological Engineering from New Zealand.

When we assembled at the dinner we were miserably tired and worn—but we were posted. Yes, it is fair to claim that. In fact, erudition is a pale name for it. New Zealand was the only subject; and it was just beautiful to hear us ripple it out. And with such an air of unembarrassed ease, and unostentatious familiarity with detail, and trained and seasoned mastery of the subject—and oh, the grace and fluency of it!

Well, finally somebody happened to notice that the guest was looking dazed, and wasn't saying anything. So they stirred him up, of course. Then that man came out with a good, honest, eloquent compliment that made the Faculty blush. He said he was not worthy to sit in the company of men like these; that he had been silent from admiration; that he had been silent from another cause also—silent from shame—silent from *ignorance*! "For," said he, "I, who have lived eighteen years in New Zealand and have served five in a professorship, and ought to know much about that country, perceive, now, that I know almost nothing about it. I say it with shame, that I have learned fifty times, yes, a hundred times more about New Zealand in these two hours at this table than I ever knew before in all the eighteen years put together. I was silent because I could not help myself. What I knew about taxes, and policies, and laws, and revenue, and products, and history, and all that multitude of things, was but general, and ordinary, and vague—unscientific, in a word—and it would have been insanity to expose it here to the searching glare of your amazingly accurate and all-comprehensive knowledge of those matters, gentlemen. I beg you to let me sit silent—as becomes me. But do not change the subject; I can at least follow you, in this one; whereas, if you change to one which shall call out the full strength of your mighty erudition, I shall be as one lost. If you know all this about a remote little inconsequent patch like New Zealand, ah, what *wouldn't* you know about any other subject!"

Chapter XXVII

Man is the Only Animal that Blushes. Or needs to.
—Pudd'nhead Wilson's New Calendar.

The universal brotherhood of man is our most precious possession, what there is of it.
—Pudd'nhead Wilson's New Calendar.

FROM Diary:
Nov. 1—Noon. A fine day, a brilliant sun. Warm in the sun, cold in the shade—an icy breeze blowing out of the south. A solemn long swell rolling up northward. It comes from the South Pole, with nothing in the way to obstruct its march and tone its energy down. I have read somewhere that an acute observer among the early explorers—Cook? or Tasman?—accepted this majestic swell as trustworthy circumstantial evidence that no important land lay to the southward, and so did not waste time on a useless quest in that direction, but changed his course and went searching elsewhere.

Afternoon. Passing between Tasmania (formerly Van Diemen's Land) and neighboring islands—islands whence the poor exiled Tasmanian savages used to gaze at their lost homeland and cry; and die of broken hearts. How glad I am that all these native races are dead and gone, or nearly so. The work was mercifully swift and horrible in some portions of Australia. As far as Tasmania is concerned, the extermination was complete: not a native is left. It was a strife of years, and decades of years. The Whites and the Blacks hunted each other, ambushed each other, butchered each other. The Blacks were not numerous. But they were wary, alert, cunning, and they knew their country well. They lasted a long time, few as they were, and inflicted much slaughter upon the Whites.

The government wanted to save the Blacks from ultimate extermination, if possible. One of its schemes was to capture them and coop them up, on a neighboring island, under guard. Bodies of Whites volunteered for the hunt, for the pay was good—five pounds for each Black captured and delivered; but the success achieved was not very satisfactory. The Black was naked, and his body was greased. It was hard to get a grip on him that would hold. The Whites moved about in armed bodies, and surprised little families of natives, and did make captures; but it was suspected that in these surprises half a dozen natives were killed to one caught—and that was not what the government desired.

Another scheme was to drive the natives into a corner of the island and fence them in by a cordon of men placed in line across the country; but the natives managed to slip through, constantly, and continue their murders and arsons.

The Governor warned these unlettered savages *by printed proclamation* that they must stay in the desolate region officially appointed for them! The proclamation was a dead letter; the savages could not read it. Afterward a *picture*-proclamation was issued. It was painted upon boards, and these were nailed to trees in the forest. Herewith is a photographic reproduction of this fashion-plate. Substantially it means:

THE GOVERNOR'S PROCLAMATION

1. The Governor wishes the Whites and the Blacks to love each other;
2. He loves his black subjects;
3. Blacks who kill Whites will be hanged;
4. Whites who kill Blacks will be hanged.

Upon its several schemes the government spent thirty thousand pounds and employed the labors and ingenuities of several thousand Whites for a long time—with failure as a result. Then, at last, a quarter of a century after the beginning of the troubles between the two races, the right man was found. No, he found himself. This was George Augustus Robinson, called in history "The Conciliator." He was not educated, and not conspicuous in any way. He was a working bricklayer, in Hobart Town. But he must have been an amazing personality; a man worth traveling far to see. It may be his counterpart appears in history, but I do not know where to look for it.

He set himself this incredible task: to go out into the wilderness, the jungle, and the mountain retreats where the hunted and implacable savages were hidden, and appear among them unarmed, speak the language of love and of kindness to them, and persuade them to forsake their homes and the wild free life that was so dear to them, and go with him and surrender to the hated Whites and live under their watch and ward, and upon their charity the rest of their lives! On its face it was the dream of a madman.

In the beginning, his moral-suasion project was sarcastically dubbed the *sugar-plum speculation*. If the scheme was striking, and new to the world's experience, the situation was not less so. It was this. The White population numbered forty thousand in 1831; the Black population numbered *three hundred*. Not three hundred warriors, but three hundred men, women, and children. The Whites were armed with guns, the Blacks with clubs and spears. The Whites had fought the Blacks for a quarter of a century, and had tried every thinkable way to capture, kill, or subdue them; and could not do it. If white men of any race *could* have done it, these would have accomplished it. But every scheme had failed, the splendid three hundred, the matchless three hundred were uncon- quered, and manifestly unconquerable. They would not yield, they would listen to no terms, they would fight to the bitter end. Yet they had no poet to keep up their heart, and sing the marvel of their magnificent patriotism.

At the end of five-and-twenty years of hard fighting, the surviving three hundred naked patriots were still defiant, still persistent, still efficacious with their rude weapons, and the Governor and the forty thousand knew not which way to turn, nor what to do.

Then the Bricklayer—that wonderful man—proposed to go out into the wilderness, with no weapon but his tongue, and no protection but his honest eye and his humane heart, and track those embittered savages to their lairs in the gloomy forests and among the mountain snows. Naturally, he was considered a crank. But he was not quite that. In fact, he was a good way short of that. He was building upon his long and intimate knowledge of the native character. The deriders of his project were right—from their standpoint—for they be- lieved the natives to be mere wild beasts; and Robinson was right, from his standpoint—for he believed the natives to be human beings. The truth did really lie between the two. The event proved that Robinson's judgment was soundest; but about once a month for four years the event came near to giving the verdict to the deriders, for about that frequently Robinson barely escaped falling under the native spears.

But history shows that he had a thinking head, and was not a mere wild sentimentalist. For instance, he wanted the war parties called in before he started unarmed upon his mission of peace. He wanted the best chance of success—not a half-chance. And he was very willing to have help; and so, high rewards were advertised, for any who would go unarmed with him. This opportunity was declined. Robinson persuaded some tamed natives of both sexes to go with him—a strong evidence of his persuasive powers, for those natives well knew that their destruction would be almost certain. As it turned out, they had to face death over and over again.

Robinson and his little party had a difficult undertaking upon their hands. They could not ride off, horseback, comfortably into the woods and call Leonidas and his three hundred together for a talk and a treaty the following day; for the wild men were not in a body; they were scattered, immense distances apart, over regions so desolate that even the birds could not make a living with the chances offered—scattered in groups of twenty, a dozen, half a dozen, even in groups of three. And the mission must go on foot. Mr. Bonwick furnishes a description of those horrible regions, whereby it will be seen that even fugitive gangs of the hardiest and choicest human devils the world has seen—the convicts set apart to people the "Hell of Macquarrie Harbor Station"—were never able, but once, to survive the horrors of a march through them, but, starving and struggling, and fainting and failing, ate each other, and died:

> Onward, still onward, was the order of the indomitable Robinson. No one ignorant of the western country of Tasmania can form a correct idea of the traveling difficulties. While I was resident in Hobart Town, the Governor, Sir John Franklin, and his lady, undertook the western journey to Macquarrie Harbor, and suffered terribly. One man who assisted to carry her ladyship through the swamps, gave me this bitter experience of its miseries. Several were disabled for life. No wonder that but one party, escaping from Macquarrie Harbor convict

settlement, arrived at the civilized region in safety. Men perished in the scrub, were lost in snow, or were devoured by their companions. This was the territory traversed by Mr. Robinson and his Black guides. All honor to his intrepidity, and their wonderful fidelity! When they had, in the depth of winter, to cross deep and rapid rivers, pass among mountains six thousand feet high, pierce dangerous thickets, and find food in a country forsaken even by birds, we can realize their hardships.

After a frightful journey by Cradle Mountain, and over the lofty plateau of Middlesex Plains, the travelers experienced unwonted misery, and the circumstances called forth the best qualities of the noble little band. Mr. Robinson wrote afterward to Mr. Secretary Burnett some details of this passage of horrors. In that letter, of October 2, 1834, he states that his Natives were very reluctant to go over the dreadful mountain passes; that "for seven successive days we continued traveling over one solid body of snow"; that "the snows were of incredible depth"; that "the Natives were frequently up to their middle in snow." But still the ill-clad, ill-fed, diseased, and wayworn men and women were sustained by the cheerful voice of their unconquerable friend, and responded most nobly to his call.

Mr. Bonwick says that Robinson's friendly capture of the Big River tribe—remember, it was a whole tribe—"was by far the grandest feature of the war, and the crowning glory of his efforts." The word "war" was not well chosen, and is misleading. There *was* war still, but only the Blacks were conducting it—the Whites were holding off until Robinson could give his scheme a fair trial. I think that we are to understand that the friendly capture of that tribe was by far the most important thing, the highest in value, that happened during the whole thirty years of truceless hostilities; that it was a decisive thing, a peaceful Waterloo, the surrender of the native Napoleon and his dreaded forces, the happy ending of the long strife. For "that tribe was the terror of the colony," its chief "the Black Douglas of Bush households."

Robinson knew that these formidable people were lurking somewhere, in some remote corner of the hideous regions just described, and he and his unarmed little party started on a tedious and perilous hunt for them. At last, "there, under the shadows of the Frenchman's Cap, whose grim cone rose five thousand feet in the uninhabited westward interior," they were found. It was a serious moment. Robinson himself believed, for once, that his mission, successful until now, was to end here in failure, and that his own death-hour had struck.

The redoubtable chief stood in menacing attitude, with his eighteen-foot spear poised; his warriors stood massed at his back, armed for battle, their faces eloquent with their long-cherished loathing for white men. "They rattled their spears and shouted their war-cry." Their women were back of them, laden with supplies of weapons, and keeping their one hundred and fifty eager dogs quiet until the chief should give the signal to fall on.

"I think we shall soon be in the resurrection," whispered a member of Robinson's little party.

"I think we shall," answered Robinson; then plucked up heart and began his persuasions—in the tribe's own dialect, which surprised and pleased the chief. Presently there was an interruption by the chief:

"Who are you?"

"We are gentlemen."

"Where are your guns?"

"We have none."

The warrior was astonished.

"Where your little guns?" (pistols.)

"We have none."

A few minutes passed—in by-play—suspense—discussion among the tribesmen—Robinson's tamed squaws ventured to cross the line and begin persuasions upon the wild squaws. Then the chief stepped back "to confer with the old women—the real arbiters of savage war." Mr. Bonwick continues:

> As the fallen gladiator in the arena looks for the signal of life or death from the president of the amphitheater, so waited our friends in anxious suspense while the conference continued. In a few minutes, before a word was uttered, the women of the tribe threw up their arms three times. This was the inviolable sign of peace! Down fell the spears. Forward, with a heavy sigh of relief, and upward glance of gratitude, came the friends of peace. The impulsive natives rushed forth with tears and cries, as each saw in the other's ranks a loved one of the past. . . .
>
> It was a jubilee of joy. A festival followed. And, while tears flowed at the recital of woe, a corroboree of pleasant laughter closed the eventful day.

In four years, without the spilling of a drop of blood, Robinson brought them all in, willing captives, and delivered them to the white governor, and ended the war which powder and bullets, and thousands of men to use them, had prosecuted without result since 1804.

Marsyas charming the wild beasts with his music—that is fable; but the miracle wrought by Robinson is fact. It is history—and authentic; and surely, there is nothing greater, nothing more reverence-compelling in the history of any country, ancient or modern.

And in memory of the greatest man Australasia ever developed or ever will develop, there is a stately monument to George Augustus Robinson, the Conciliator, in—no, it is to another man, I forget his name.

However, Robinson's own generation honored him, and in manifesting it honored themselves. The government gave him a money reward and a thousand acres of land; and the people held mass-meetings and praised him and emphasized their praise with a large subscription of money.

A good dramatic situation; but the curtain fell on another:

> When this desperate tribe was thus captured, there was much surprise to find that the thirty thousand pounds of a little earlier day had been spent, and the whole population of the colony placed under arms, in contention with an opposing force of *sixteen men with wooden spears!* Yet such was the fact. The celebrated Big River tribe, that had been raised by European fears to a host, consisted of *sixteen men, nine women, and one child.* With a knowledge of the mischief done by these few, their wonderful marches and their wide-spread aggressions, their enemies cannot deny to them the attributes of courage and military tact. A Wallace might harass a large army with a small and determined band; but the contending parties were at least equal in arms and civilization. The Zulus who fought us in Africa, the Maoris in New Zealand, the Arabs in the Soudan, were far better provided with weapons, more advanced in the science of war, and considerably more numerous, than the naked Tasmanians. Governor Arthur rightly termed them a *noble race.*

These were indeed wonderful people, the natives. They ought not to have been wasted. They should have been crossed with the Whites. It would have improved the Whites and done the Natives no harm.

But the Natives *were* wasted, poor heroic wild creatures.

They were gathered together in little settlements on neighboring islands, and paternally cared for by the government, and instructed in religion, and deprived of tobacco, because the superintendent of the Sunday-school was not a smoker, and so considered smoking immoral.

The Natives were not used to clothes, and houses, and regular hours, and church, and school, and Sunday-school, and work, and the other misplaced persecutions of civilization, and they pined for their lost home and their wild, free life. Too late they repented that they had traded that heaven for this hell. They sat homesick on their alien crags, and day by day gazed out through their tears over the sea with unappeasable longing toward the hazy bulk which was the specter of what had been their paradise; one by one their hearts broke and they died.

In a very few years nothing but a scant remnant remained alive. A handful lingered along into age. In 1864 the last man died, in 1876 the last woman died, and the Spartans of Australasia were extinct.

The Whites always mean well when they take human fish out of the ocean and try to make them dry and warm and happy and comfortable in a chicken-coop; but the kindest-hearted white man can always be depended on to prove himself inadequate when he deals with savages. He cannot turn the situation around and imagine how he would like it to have a well-meaning savage transfer him from his house and his church and his clothes and his books and his choice food to a hideous wilderness of sand and rocks and snow, and ice and sleet and storm and blistering sun, with no shelter, no bed, no covering for his and his family's naked bodies, and nothing to eat but snakes and grubs and offal. This would be a hell to him; and if he had any wisdom he would know that his own civilization is a hell to the savage—but he hasn't any, and has never had any; and for lack of it he shut up those poor natives in the unimaginable perdition of his civilization, committing his crime with the very best intentions, and saw those poor creatures waste away under his tortures; and gazed at it, vaguely troubled and sorrowful, and wondered what could be the matter with them. One is almost betrayed into respecting those criminals, they were so sincerely kind, and tender, and humane, and well-meaning.

They didn't know why those exiled savages faded away, and they did their honest best to reason it out. And one man, in a like case, in New South Wales, *did* reason it out and arrive at a solution:

"It is from the wrath of God, which is revealed from heaven against all ungodliness and unrighteousness of men."

That settles it.

Chapter XXVIII

Let us be thankful for the fools. But for them the rest of us could not succeed.
> —*Pudd'nhead Wilson's New Calendar.*

THE aphorism does really seem true: "Given the Circumstances, the Man will appear." But the man mustn't appear ahead of time, or it will spoil everything. In Robinson's case the Moment had been approaching for a quarter of a century—and meantime the future Conciliator was tranquilly laying bricks in Hobart. When all other means had failed, the Moment had arrived, and the Bricklayer put down his trowel and came forward. Earlier he would have been jeered back to his trowel again. It reminds me of a tale that was told me by a Kentuckian on the train when we were crossing Montana. He said the tale was current in Louisville years ago. He thought it had been in print, but could not remember. At any rate, in substance it was this, as nearly as I can call it back to mind.

A few years before the outbreak of the Civil War it began to appear that Memphis, Tennessee, was going to be a great tobacco *entrepôt*—the wise could see the signs of it. At that time Memphis had a wharfboat, of course. There was a paved sloping wharf, for the accommodation of freight, but the steamers landed on the outside of the wharfboat, and all loading and unloading was done across it, between steamer and shore. A number of wharfboat clerks were needed, and part of the time, every day, they were very busy, and part of the time tediously idle. They were boiling over with youth and spirits, and they had to make the intervals of idleness endurable in some way; and as a rule, they did it by contriving practical jokes and playing them upon each other.

The favorite butt for the jokes was Ed Jackson, because he played none himself, and was easy game for other people's—for he always believed whatever was told him.

One day he told the others his scheme for his holiday. He was not going fishing or hunting this time—no, he had thought out a better plan. Out of his forty dollars a month he had saved enough for his purpose, in an economical way, and he was going to have a look at New York.

It was a great and surprising idea. It meant travel—immense travel—in those days it meant seeing the world; it was the equivalent of a voyage around it in ours. At first the other youths thought his mind was affected, but when they found that he was in earnest, the next thing to be thought of was, what sort of opportunity this venture might afford for a practical joke.

The young men studied over the matter, then held a secret consultation and made a plan. The idea was, that one of the conspirators should offer Ed a letter of introduction to Commodore Vanderbilt, and trick him into delivering it. It would be easy to do this. But what would Ed do when he got back to Memphis? That was a serious matter. He was good-hearted, and had always taken the jokes patiently; but they had been jokes which did not humiliate him, did not bring him to shame; whereas, this would be a cruel one in that way, and to play it was to meddle with fire; for with all his good nature, Ed was a Southerner—and the English of that was, that when he came back he would kill as many of the conspirators as he could before falling himself. However, the chances must be taken—it wouldn't do to waste such a joke as that.

So the letter was prepared with great care and elaboration. It was signed Alfred Fairchild, and was written in an easy and friendly spirit. It stated that the bearer was the bosom friend of the writer's son, and was of good parts and sterling character, and it begged the Commodore to be kind to the young stranger for the writer's sake. It went on to say, "You may have forgotten me, in this long stretch of time, but you will easily call me back out of your boyhood memories when I remind you of how we robbed old Stevenson's orchard that night; and how, while he was chasing down the road after us, we cut across the field and doubled back and sold his own apples to his own cook for a hatful of doughnuts; and the time that we—" and so forth and so on, bringing in names of imaginary comrades, and detailing all sorts of wild and absurd and, of course, wholly imaginary school-boy pranks and adventures, but putting them into lively and telling shape.

With all gravity Ed was asked if he would like to have a letter to Commodore Vanderbilt, the great millionaire. It was expected that the question would astonish Ed, and it did.

"What? Do *you* know that extraordinary man?"

"No; but my father does. They were schoolboys together. And if you like, I'll write and ask father. I know he'll be glad to give it to you for my sake."

Ed could not find words capable of expressing his gratitude and delight. The three days passed, and the letter was put into his hands. He started on his trip, still pouring out his thanks while he shook good-by all around. And when he was out of sight his comrades let fly their laughter in a storm of happy satisfaction—and then quieted down, and were less happy, less satisfied. For the old doubts as to the wisdom of this deception began to intrude again.

Arrived in New York, Ed found his way to Commodore Vanderbilt's business quarters, and was ushered into a large anteroom, where a score of people were patiently awaiting their turn for a two-minute interview with the millionaire in his private office. A servant asked for Ed's card, and got the letter instead. Ed was sent for a moment later, and found Mr. Vanderbilt alone, with the letter—open—in his hand.

"Pray sit down, Mr.—er—"

"Jackson."

"Ah—sit down, Mr. Jackson. By the opening sentences it seems to be a letter from an old friend. Allow me—I will run my eye through it. He says—he says—why, who *is* it?" He turned the sheet and found the signature. "Alfred Fairchild—h'm—Fairchild—I don't recall the name. But that is nothing—a thousand names have gone from me. He says— he says—h'm—h'm—oh, dear, but it's good! Oh, it's rare! I don't *quite* remember it, but I *seem* to—it'll all come back to me presently. He says—he says—h'm—h'm—oh, but that was a game! Oh, spl-endid! How it carries me back! It's all dim, of course—it's a long time ago—and the names—*some* of the names are wavery and indistinct—but sho', I know it happened—I can *feel* it! and lord, how it warms my heart, and brings back my lost youth! Well, well, well, I've got to come back into this workaday world now—business presses and people are waiting—I'll keep the rest for bed to-night, and live my youth over again. And you'll thank Fairchild for me when you see him—I used to call him Alf, I think—and you'll give him my gratitude for what this letter has done for the tired spirit of a hard-worked man; and tell him there isn't anything that I can do for him or any friend of his that I won't do. And as for you, my lad, you are my guest; you can't stop at any hotel in New York. Sit where you are a little while, till I get through with these people, then we'll go home. I'll take care of *you*, my boy—make yourself easy as to that."

Ed stayed a week, and had an immense time—and never suspected that the Commodore's shrewd eyes were on him, and that he was daily being weighed and measured and analyzed and tried and tested.

Yes, he had an immense time; and never wrote home, but saved it all up to tell when he should get back. Twice, with proper modesty and decency, he proposed to end his visit, but the Commodore said, "No—wait; leave it to me; I'll tell you when to go."

In those days the Commodore was making some of those vast combinations of his—consolidations of warring odds and ends of railroads into harmonious systems, and concentrations of floating and rudderless commerce in effective centers—and among other things his far-seeing eye had detected the convergence of that huge tobacco-commerce, already spoken of, toward Memphis, and he had resolved to set his grasp upon it and make it his own.

The week came to an end. Then the Commodore said:

"Now you can start home. But first we will have some more talk about that tobacco matter. I know you now. I know your abilities as well as you know them yourself—perhaps better. You understand that tobacco matter; you understand that I am going to take possession of it, and you also understand the plans which I have matured for doing it. What I want is a man who knows my mind, and is qualified to represent me in Memphis, and be in supreme command of that important business—and I appoint you."

"Me!"

"Yes. Your salary will be high—of course—for you are representing me. Later you will earn increases of it, and will get them. You will need a small army of assistants; choose them yourself—and carefully. Take no man for friendship's sake; but, all things being equal, take the man you know, take your friend, in preference to the stranger."

After some further talk under this head, the Commodore said: "Good-by, my boy, and thank Alf for me, for sending you to me."

When Ed reached Memphis he rushed down to the wharf in a fever to tell his great news and thank the boys over and over again for thinking to give him the letter to Mr. Vanderbilt. It happened to be one of those idle times. Blazing hot noonday, and no sign of life on the wharf. But as Ed threaded his way among the freight-piles, he saw a white linen figure stretched in slumber upon a pile of grain-sacks under an awning, and said to himself, "That's one of them," and hastened his step; next, he said, "It's Charley—it's Fairchild—good"; and the next moment laid an affectionate hand on the sleeper's shoulder. The eyes opened lazily, took one glance, the face blanched, the form whirled itself from the sack-pile, and in an instant Ed was alone and Fairchild was flying for the wharfboat like the wind!

Ed was dazed, stupefied. Was Fairchild crazy? What could be the meaning of this? He started slow and dreamily down toward the wharfboat; turned the corner of a freight-pile and came suddenly upon two of the boys. They were lightly laughing over some pleasant matter; they heard his step, and glanced up just as he discovered them; the laugh died abruptly; and before Ed could speak they were off, and sailing over barrels and bales like hunted deer. Again Ed was paralyzed. Had the boys all gone mad? What *could* be the explanation of this extraordinary conduct? And so, dreaming along, he reached the wharfboat, and stepped aboard—nothing but silence there, and vacancy. He crossed the deck, turned the corner to go down the outer guard, heard a fervent—

"O Lord!" and saw a white linen form plunge overboard.

The youth came up coughing and strangling, and cried out:

"Go 'way from here! You let me alone. *I* didn't do it, I swear I didn't!"

"Didn't do *what*?"

"Give you the—"

"Never mind what you didn't do—come out of that! What makes you all act so? What have *I* done?"

"You? Why, *you* haven't done anything. But—"

"Well, then, what have you got against me? What do you all treat me so for?"

"I—er—but haven't you got anything against *us*?"

"Of course not. What put such a thing into your head?"

"Honor bright—you haven't?"

"Honor bright."

"Swear it!"

"I don't know what in the *world* you mean, but I swear it, anyway."

"And you'll shake hands with me?"

"Goodness knows I'll be *glad* to! Why, I'm just starving to shake hands with *somebody*!"

The swimmer muttered, "Hang him, he smelt a rat and never delivered the letter!—but it's all right, I'm not going to fetch up the subject." And he crawled out and came dripping and draining to shake hands. First one and then another of the conspirators showed up cautiously—armed to the teeth—took in the amicable situation, then ventured warily forward and joined the love-feast.

And to Ed's eager inquiry as to what made them act as they had been acting, they answered evasively and pretended that they had put it up as a joke, to see what he would do. It was the best explanation they could invent at such short notice. And each said to himself, "He never delivered that letter, and the joke is on *us*, if he only knew it or we were dull enough to come out and tell."

Then, of course, they wanted to know all about the trip; and he said:

"Come right up on the boiler deck and order the drinks—it's my treat. I'm going to tell you all about it. And to-night it's my treat again—and we'll have oysters and a time!"

When the drinks were brought and cigars lighted, Ed said:

"Well, when I delivered the letter to Mr. Vanderbilt—"

"Great Scott!"

"Gracious, how you scared me. What's the matter?"

"Oh—er—nothing. Nothing—it was a tack in the chair-seat," said one.

"But you *all* said it. However, no matter. When I delivered the letter—"

"*Did* you deliver it?" And they looked at each other as people might who thought that maybe they were dreaming.

Then they settled to listening; and as the story deepened and its marvels grew, the amazement of it made them dumb, and the interest of it took their breath. They hardly uttered a whisper during two hours, but sat like petrifactions and drank in the immortal romance. At last the tale was ended, and Ed said:

"And it's all owing to *you*, boys, and you'll never find *me* ungrateful—bless your hearts, the best friends a fellow ever had! You'll all have places; I want every one of you. I *know* you—I know you 'by the *back*,' as the gamblers say. You're jokers, and all that, but you're *sterling*, with the hall-mark *on*. And Charley Fairchild, you shall be my first assistant and right hand, because of your first-class ability, and because you got me the letter, and for your father's sake who wrote it for me, and to please Mr. Vanderbilt, who *said* it would! And here's to that great man—drink hearty!"

Yes, when the Moment comes, the Man appears—even if he is a thousand miles away, and has to be discovered by a practical joke.

Chapter XXIX

NECESSARILY, the human interest is the first interest in the log-book of any country. The annals of Tasmania, in whose shadow we were sailing, are lurid with that feature. Tasmania was a convict-dump, in old times; this has been indicated in the account of the Conciliator, where reference is made to vain attempts of desperate convicts to win to permanent freedom, after escaping from Macquarrie Harbor and the "Gates of Hell." In the early days Tasmania had a great population of convicts, of both sexes and all ages, and a bitter hard life they had. In one spot there was a settlement of juvenile convicts—children—who had been sent thither from their home and their friends on the other side of the globe to expiate their "crimes."

In due course our ship entered the estuary called the Derwent, at whose head stands Hobart, the capital of Tasmania. The Derwent's shores furnish scenery of an interesting sort. The historian Laurie, whose book, *The Story of Australasia,* is just out, invoices its features with considerable truth and intemperance: "The marvelous picturesqueness of every point of view, combined with the clear balmy atmosphere and the transparency of the ocean depths, must have delighted and deeply impressed" the early explorers. "If the rock-bound coasts, sullen, defiant, and lowering, seemed uninviting, these were occasionally broken into charmingly alluring coves floored with golden sand, clad with evergreen shrubbery, and adorned with every variety of indigenous wattle, she-oak, wild flower, and fern, from the delicately graceful 'maiden-hair' to the palm-like 'old man'; while the majestic gum tree, clean and smooth as the mast of 'some tall ammiral,' pierces the clear air to the height of two hundred and thirty feet or more."

It looks so to me. "Coasting along Tasman's Peninsula, what a shock of pleasant wonder must have struck the early mariner on suddenly sighting Cape Pillar, with its cluster of black-ribbed basaltic columns rising to a height of nine hundred feet, the hydra heads wreathed in a turban of fleecy cloud, the base lashed by jealous waves spouting angry fountains of foam."

That is well enough, but I did not suppose those snags were nine hundred feet high. Still they were a very fine show. They stood boldly out by themselves, and made a fascinatingly odd spectacle. But there was nothing about their appearance to suggest the heads of a hydra. They looked like a row of lofty slabs with their upper ends tapered to the shape of a carving-knife point; in fact, the early voyager, ignorant of their great height, might have mistaken them for a rusty old rank of piles that had sagged this way and that out of the perpendicular.

The Peninsula is lofty, rocky, and densely clothed with scrub, or brush, or both. It is joined to the main by a low neck. At this junction was formerly a convict station called Port Arthur—a place hard to escape from. Behind it was the wilderness of scrub, in which a fugitive would soon starve; in front was the narrow neck, with a cordon of chained dogs across it, and a line of lanterns, and a fence of living guards, armed. We saw the place as we swept by—that is, we had a glimpse of what we were told was the entrance to Port Arthur. The glimpse was worth something, as a remembrancer, but that was all.

"The voyage thence up the Derwent Frith displays a grand succession of fairy visions, in its entire length elsewhere unequaled. In gliding over the deep blue sea studded with lovely islets luxuriant to the water's edge, one is at a loss which scene to choose for contemplation and to admire most. When the Huon and Bruni have been passed, there seems no possible chance of a rival; but suddenly Mount Wellington, massive and noble like his brother Etna, literally heaves in sight, sternly guarded on either hand by Mounts Nelson and Rumney; presently we arrive at Sullivan's Cove—Hobart!"

It is an attractive town. It sits on low hills that slope to the harbor—a harbor that looks like a river, and is as smooth as one. Its still surface is pictured with dainty reflections of boats and grassy banks and luxuriant foliage. Back of the town rise highlands that are clothed in woodland loveliness, and over the way is that noble mountain, Wellington, a stately bulk, a most majestic pile. How beautiful is the whole region, for form, and grouping, and opulence, and freshness of foliage, and variety of color, and grace and shapeliness of the hills, the capes, the promontories; and then, the splendor of the sunlight, the dim rich distances, the charm of the water-glimpses! And it was in this paradise that the yellow-liveried convicts were landed, and the Corps-bandits quartered, and the wanton slaughter of the kangaroo-chasing black innocents consummated on that autumn day in May, in the brutish old time. It was all out of keeping with the place, a sort of bringing of heaven and hell together.

The remembrance of this paradise reminds me that it was at Hobart that we struck the head of the procession of Junior Englands. We were to encounter other sections of it in New Zealand, presently, and others later in Natal. Wherever the exiled Englishman can find in his new home resemblances to his old one, he is touched to the marrow of his being; the love that is in his heart inspires his imagination, and these allied forces transfigure those resemblances into authentic duplicates of the revered originals. It is beautiful, the feeling which works this enchantment, and it compels one's homage; compels it, and also compels one's assent—compels it always—even when, as happens sometimes, one does not see the resemblances as clearly as does the exile who is pointing them out.

The resemblances do exist, it is quite true; and often they cunningly approximate the originals—but after all, in the matter of certain physical patent rights there is only one England. Now that I have sampled the globe, I am not in doubt. There is a beauty of Switzerland, and it is repeated in the glaciers and snowy ranges of many parts of the earth; there is a beauty of the fiord, and it is repeated in New Zealand and Alaska; there is a beauty of Hawaii, and it is repeated in ten thousand islands of the Southern seas; there is a beauty of the prairie and the plain, and it is repeated here and there in the earth; each of these is worshipful, each is perfect in its way, yet holds no monopoly of its beauty; but that beauty which is England is alone—it has no duplicate. It is made up of very simple details—just grass, and trees, and shrubs, and roads, and hedges, and gardens, and houses, and vines, and churches, and castles, and here and there a ruin—and over it all a mellow dream-haze of history. But its beauty is incomparable, and all its own.

Hobart has a peculiarity—it is the neatest town that the sun shines on; and I incline to believe that it is also the cleanest. However that may be, its supremacy in neatness is not to be questioned. There cannot be another town in the world that has no shabby exteriors; no rickety gates and fences, no neglected houses crumbling to ruin, no crazy and unsightly sheds, no weed-grown front yards of the poor, no back yards littered with tin cans and old boots and empty bottles, no rubbish in the gutters, no clutter on the sidewalks, no outer borders fraying out into dirty lanes and tin-patched huts. No, in Hobart all the aspects are tidy, and all a comfort to the eye; the modestest cottage looks combed and brushed, and has its vines, its flowers, its neat fence, its neat gate, its comely cat asleep on the window ledge.

We had a glimpse of the museum, by courtesy of the American gentleman who is curator of it. It has samples of half a dozen different kinds of marsupials[1]—one, the "Tasmanian devil"; that is, I *think* he was one of them. And there was a fish with lungs. When the water dries up it can live in the mud. Most curious of all was a parrot that kills sheep. On one great sheep-run this bird killed a thousand sheep in a whole year. He doesn't want the whole sheep, but only the kidney-fat. This restricted taste makes him an expensive bird to support. To get the fat he drives his beak in and rips it out; the wound is mortal. This parrot furnishes a notable example of evolution brought about by changed conditions. When the

[1] A marsupial is a plantigrade vertebrate whose specialty is its pocket. In some countries it is extinct, in the others it is rare. The first American marsupials were Stephen Girard, Mr. Astor, and the opossum; the principal marsupials of the Southern Hemisphere are Mr. Rhodes and the kangaroo. I, myself, am the latest marsupial. Also, I might boast that I have the largest pocket of them all. But there is nothing in that.

sheep culture was introduced, it presently brought famine to the parrot by exterminating a kind of grub which had always hitherto been the parrot's diet. The miseries of hunger made the bird willing to eat raw flesh, since it could get no other food, and it began to pick remnants of meat from sheep-skins hung out on the fences to dry. It soon came to prefer sheep meat to any other food, and by and by it came to prefer the kidney-fat to any other detail of the sheep. The parrot's bill was not well shaped for digging out the fat, but Nature fixed that matter; she altered the bill's shape, and now the parrot can dig out kidney-fat better than the Chief Justice of the Supreme Court, or anybody else, for that matter—even an Admiral.

And there was another curiosity—quite a stunning one, I thought: Arrow-heads and knives just like those which Primeval Man made out of flint, and thought he had done such a wonderful thing—yes, and has been humored and coddled in that superstition by this age of admiring scientists until there is probably no living with him in the other world by now. Yet here is his finest and nicest work exactly duplicated in our day; and by people who have never heard of him or his works: by aborigines who lived in the islands of these seas, within our time. And they not only duplicated those works of art but did it in the brittlest and most treacherous of substances—*glass*: made them out of old brandy bottles flung out of the British camps; millions of tons of them. It is time for Primeval Man to make a little less noise, now. He has had his day. He is not what he used to be.

We had a drive through a bloomy and odorous fairy-land, to the Refuge for the Indigent—a spacious and comfortable home, with hospitals, etc., for both sexes. There was a crowd there, of the oldest people I have ever seen. It was like being suddenly set down in a new world—a weird world where Youth has never been, a world sacred to Age, and bowed forms, and wrinkles. Out of the 359 persons present, 223 were ex-convicts, and could have told stirring tales, no doubt, if they had been minded to talk; 42 of the 359 were past 80, and several were close upon 90; the average age at death there is 76 years. As for me, I have no use for that place; it is too healthy. Seventy is old enough—after that, there is too much risk. Youth and gaiety might vanish, any day—and then, what is left? Death in life; death without its privileges, death without its benefits. There were 185 women in that Refuge, and 81 of them were ex-convicts.

The steamer disappointed us. Instead of making a long visit at Hobart, as usual, she made a short one. So we got but a glimpse of Tasmania, and then moved on.

Chapter XXX

Nature makes the locust with an appetite for crops;
man would have made him with an appetite for sand.
                    —Pudd'nhead Wilson's New Calendar.

WE spent part of an afternoon and a night at sea, and reached Bluff, in New Zealand, early in the morning. Bluff is at the bottom of the middle island, and is away down south, nearly forty-seven degrees below the equator. It lies as far south of the line as Quebec lies north of it, and the climates of the two should be alike; but for some reason or other it has not been so arranged. Quebec is hot in the summer and cold in the winter, but Bluff's climate is less intense; the cold weather is not very cold, the hot weather is not very hot; and the difference between the hottest month and the coldest is but seventeen degrees Fahrenheit.

In New Zealand the rabbit plague began at Bluff. The man who introduced the rabbit there was banqueted and lauded; but they would hang him, now, if they could get him. In England the natural enemy of the rabbit is detested and persecuted; in the Bluff region the natural enemy of the rabbit is honored, and his person is sacred. The rabbit's natural enemy in England is the poacher; in Bluff its natural enemy is the stoat, the weasel, the ferret, the cat, and the mongoose. In England any person below the Heir who is caught with a rabbit in his possession must satisfactorily explain how it got there, or he will suffer fine and imprisonment, together with extinction of his peerage; in Bluff, the cat found with a rabbit in its possession does not have to explain—everybody looks the other way; the person caught noticing would suffer fine and imprisonment, with extinction of peerage. This is a sure way to undermine the moral fabric of a cat. Thirty years from now there will not be a moral cat in New Zealand. Some think there is none there now. In England the poacher is watched, tracked, hunted—he dare not show his face; in Bluff the cat, the weasel, the stoat, and the mongoose go up and down, whither they will, unmolested. By a law of the legislature, posted where all may read, it is decreed that any person found in possession of one of these creatures (dead) must satisfactorily explain the circumstances or pay a fine of not less than five pounds, nor more than twenty pounds. The revenue from this source is not large. Persons who want to pay a hundred dollars for a dead cat are getting rarer and rarer every day. This is bad, for the revenue was to go to the endowment of a university. All governments are more or less short-sighted: in England they fine a poacher, whereas he ought to be banished to New Zealand. New Zealand would pay his way, and give him wages.

It was from Bluff that we ought to have cut across to the west coast and visited the New Zealand Switzerland, a land of superb scenery, made up of snowy grandeurs, and mighty glaciers, and beautiful lakes; and over there, also, are the wonderful rivals of the Norwegian and Alaskan fiords; and for neighbor, a waterfall of nineteen hundred feet; but we were obliged to postpone the trip to some later and indefinite time.

November 6. A lovely summer morning; brilliant blue sky. A few miles out from Invercargill, passed through vast level green expanses snowed over with sheep. Fine to see. The green, deep and very vivid sometimes; at other times less so, but delicate and lovely. A passenger reminds me that I am in "the England of the Far South."

Dunedin, same date. The town justifies Michael Davitt's praises. The people are Scotch. They stopped here on their way from home to heaven—thinking they had arrived. The population is stated at forty thousand, by Malcolm Ross, journalist; stated by an M.P. at sixty thousand. A journalist cannot lie.

To the residence of Dr. Hockin. He has a fine collection of books relating to New Zealand; and his house is a museum of Maori art and antiquities. He has pictures and prints in color of many native chiefs of the past—some of them of note in history. There is nothing of the savage in the faces; nothing could be finer than these men's features, nothing more intellectual than these faces, nothing more masculine, nothing nobler than their aspect. The aboriginals of Australia and Tasmania looked the savage, but these chiefs looked like Roman patricians. The tattooing in these portraits ought to suggest the savage, of course, but it does not. The designs are so flowing and graceful and beautiful that they are a most satisfactory decoration. It takes but fifteen minutes to get reconciled to the tattooing, and but fifteen more to perceive that it is just the thing. After that, the undecorated European face is unpleasant and ignoble.

Dr. Hockin gave us a ghastly curiosity—a lignified caterpillar with a plant growing out of the back of its neck—a plant with a slender stem four inches high. It happened not by accident, but by design—Nature's design. This caterpillar was in the act of loyally carrying out a law inflicted upon him by Nature—a law purposely inflicted upon him to get him into trouble—a law which was a trap; in pursuance of this law he made the proper preparations for turning himself into a night-moth; that is to say, he dug a little trench, a little grave, and then stretched himself out in it on his stomach and partially buried himself—then Nature was ready for him. She blew the spores of a peculiar fungus through the air—with a purpose. Some of them fell into a crease in the back of the caterpillar's neck, and began to sprout and grow—for there was soil there—he had not washed his neck. The roots forced themselves down into the worm's person, and rearward along through its body, sucking up the creature's juices for sap; the worm slowly died, and turned to wood. And here he was now, a wooden caterpillar, with every detail of his former physique delicately and exactly preserved and perpetuated, and with that stem standing up out of him for his monu- ment—monument commemorative of his own loyalty and of Nature's unfair return for it.

Nature is always acting like that. Mrs. X said (of course) that the caterpillar was not conscious and didn't suffer. She should have known better. No caterpillar can deceive Nature. If this one couldn't suffer, Nature would have known it and would have hunted up another caterpillar. Not that she would have let this one go, merely because it was defective. No. She would have waited and let him turn into a night-moth; and then fried him in the candle.

Nature cakes a fish's eyes over with parasites, so that it sha'n't be able to avoid its enemies or find its food. She sends parasites into a starfish's system, which clog up its prongs and swell them and make them so uncomfortable that the poor creature delivers itself from the prong to ease its misery; and presently it has to part with another prong for the sake of comfort, and finally with a third. If it regrows the prongs, the parasite returns and the same thing is repeated. And fi- nally, when the ability to reproduce prongs is lost through age, that poor old starfish can't get around any more, and so it dies of starvation.

In Australia is prevalent a horrible disease due to an "unperfected tape-worm." Unperfected—that is what they call it, I do not know why, for it transacts business just as well as if it were finished and frescoed and gilded, and all that.

November 9. To the museum and public picture-gallery with the president of the Society of Artists. Some fine pictures there, lent by the S. of A.—several of them they bought, the others came to them by gift. Next, to the gallery of the S. of A.—annual exhibition—just opened. Fine. Think of a town like this having two such collections as this, and a Society of Artists. It is so all over Australasia. If it were a monarchy one might understand it. I mean an absolute monarchy, where it isn't necessary to vote money, but take it. Then art flourishes. But these colonies are republics—republics with a wide suffrage; voters of both sexes, this one of New Zealand. In republics, neither the government nor the rich private citizen is much given to propagating art. All over Australasia pictures by famous European artists are bought for the public galleries by the state and by societies of citizens. Living citizens—not dead ones. They rob *themselves* to give, not their heirs. This S. of A. here owns its building—built it by subscription.

Chapter XXXI

The spirit of wrath—not the words—is the sin;
and the spirit of wrath is cursing. We begin to swear
before we can talk.
       —Pudd'nhead Wilson's New Calendar.

NOVEMBER 11. On the road. This train—express—goes twenty and one-half miles an hour, schedule time; but it is fast enough, the outlook upon sea and land is so interesting, and the cars so comfortable. They are not English, and not American; they are the Swiss combination of the two. A narrow and railed porch along the side, where a person can walk up and down. A lavatory in each car. This is progress; this is nineteenth-century spirit. In New Zealand, these fast expresses run twice a week. It is well to know this if you want to be a bird and fly through the country at a twenty-mile gait; otherwise you may start on one of the five wrong days, and then you will get a train that can't overtake its own shadow.

By contrast, these pleasant cars call to mind the branch-road cars at Maryborough, Australia, and a passenger's talk about the branch-road and the hotel.

Somewhere on the road to Maryborough I changed for

a while to a smoking-carriage. There were two gentlemen there; both riding backward, one at each end of the compartment. They were acquaintances of each other. I sat down facing the one that sat at the starboard window. He had a good face, and a friendly look, and I judged from his dress that he was a dissenting minister. He was along toward fifty. Of his own motion he struck a match, and shaded it with his hand for me to light my cigar. I take the rest from my diary:

In order to start conversation I asked him something about Maryborough. He said, in a most pleasant—even musical—voice, but with quiet and cultured decision:

"It's a charming town, with a hell of a hotel."

I was astonished. It seemed so odd to hear a minister swear out loud. He went placidly on:

"It's the worst hotel in Australia. Well, one may go further, and say in Australasia."

"Bad beds?"

"No—none at all. Just sand-bags."

"The pillows, too?"

"Yes, the pillows, too. Just sand. And not a good quality of sand. It packs too hard, and has never been screened. There is too much gravel in it. It is like sleeping on nuts."

"Isn't there any good sand?"

"Plenty of it. There is as good bed-sand in this region as the world can furnish. Aerated sand—and loose; but they won't buy it. They want something that will pack solid, and petrify."

"How are the rooms?"

"Eight feet square; and a sheet of iced oil-cloth to step on in the morning when you get out of the sand-quarry."

"As to lights?"

"Coal-oil lamp."

"A good one?"

"No. It's the kind that sheds a gloom."

"I like a lamp that burns all night."

"This one won't. You must blow it out early."

"That is bad. One might want it again in the night. Can't find it in the dark."

"There's no trouble; you can find it by the stench."

"Wardrobe?"

"Two nails on the door to hang seven suits of clothes on—if you've got them."

"Bells?"

"There aren't any."

"What do you do when you want service?"

"Shout. But it won't fetch anybody."

"Suppose you want the chambermaid to empty the slop-jar?"

"There isn't any slop-jar. The hotels don't keep them. That is, outside of Sydney and Melbourne."

"Yes, I knew that. I was only talking. It's the oddest thing in Australia. Another thing: I've got to get up in the dark, in the morning, to take the five-o'clock train. Now if the boots—"

"There isn't any."

"Well, the porter."

"There isn't any."

"But who will call me?"

"Nobody. You'll call yourself. And you'll light yourself, too. There'll not be a light burning in the halls or anywhere. And if you don't carry a light, you'll break your neck."

"But who will help me down with my baggage?"

"Nobody. However, I will tell you what to do. In Maryborough there's an American who has lived there half a lifetime; a fine man, and prosperous and popular. He will be on the lookout for you; you won't have any trouble. Sleep in peace; he will rout you out, and you will make your train. Where is your manager?"

"I left him at Ballarat, studying the language. And besides, he had to go to Melbourne and get us ready for New Zealand. I've not tried to pilot myself before, and it doesn't look easy."

"Easy! You've selected the very most difficult piece of railroad in Australia for your experiment. There are twelve miles of this road which no man without good executive ability can ever hope—tell me, have you good executive ability?—first-rate executive ability?"

"I—well, I think so, but—"

"That settles it. The tone of —oh, *you* wouldn't ever make it in the world. However, that American will point you right, and you'll go. You've got tickets?"

"Yes—round trip; all the way to Sydney."

"Ah, there it is, you see! You are going in the five o'clock by Castlemaine—twelve miles—instead of the seven-fifteen by Ballarat—in order to save two hours of fooling along the road. Now then, don't interrupt—let me have the floor. You're going to save the government a deal of hauling, but that's nothing; your ticket is by Ballarat, and it isn't good over that twelve miles, and so—"

"But why should the government care which way I go?"

"Goodness knows! Ask of the winds that far away with fragments strewed the sea, as the boy that stood on the burning deck used to say. The government chooses to do its railway business in its own way, and it doesn't know as much about it as the French. In the beginning they tried idiots; then they imported the French—which was going backward, you see; now it runs the roads itself—which is going backward again, you see. Why, do you know, in order to curry favor with the voters, the government puts down a road wherever anybody wants it—anybody that owns two sheep and a dog; and by consequence we've got, in the colony of Victoria, eight hundred railway-stations, and the business done at eighty of them doesn't foot up twenty shillings a week."

"Five dollars? Oh, come!"

"It's true. It's the absolute truth."

"Why, there are three or four men on wages at every station."

"I know it. And the station business doesn't pay for the sheep-dip to sanctify their coffee with. It's just as I say. And accommodating? Why, if you shake a rag the train will stop in the midst of the wilderness to pick you up. All that kind of politics costs, you see. And then, besides, any town that has a good many votes and wants a fine station, gets it. Don't you overlook that Maryborough station, if you take an interest in governmental curiosities. Why, you can put the whole population of Maryborough into it, and give them a sofa apiece, and have room for more. You haven't fifteen stations in America that are as big, and you probably haven't five that are half as fine. Why, it's perfectly elegant. And the clock! Everybody will show you the clock. There isn't a station in Europe that's got such a clock. It doesn't strike—and that's one mercy. It hasn't any bell; and as you'll have cause to remember, if you keep your reason, all Australia is simply bedamned with bells. On every quarter-hour, night and day, they jingle a tiresome chime of half a dozen notes—all the clocks in town at once, all the clocks in Australasia at once, and all the *very same* notes; first, downward scale: *mi, re, do, sol*—then upward scale: *sol, si, re, do*—down again: *mi, re, do, sol*—up again: *sol, si, re, do*—then the clock—say at midnight: *clang—clang—clang—clang—clang—clang—clang—clang—clang—clang—clang—clang!—and*, by that time you're—hello, what's all this excitement about? Oh, I see—a runaway—scared by the train; why, you wouldn't think *this* train could scare anything. Well, of course, when they build and run eighty stations at a loss, and a lot of palace-stations and clocks like Maryborough's at another loss, the government has got to economize somewhere, hasn't it? Very well—look at the rolling stock! That's where they save the money. Why, that train from Maryborough will consist of eighteen freight-cars and two passenger-kennels; cheap, poor, shabby, slovenly; no drinking-water, no sanitary arrangements, every imaginable inconvenience; and slow?—oh, the gait of cold molasses; no air-brake, no springs, and they'll jolt your head off every time they start or stop. That's where they make their little economies, you see. They spend tons of money to house you palatially while you wait fifteen minutes for a train, then degrade you to six hours' convict-transportation to get the foolish outlay back. What a rational man really needs is discomfort while he's waiting, then his journey in a nice train would be a grateful change. But no, that would be common sense—and out of place in a government. And then, besides, they save in that other little detail, you know—repudiate their own tickets, and collect a poor little illegitimate extra shilling out of you for that twelve miles, and—"

"Well, in any case—"

"Wait—there's more. Leave that American out of the account and see what would happen. There's nobody on hand to examine your ticket when you arrive. But the conductor will come and examine it when the train is ready to start. It is too late to buy your extra ticket now; the train can't wait, and won't. You must climb out."

"But can't I pay the conductor?"

"No, he is not authorized to receive the money, and he won't. You must climb out. There's no other way. I tell you, the railway management is about the only thoroughly European thing here—continentally European I mean, not English. It's the continental business in perfection; down *fine*.

Oh, yes, even to the peanut-commerce of weighing bag-gage."

The train slowed up at his place. As he stepped out he said:

"Yes, you'll like Maryborough. Plenty of intelligence there. It's a charming place—with a hell of a hotel."

Then he was gone. I turned to the other gentleman:

"Is your friend in the ministry?"

"No—studying for it."

Chapter XXXII

The man with a new idea is a Crank until the idea succeeds.

—Pudd'nhead Wilson's New Calendar.

IT was Junior England all the way to Christchurch—in fact, just a garden. And Christchurch is an English town, with an English-park annex, and a winding English brook just like the Avon—and named the Avon; but from a man, not from Shakespeare's river. Its grassy banks are bordered by the stateliest and most impressive weeping willows to be found in the world, I suppose. They continue the line of a great ancestor; they were grown from sprouts of the willow that sheltered Napoleon's grave in St. Helena. It is a settled old community, with all the serenities, the graces, the conveniences, and the comforts of the ideal home-life. If it had an established Church and social inequality it would be England over again with hardly a lack.

In the museum we saw many curious and interesting things; among others a fine native house of the olden time, with all the details true to the facts, and the showy colors right and in their proper places. All the details: the fine mats and rugs and things; the elaborate and wonderful wood-carvings—wonderful, surely, considering who did them—wonderful in design and particularly in execution, for they were done with admirable sharpness and exactness, and yet with no better tools than flint and jade and shell could furnish; and the totem-posts were there, ancestor above ancestor, with tongues protruded and hands clasped comfortably over bellies containing other people's ancestors—grotesque and ugly devils, every one, but lovingly carved, and ably; and the stuffed natives were present, in their proper places, and looking as natural as life; and the housekeeping utensils were there, too, and close at hand the carved and finely ornamented war-canoe.

And we saw little jade gods, to hang around the neck—not everybody's, but sacred to the necks of natives of rank. Also jade weapons, and many kinds of jade trinkets—all made out of that excessively hard stone without the help of any tool of iron. And some of these things had small round holes bored through them—nobody knows how it was done; a mystery, a lost art. I think it was said that if you want such a hole bored in a piece of jade now, you must send it to London or Amsterdam where the lapidaries are.

Also we saw a complete skeleton of the giant Moa. It stood ten feet high, and must have been a sight to look at when it was a living bird. It was a kicker, like the ostrich; in fight it did not use its beak, but its foot. It must have been a convincing kind of kick. If a person had his back to the bird and did not see who it was that did it, he would think he had been kicked by a wind-mill.

There must have been a sufficiency of moas in the old forgotten days when his breed walked the earth. His bones are found in vast masses, all crammed together in huge graves. They are not in caves, but in the ground. Nobody knows how they happened to get concentrated there. Mind, they are bones, not fossils. This means that the moa has not been extinct very long. Still, this is the only New Zealand creature which has no mention in that otherwise comprehensive literature, the native legends. This is a significant detail, and is good circumstantial evidence that the moa has been extinct five hundred years, since the Maori has himself—by tradition—been in New Zealand since the end of the fifteenth century. He came from an unknown land—the first Maori did—then sailed back in a canoe and brought his tribe, and they removed the aboriginal peoples into the sea and into the ground and took the land. That is the tradition. That that first Maori could come is understandable, for anybody can come to a place when he isn't trying to; but how that discoverer found his way back home again without a compass is his secret, and he died with it in him. His language indicates that he came from Polynesia. He *told* where he came from, but he couldn't spell well, so one can't find the place on the map, because people who could spell better than he could spelled the resemblance all out of it when they made the map. However, it is better to have a map that is spelled right than one that has information in it.

In New Zealand women have the right to vote for members of the legislature, but they cannot be members themselves. The law extending the suffrage to them went into effect in 1893. The population of Christchurch (census of 1891) was 31,454. The first election under the law was held in November of that year. Number of men who voted, 6,313; number of women who voted, 5,989. These figures ought to convince us that women are not as indifferent about politics as some people would have us believe. In New Zealand as a whole, the estimated adult female population was 139,915; of those 109,461 qualified and registered their names on the rolls—78.23 per cent. of the whole. Of these, 90,290 went to the polls and voted—85.18 per cent. Do men ever turn out better than that—in America or elsewhere? Here is a remark to the other sex's credit, too—I take it from the official report:

"A feature of the election was the orderliness and sobriety of the people. Women were in no way molested."

At home, a standing argument against woman suffrage has always been that women could not go to the polls without being insulted. The arguments against woman suffrage have always taken the easy form of prophecy. The prophets have been prophesying ever since the woman's rights movement began in 1848—and in forty-seven years they have never scored a hit.

Men ought to begin to feel a sort of respect for their mothers and wives and sisters by this time. The women deserve a change of attitude like that, for they have wrought well. In forty-seven years they have swept an imposingly large number of unfair laws from the statute-books of America. In that brief time these serfs have set themselves free—essentially. Men could not have done so much for themselves in that time without bloodshed—at least they never have; and that is argument that they didn't know how. The women have accomplished a peaceful revolution, and a very beneficent one; and yet that has not convinced the average man that they are intelligent, and have courage and energy and perseverance and fortitude. It takes much to convince the average man of anything; and perhaps nothing can ever make him realize that he is the average woman's inferior—yet in several important details the evidence seems to show that that is what he is. Man has ruled the human race from the beginning—but he should remember that up to the middle of the present century it was a dull world, and ignorant and stupid; but it is not such a dull world now, and is growing less and less dull all the time. This is woman's opportunity—she has had none before. I wonder where man will be in another forty-seven years?

In New Zealand law occurs this; "The word *person* wherever it occurs throughout the Act includes *woman*."

That is promotion, you see. By that enlargement of the word, the matron with the garnered wisdom and experience of fifty years becomes at one jump the political equal of her callow kid of twenty-one. The white population of the colony is six hundred and twenty-six thousand, the Maori population is forty-two thousand. The whites elect seventy members of the House of Representatives, the Maoris four. The Maori women vote for their four members.

November 16. After four pleasant days in Christchurch, we are to leave at midnight to-night. Mr. Kinsey gave me an ornithorhyncus, and I am taming it.

Sunday, 17. Sailed last night in the *Flora*, from Lyttelton.

So we did. I remember it yet. The people who sailed in the *Flora* that night may forget some other things if they live a good while, but they will not live long enough to forget that. The *Flora* is about the equivalent of a cattle-scow; but when the Union Company find it inconvenient to keep a contract and lucrative to break it, they smuggle her into passenger service, and "keep the change."

They give no notice of their projected depredation; you innocently buy tickets for the advertised passenger-boat, and when you get down to Lyttelton at midnight, you find that they have substituted the scow. They have plenty of good boats, but no competition—and that is the trouble. It is too late now to make other arrangements if you have engagements ahead.

It is a powerful company, it has a monopoly, and everybody is afraid of it—including the government's representative, who stands at the end of the stage-plank to tally the passengers and see that no boat receives a greater number than the law allows her to carry. This conveniently blind representative saw the scow receive a number which was far in excess of its privilege, and winked a politic wink and said nothing. The passengers bore with meekness the cheat which had been put upon them, and made no complaint.

It was like being at home in America, where abused passengers act in just the same way. A few days before, the Union Company had discharged a captain for getting a boat into danger, and had advertised this act as evidence of its vigilance in looking after the safety of the passengers—for thugging a captain costs a company nothing; but when opportunity offered to send this dangerously overcrowded tub to sea and save a little trouble and a tidy penny by it, it forgot to worry about the passengers' safety.

The first officer told me that the *Flora* was privileged to carry one hundred and twenty-five passengers. She must have had all of two hundred on board. All the cabins were full, all the cattle-stalls in the main stable were full, the spaces at the heads of companionways were full, every inch of floor and table in the swill-room was packed with sleeping men and remained so until the place was required for breakfast, all the chairs and benches on the hurricane-deck were occupied, and *still* there were people who had to walk about all night!

If the *Flora* had gone down that night, half of the people on board would have been wholly without means of escape.

The owners of that boat were not technically guilty of conspiracy to commit murder, but they were morally guilty of it.

I had a cattle-stall in the main stable—a cavern fitted up with a long double file of two-storied bunks, the files separated by a calico partition—twenty men and boys on one side of it, twenty women and girls on the other. The place was as dark as the soul of the Union Company, and smelt like a kennel. When the vessel got out into the heavy seas and began to pitch and wallow, the cavern prisoners became immediately seasick, and then the peculiar results that ensued laid all my previous experiences of the kind well away in the shade. And the wails, the groans, the cries, the shrieks, the strange ejaculations—it was wonderful.

The women and children and some of the men and boys spent the night in that place, for they were too ill to leave it; but the rest of us got up, by and by, and finished the night on the hurricane-deck.

That boat was the foulest I was ever in; and the smell of the breakfast saloon when we threaded our way among the layers of steaming passengers stretched upon its floor and its tables was incomparable for efficiency.

A good many of us got ashore at the first way-port to seek another ship. After a wait of three hours we got good rooms in the *Mahinapua*, a wee little bridal parlor of a boat—only two hundred and five tons burthen; clean and comfortable; good service; good beds; good table, and no crowding. The seas danced her about like a duck, but she was safe and capable.

Next morning early she went through the French Pass—a narrow gateway of rock, between bold headlands—so narrow, in fact, that it seemed no wider than a street. The current tore through there like a mill-race, and the boat darted through like a telegram. The passage was made in half a minute; then we were in a wide place where noble vast eddies swept grandly round and round in shoal-water, and I wondered what they would do with the little boat. They did as they pleased with her. They picked her up and flung her around like nothing and landed her gently on the solid, smooth bottom of sand—so gently, indeed, that we barely felt her touch it, barely felt her quiver when she came to a standstill. The water was as clear as glass, the sand on the bottom was vividly distinct, and the fishes seemed to be swimming about in nothing. Fishinglines were brought out, but before we could bait the hooks the boat was off and away again.

Chapter XXXIII

Let us be grateful to Adam our benefactor. He cut us out of the "blessing" of idleness and won for us the "curse" of labor.
— *Pudd'nhead Wilson's New Calendar.*

WE soon reached the town of Nelson, and spent the most of the day there, visiting acquaintances and driving with them about the garden—the whole region is a garden, excepting the scene of the "Maungatapu Murders," of thirty years ago. That is a wild place—wild and lonely; an ideal place for a murder. It is at the base of a vast, rugged, densely timbered mountain. In the deep twilight of that forest solitude four desperate rascals—Burgess, Sullivan, Levy, and Kelley—ambushed themselves beside the mountain trail to murder and rob four travelers—Kempthorne, Mathieu, Dudley, and De Pontius, the latter a New-Yorker. A harmless old laboring-man came wandering along, and, as his presence was an embarrassment, they choked him, hid him, and then resumed their watch for the four. They had to wait awhile, but eventually everything turned out as they desired.

That dark episode is the one large event in the history of Nelson. The fame of it traveled far. Burgess made a confession. It is a remarkable paper. For brevity, succinctness, and concentration, it is perhaps without its peer in the literature of murder. There are no waste words in it; there is no obtrusion of matter not pertinent to the occasion, nor any departure from the dispassionate tone proper to a formal business statement—for that is what it is: a business statement of a murder, by the chief engineer of it, or superintendent, or foreman, or whatever one may prefer to call him.

We were getting impatient, when we saw four men and a pack-horse coming. I left my cover and had a look at the men, for Levy had told me that Mathieu was a small man and wore a large beard, and that it was a chestnut horse. I said, "Here they come." They were then a good distance away; I took the caps off my gun, and put fresh ones on. I said, "You keep where you are, I'll put them up, and you give me your gun while you tie them." It was arranged as I have described. The men came; they arrived within about fifteen yards, when I stepped up and said, "Stand! bail up!" That means all of them to get together. I made them fall back on the upper side of the road with their faces up the range, and Sullivan brought me his gun, and then tied their hands behind them. The horse was very quiet all the time, he did not move. When they were all tied, Sullivan took the horse up the hill, and put him in the bush; he cut the rope and let the swags[1] fall on the ground, and then came to me. We then marched the men down the incline to the creek; the water at this time barely running. Up this creek we took the men; we went, I dare say, five or six hundred yards up it, which took us nearly half an hour to accomplish. Then we turned to the right up the range; we went, I dare say, one hundred and fifty yards from the creek, and there we sat down with the men. I said to Sullivan, "Put down your gun and search these men," which he did. I asked them their several names; they told me. I asked them if they

[1] A "swag" is a kit, a pack, small baggage.

were expected at Nelson. They said, "No." If such their lives would have been spared. In money we took sixty pounds odd. I said, "Is this all you have? You had better tell me." Sullivan said, "Here is a bag of gold." I said, "What's on that pack-horse? Is there any gold?" when Kempthorne said, "Yes, my gold is in the portmanteau, and I trust you will not take it all." "Well," I said, "we must take you away one at a time, because the range is steep just here, and then we will let you go." They said, "All right," most cheerfully. We tied their feet, and took Dudley with us; we went about sixty yards with him. This was through a scrub. It was arranged the night previously that it would be best to choke them, in case the report of the arms might be heard from the road, and if they were missed they never would be found. So we tied a handkerchief over his eyes, when Sullivan took the sash off his waist, put it round his neck, and so strangled him. Sullivan, after I had killed the old laboring-man, found fault with the way he was choked. He said, "The *next* we do I'll show you *my* way." I said, "I have never done such a thing before. I have shot a man, but never choked one." We returned to the others, when Kemp-thorne said, "What noise was that?" I said it was caused by breaking through the scrub. This was taking too much time, so it was agreed to shoot them. With that I said, "We'll take you no further, but separate you, and then loose one of you, and he can relieve the others." So with that, Sullivan took De Pontius to the left of where Kempthorne was sitting. I took Mathieu to the right. I tied a strap round his legs, and shot him with a revolver. He yelled, I ran from him with my gun in my hand, I sighted Kempthorne, who had risen to his feet. I presented the gun, and shot him behind the right ear; his life's blood welled from him, and he died instantaneously. Sullivan had shot De Pontius in the mean time, and then came to me. I said, "Look to Mathieu," indicating the spot where he lay. He shortly returned and said, "I had to 'chiv' that fellow, he was not dead," a cant word, meaning that he had to stab him. Returning to the road we passed where De Pontius lay and was dead. Sullivan said, "This is the digger, the others were all storekeepers; this is the digger, let's cover him up, for should the others be found, they'll think he done it and sloped," meaning he had gone. So with that we threw all the stones on him, and then left him. This bloody work took nearly an hour and a half from the time we stopped the men.

Any one who reads that confession will think that the man who wrote it was destitute of emotions, destitute of feeling. That is partly true. As regarded others he was plainly without feeling—utterly cold and pitiless; but as regarded himself the case was different. While he cared nothing for the future of the murdered men, he cared a great deal for his own. It makes one's flesh creep to read the introduction to his confession. The judge on the bench characterized it as "scandalously blasphemous," and it certainly reads so, but Burgess meant no blasphemy. He was merely a brute, and whatever he said or wrote was sure to expose the fact. His redemption was a very real thing to him, and he was as jubilantly happy on the gallows as ever was Christian martyr at the stake. We dwellers in this world are strangely made, and mysteriously circumstanced. We have to suppose that the murdered men are lost, and that Burgess is saved; but we cannot suppress our natural regrets:

> Written in my dungeon drear this 7th of August, in the year of Grace, 1866. To God be ascribed all power and glory in subduing the rebellious spirit of a most guilty wretch, who has been brought, through the instrumentality of a faithful follower of Christ, to see his wretched and guilty state, inasmuch as hitherto he has led an awful and wretched life, and through the assurance of this faithful soldier of Christ, he has been led and also believes that Christ will yet receive and cleanse him from all his deep-dyed and bloody sins. I lie under the imputation which says, "Come now and let us reason

together, saith the Lord; though your sins be as scarlet, they shall be as white as snow; though they be red like crimson, they shall be as wool." On this promise I rely.

We sailed in the afternoon late, spent a few hours at New Plymouth, then sailed again and reached Auckland the next day, November 20th, and remained in that fine city several days. Its situation is commanding, and the sea view is superb. There are charming drives all about, and by courtesy of friends we had opportunity to enjoy them. From the grassy crater-summit of Mount Eden one's eye ranges over a grand sweep and variety of scenery—forests clothed in luxuriant foliage, rolling green fields, conflagrations of flowers, receding and dimming stretches of green plain, broken by lofty and symmetrical old craters—then the blue bays twinkling and sparkling away into the dreamy distances where the mountains loom spiritual in their veils of haze.

It is from Auckland that one goes to Rotorua, the region of the renowned hot lakes and geysers—one of the chief wonders of New Zealand; but I was not well enough to make the trip. The government has a sanitarium there, and everything is comfortable for the tourist and the invalid. The government's official physician is almost over-cautious in his estimates of the efficacy of the baths, when he is talking about rheumatism, gout, paralysis, and such things; but when he is talking about the effectiveness of the waters in eradicating the whisky-habit, he seems to have no reserves. The baths will cure the drinking-habit no matter how chronic it is—and cure it so effectually that even the *desire* to drink intoxicants will come no more. There should be a rush from Europe and America to that place; and when the victims of alcoholism find out what they can get by going there, the rush will begin.

The Thermal-springs District of New Zealand comprises an area of upward of six hundred thousand acres, or close on one thousand square miles. Rotorua is the favorite place. It is the center of a rich field of lake and mountain scenery; from Rotorua as a base the pleasure-seeker makes excursions. The crowd of sick people is great, and growing. Rotorua is the Carlsbad of Australasia.

It is from Auckland that the Kauri gum is shipped. For a long time now about eight thousand tons of it have been brought into the town per year. It is worth about three hundred dollars per ton, unassorted; assorted, the finest grades are worth about one thousand dollars. It goes to America, chiefly. It is in lumps, and is hard and smooth, and looks like amber—the light colored like new amber, and the dark brown like rich old amber. And it has the pleasant feel of amber, too. Some of the light-colored samples were a tolerably fair counterfeit of uncut South African diamonds, they were so perfectly smooth and polished and transparent. It is manufactured into varnish; a varnish which answers for copal varnish and is cheaper.

The gum is dug up out of the ground; it has been there for ages. It is the sap of the Kauri tree. Dr. Campbell of Auckland told me he sent a cargo of it to England fifty years ago, but nothing came of the venture. Nobody knew what to do with it; so it was sold at five pounds a ton, to light fires with.

November 26—3 P.M., sailed. Vast and beautiful harbor. Land all about for hours. Tangariwa, the mountain that "has the same shape from *every* point of view." That is the common belief in Auckland. And so it has—from every point of view except thirteen. . . . Perfect summer weather. Large school of whales in the distance. Nothing could be daintier than the puffs of vapor they spout up, when seen against the pink glory of the sinking sun, or against the dark mass of an island reposing in the deep blue shadow of a storm-cloud. . . . Great Barrier rock standing up out of the sea away to the left. Some time ago a ship hit it full speed in a fog—twenty miles out of her course—one hundred and forty lives lost; the captain committed suicide without waiting a moment. He knew that, whether he was to blame or not, the company owning the vessel would discharge him and make a devotion-to-passengers'-safety advertisement out of it, and his chance to make a livelihood would be permanently gone.

Chapter XXXIV

Let us not be too particular. It is better to have old second-hand diamonds than none at all.
—Pudd'nhead Wilson's New Calendar.

*N*OVEMBER 27. To-day we reached Gisborne, and anchored in a big bay; there was a heavy sea on, so we remained on board.

We were a mile from shore; a little steam-tug put out from the land; she was an object of thrilling interest; she would climb to the summit of a billow, reel drunkenly there a moment, dim and gray in the driving storm of spindrift, then make a plunge like a diver, and remain out of sight until one had given her up, then up she would dart again, on a steep slant toward the sky, shedding Niagaras of water from her forecastle—and this she kept up, all the way out to us. She brought twenty-five passengers in her stomach—men and women—mainly a traveling dramatic company. In sight on deck were the crew, in sou'westers, yellow waterproof canvas suits, and boots to the thigh. The deck was never quiet for a moment, and seldom nearer level than a ladder, and noble were the seas which leaped aboard and went flooding aft. We rove a long line to the yard-arm, hung a most primitive basket-chair to it, and swung it out into the spacious air of heaven, and there it swayed, pendulum-fashion, waiting for its chance—then down it shot, skilfully aimed, and was grabbed by the two men on the forecastle. A young fellow belonging to our crew was in the chair, to be a protection to the lady-comers. At once a couple of ladies appeared from below, took seats in his lap, we hoisted them into the sky, waited a moment till the roll of the ship brought them in, overhead, then we lowered suddenly away, and seized the chair as it struck the deck. We took the twenty-five aboard, and delivered twenty-five into the tug—among them several aged ladies, and one blind one—and all without accident. It was a fine piece of work.

Ours is a nice ship, roomy, comfortable, well ordered, and satisfactory. Now and then we step on a rat in a hotel, but we have had no rats on shipboard lately; unless, perhaps, in the *Flora*; we had more serious things to think of there, and did not notice. I have noticed that it is only in ships and hotels which still employ the odious Chinese gong, that you find rats. The reason would seem to be, that as a rat cannot tell the time of day by a clock, he won't stay where he cannot find out when dinner is ready.

November 29. The doctor tells me of several old drunkards, one spiritless loafer, and several far-gone moral wrecks who have been reclaimed by the Salvation Army and have remained stanch people and hard workers these two years. Wherever one goes, these testimonials to the Army's efficiency are forthcoming. . . . This morning we had one of those whizzing green Ballarat flies in the room, with his stunning buzz-saw noise—the swiftest creature in the world except the lightning-flash. It is a stupendous force that is stored up in that little body. If we had it in a ship in the same proportion, we could spin from Liverpool to New York in the space of an hour—the time it takes to eat luncheon. The New Zealand express train is called the Ballarat Fly. . . . Bad teeth in the colonies. A citizen told me they don't have teeth filled, but pull them out and put in false ones, and that now and then one sees a young lady with a full set. She is fortunate. I wish I had been born with false teeth and a false liver and false carbuncles. I should get along better.

December 2—Monday. Left Napier in the Ballarat Fly— the one that goes twice a week. From Napier to Hastings, twelve miles; time, fifty-five minutes—not so far short of thirteen miles an hour. . . . A perfect summer day; cool breeze, brilliant sky, rich vegetation. Two or three times during the afternoon we saw wonderfully dense and beautiful forests, tumultuously piled skyward on the broken highlands—not the customary rooflike slant of a hillside, where the trees are all the same height. The noblest of these trees were of the Kauri breed, we were told—the timber that is now furnishing the wood-paving for Europe, and is the best of all wood for that purpose. Sometimes these towering upheavals of forestry were festooned and garlanded with vine-cables, and sometimes the masses of undergrowth were cocooned in another sort of vine of a delicate cobwebby texture—they call it the "supple-jack," I think. Tree-ferns everywhere—a stem fifteen feet high, with a graceful chalice of fern-fronds sprouting from its top—a lovely forest ornament. And there was a ten-foot reed with a flowing suit of what looked like yellow hair hanging from its upper end. I do not know its name, but if there is such a thing as a scalp plant, this is it. A romantic gorge, with a brook flowing in its bottom, approaching Palmerston North.

Waitukurau. Twenty minutes for luncheon. With me sat my wife and daughter, and my manager, Mr. Carlyle Smythe. I sat at the head of the table, and could see the right-hand wall; the others had their backs to it. On that wall, at a good distance away, were a couple of framed pictures. I could not see them clearly, but from the groupings of the figures I fancied that they represented the killing of Napoleon III.'s son by the Zulus in South Africa. I broke into the conversation, which was about poetry and cabbage and art, and said to my wife:

"Do you remember when the news came to Paris—"

"Of the killing of the Prince?"

(Those were the very words I had in my mind.)

"Yes, but *what* Prince?"

"Napoleon. Lulu."

"What made you think of that?"

"I don't know."

There was no collusion. She had not seen the pictures, and they had not been mentioned. She ought to have thought of some *recent* news that came to Paris, for we were but seven months from there and had been living there a couple of years when we started on this trip; but instead of that she thought of an incident of our brief sojourn in Paris of sixteen years before.

Here was a clear case of mental telegraphy; of mind-transference; of my mind telegraphing a thought into hers. How do I know? Because I telegraphed an *error*. For it turned out that the pictures did not represent the killing of Lulu at all, nor anything connected with Lulu. She had to get the error from my head—it existed nowhere else.

Chapter XXXV

*The Autocrat of Russia possesses more power than
any other man in the earth; but he cannot stop a sneeze.*
—Pudd'nhead Wilson's New Calendar.

WANGANUI, *December 3*. A pleasant trip, yesterday,
per Ballarat Fly. Four hours. I do not know the distance, but it must have been well along toward fifty miles.
The Fly could have spun it out to eight hours and not discom-
moded me; for where there is comfort, and no need for hurry,
speed is of no value—at least to me; and nothing that goes
on wheels can be more comfortable, more satisfactory, than
the New Zealand trains. Outside of America there are no cars
that are so rationally devised. When you add the constant
presence of charming scenery and the nearly constant absence
of dust—well, if one is not content then, he ought to get out
and walk. That would change his spirit, perhaps; I think so.
At the end of an hour you would find him waiting humbly
beside the track, and glad to be taken aboard again.

Much horseback-riding in and around this town; many
comely girls in cool and pretty summer gowns; much Salvation Army; lots of Maoris; the faces and bodies of some of

the old ones very tastefully frescoed. Maori Council House over the river—large, strong, carpeted from end to end with matting, and decorated with elaborate wood-carvings, artistically executed. The Maoris were very polite.

I was assured by a member of the House of Representatives that the native race is not decreasing, but actually increasing slightly. It is another evidence that they are a superior breed of savages. I do not call to mind any savage race that built such good houses, or such strong and ingenious and scientific fortresses, or gave so much attention to agriculture, or had military arts and devices which so nearly approached the white man's. These, taken together with their high abilities in boat-building, and their tastes and capacities in the ornamental arts, modify their savagery to a semi-civilization— or at least to a quarter-civilization.

It is a compliment to them that the British did not exterminate them, as they did the Australians and the Tasmanians, but were content with subduing them, and showed no desire to go further. And it is another compliment to them that the British did not take the whole of their choicest lands, but left them a considerable part, and then went further and protected them from the rapacities of land-sharks—a protection which the New Zealand Government still extends to them. And it is still another compliment to the Maoris that the government allows native representation in both the legislature and the cabinet, and gives both sexes the vote. And in doing these things the government also compliments itself. It has not been the custom of the world for conquerors to act in this large spirit toward the conquered.

The highest-class white men who lived among the Maoris in the earliest time had a high opinion of them and a strong affection for them. Among the whites of this sort was the author of *Old New Zealand* and Dr. Campbell of Auckland was another. Dr. Campbell was a close friend of several chiefs, and has many pleasant things to say of their fidelity, their magnanimity, and their generosity. Also of their quaint notions about the white man's queer civilization, and their equally quaint comments upon it. One of them thought the missionary had got everything wrong end first and upside down. "Why, he wants us to stop worshiping and supplicating the evil gods, and go to worshiping and supplicating the Good One! There is no sense in that. A *good* god is not going to do us any harm."

The Maoris had the *tabu*; and had it on a Polynesian scale of comprehensiveness and elaboration. Some of its features could have been importations from India and Judea. Neither the Maori nor the Hindu of common degree could cook by a fire that a person of higher caste had used, nor could the high Maori or high Hindu employ fire that had served a man of low grade; if a low-grade Maori or Hindu drank from a vessel belonging to a high-grade man, the vessel was defiled, and had to be destroyed. There were other resemblances between Maori *tabu* and Hindu caste-custom.

Yesterday a lunatic burst into my quarters and warned me that the Jesuits were going to "cook" (poison) me in my food, or kill me on the stage at night. He said a mysterious sign ☿ was visible upon my posters and meant my death. He said he saved Rev. Mr. Haweis's life by warning him that there were three men on his platform who would kill him if he took his eyes off them for a moment during his lecture. The same men were in my audience last night, but they saw that *he* was there. "Will they be here again to-night?" He hesitated; then said no, *he thought they would rather take a rest* and chance the poison. This lunatic has no delicacy. But he was not uninteresting. He told me a lot of things. He said he had "saved so many *lecturers* in twenty years, that *they put him in the asylum.*" I think he has less refinement than any lunatic I have met.

December 8. A couple of curious war-monuments here at Wanganui. One is in honor of white men "who fell in defense of law and order against fanaticism and barbarism." Fanaticism. We Americans are English in blood, English in speech, English in religion, English in the essentials of our governmental system, English in the essentials of our civilization; and so, let us hope, for the honor of the blend, for the honor of the blood, for the honor of the race, that that word got there through lack of heedfulness, and will not be suffered to remain. If you carve it at Thermopylæ, or where Winkelried died, or upon Bunker Hill monument, and read it again—"who fell in defense of law and order against fanaticism"—you will perceive what the word means, and how mischosen it is. Patriotism is Patriotism. Calling it Fanaticism cannot degrade it; nothing can degrade it. Even though it be a political mistake, and a thousand times a political mistake, that does not affect it; it is honorable—always honorable, always noble—and privileged to hold its head up and look the nations in the face. It is right to praise these brave white men who fell in the Maori war—they deserve it; but the presence of that word detracts from the dignity of their cause and their deeds, and makes them appear to have spilled their blood in a conflict with ignoble men, men not worthy of that costly sacrifice. But the men *were* worthy. It was no shame to fight them. They fought for their homes, they fought for their country; they bravely fought and bravely fell; and it would take nothing from the honor of the brave Englishmen who lie under the monument, but *add* to it, to say that they died in defense of English laws and English homes against men worthy of the sacrifice—the Maori patriots.

The other monument cannot be rectified. Except with dynamite. It is a mistake all through, and a strangely thoughtless one. It is a monument erected by white men to Maoris who fell fighting with the whites and *against their own people,* in the Maori war. "Sacred to the memory of the brave men who fell on the 14th of May, 1864," etc. On one side are the names of about twenty Maoris. It is not a fancy of mine; the monument exists. I saw it. It is an object-lesson to the rising generation. It invites to treachery, disloyalty, unpatriotism. Its lesson, in frank terms is, "Desert your flag, slay your people, burn their homes, shame your nationality—we honor such."

December 9. Wellington. Ten hours from Wanganui by the Fly.

December 12. It is a fine city and nobly situated. A busy place, and full of life and movement. Have spent the three days partly in walking about, partly in enjoying social privileges, and largely in idling around the magnificent garden at Hutt, a little distance away, around the shore. I suppose we shall not see such another one soon.

We are packing to-night for the return-voyage to Australia. Our stay in New Zealand has been too brief; still, we are not unthankful for the glimpse which we have had of it.

The sturdy Maoris made the settlement of the country by the whites rather difficult. Not at first—but later. At first they welcomed the whites, and were eager to trade with them—particularly for muskets; for their pastime was internecine war, and they greatly preferred the white man's weapons to their own. War *was* their pastime—I use the word advisedly. They often met and slaughtered each other just for a lark, and when there was no quarrel. The author of *Old New Zealand* mentions a case where a victorious army could have followed up its advantage and exterminated the opposing army, but declined to do it; explaining naïvely that "if we did that, there couldn't be any more fighting." In another battle one army sent word that it was out of ammunition, and would be obliged to stop unless the opposing army would send some. It was sent, and the fight went on.

In the early days things went well enough. The natives sold land without clearly understanding the terms of exchange, and the whites bought it without being much disturbed about the native's confusion of mind. But by and by the Maori began to comprehend that he was being wronged; then there was trouble, for he was not the man to swallow a wrong and go aside and cry about it. He had the Tasmanian's spirit and endurance, and a notable share of military science besides; and so he rose against the oppressor, did this gallant "fanatic," and started a war that was not brought to a definite end until more than a generation had sped.

Chapter XXXVI

*There are several good protections against tempta-
tions, but the surest is cowardice.*
  —Pudd'nhead Wilson's New Calendar.

*Names are not always what they seem. The com-
mon Welsh name Bzjxxllwcp is pronounced Jackson.*
  —Pudd'nhead Wilson's New Calendar.

*F*RIDAY, *December 13*. Sailed, at 3 P.M., in the *Mararoa.*
Summer seas and a good ship—life has nothing better.
Monday. Three days of paradise. Warm and sunny and
smooth; the sea a luminous Mediterranean blue. . . . One
lolls in a long chair all day under deck-awnings, and reads
and smokes, in measureless content. One does not read prose
at such a time, but poetry. I have been reading the poems of
Mrs. Julia A. Moore, again, and I find in them the same grace
and melody that attracted me when they were first published,
twenty years ago, and have held me in happy bonds ever
since. *The Sentimental Song Book* has long been out of print,
and has been forgotten by the world in general, but not by
me. I carry it with me always—it and Goldsmith's deathless
story. . . . Indeed, it has the same deep charm for me that
the *Vicar of Wakefield* has, and I find in it the same subtle
touch—the touch that makes an intentionally humorous episode pathetic and an intentionally pathetic one funny. In her

MARK TWAIN

time Mrs. Moore was called "the Sweet Singer of Michigan," and was best known by that name. I have read her book through twice to-day, with the purpose of determining which of her pieces has most merit, and I am persuaded that for wide grasp and sustained power, "William Upson" may claim first place:

WILLIAM UPSON

Air—"The Major's Only Son"

Come all good people far and near,
Oh, come and see what you can hear,
It's of a young man true and brave,
That is now sleeping in his grave.

Now, William Upson was his name—
If it's not that, it's all the same—
He did enlist in a cruel strife,
And it caused him to lose his life.

He was Perry Upson's eldest son,
His father loved his noble son,
This son was nineteen years of age
When first in the rebellion he engaged.

His father said that he might go,
But his dear mother she said no,
"Oh! stay at home, dear Billy," she said,
But she could not turn his head.

He went to Nashville, in Tennessee,
There his kind friends he could not see;
He died among strangers, so far away,
They did not know where his body lay.

He was taken sick and lived four weeks,
And Oh! how his parents weep,

But now they must in sorrow mourn,
For Billy has gone to his heavenly home.

Oh! if his mother could have seen her son,
For she loved him, her darling son;
If she could heard his dying prayer,
It would ease her heart till she met him there.

How it would relieve his mother's heart
To see her son from this world depart,
And hear his noble words of love,
As he left this world for that above.

Now it will relieve his mother's heart,
For her son is laid in our graveyard;
For now she knows that his grave is near,
She will not shed so many tears.

Although she knows not that it was her son,
For his coffin could not be opened—
It might be some one in his place,
For she could not see his noble face.

December 17. Reached Sydney.

December 19. In the train. Fellow of thirty with four valises; a slim creature, with teeth which made his mouth look like a neglected churchyard. He had solidified hair—solidified with pomatum; it was all one shell. He smoked the most extraordinary cigarettes—made of some kind of manure, apparently. These and his hair made him smell like the very nation. He had a low-cut vest on, which exposed a deal of frayed and broken and unclean shirt-front. Showy studs, of imitation gold—they had made black disks on the linen. Oversized sleeve-buttons of imitation gold, the copper base showing that. Ponderous watch-chain of imitation gold. I judge he couldn't tell the time by it, for he asked

Smythe what time it was, once. He wore a coat which had been gay when it was young; five-o'clock-tea trousers of a light tint, and marvelously soiled; yellow mustache with a dashing upward whirl at the ends; foxy shoes, imitation patent leather. He was a novelty—an imitation dude. He would have been a real one if he could have afforded it. But he was satisfied with himself. You could see it in his expression, and in all his attitudes and movements. He was living in a dude dreamland where all his squalid shams were genuine, and himself a sincerity. It disarmed criticism, it mollified spite, to see him so enjoy his imitation languors, and arts, and airs, and his studied daintinesses of gesture and misbegotten refinements. It was plain to me that he was imagining himself the Prince of Wales, and was doing everything the way he thought the Prince would do it. For bringing his four valises aboard and stowing them in the nettings, he gave his porter four cents, and lightly apologized for the smallness of the gratuity—just with the condescendingest little royal air in the world. He stretched himself out on the front seat and rested his pomatum-cake on the middle arm, and stuck his feet out of the window, and began to pose as the Prince and work his dreams and languors for exhibition; and he would indolently watch the blue films curling up from his cigarette, and inhale the stench, and look so grateful; and would flip the ash away with the daintiest gesture, unintentionally displaying his brass ring in the most intentional way; why, it was as good as being in Marlborough House itself to see him do it so like.

There was other scenery in the trip. That of the Hawksbury River, in the National Park region, fine—extraordinarily fine, with spacious views of stream and lake imposingly framed in woody hills; and every now and then the noblest groupings of mountains, and the most enchanting rearrangements of the water effects. Further along, green flats, thinly covered with gum forests, with here and there the huts and cabins of small farmers engaged in raising children. Still further along, arid stretches, lifeless and melancholy. Then Newcastle, a rushing town, capital of the rich coal regions. Approaching Scone, wide farming and grazing levels, with pretty frequent glimpses of a troublesome plant—a particularly devilish little prickly pear, daily damned in the orisons of the agriculturist; imported by a lady of sentiment, and contributed gratis to the colony. . . . Blazing hot, all day.

December 20. Back to Sidney. Blazing hot again. From the newspaper, and from the map, I have made a collection of curious names of Australasian towns, with the idea of making a poem out of them:

Tumut	Waitpinga	Wollongong
Takee	Goelwa	Woolloomooloo
Murriwillumba	Munno Para	Bombola
Bowral	Nangkita	Coolgardie
Ballarat	Myponga	Bendigo
Mullengudgery	Kapunda	Coonamble
Murrurundi	Kooringa	Cootamundra
Wagga-Wagga	Penola	Woolgoolga
Wyalong	Nangwarry	Mittagong
Murrumbidgee	Kongorong	Jamberoo
Goomeroo	Comaum	Kondoparinga
Wolloway	Koolywurtie	Kuitpo
Wangary	Killanoola	Tungkillo
Wanilla	Naracoorte	Oukaparinga
Worrow	Muloowurtie	Talunga
Koppio	Binnum	Yatala
Yankalilla	Wallaroo	Parawirra
Yaranyacka	Wirrega	Moorooroo
Yackamoorundie	Mundoora	Whangarei

MARK TWAIN

Kaiwaka	Hauraki	Woolundunga
Goomooroo	Rangiriri	Booleroo
Tauranga	Teawamute	Pernattyi
Geelong	Taranaki	Parramatta
Tongariro	Toowoomba	Taroom
Kaikoura	Goondiwindi	Narrandera
Wakatipu	Jerrilderie	Deniliquin
Oohipara	Whangaroa	Kawakawa

It may be best to build the poem now, and make weather help:

A SWELTERING DAY IN AUSTRALIA

(To be read soft and low, with the lights turned down)

The Bombola faints in the hot Bowral tree,
　　Where fierce Mullengudgery's smothering fires
Far from the breezes of Coolgardie
　　Burn ghastly and blue as the day expires;

And Murriwillumba complaineth in song
　　For the garlanded bowers of Woolloomooloo,
And the Ballarat Fly and the lone Wollongong
　　They dream of the gardens of Jamberoo;

The wallabi sighs for the Murrumbidgee,
　　For the velvety sod of the Munno Parah,
Where the waters of healing from Muloowurtie
　　Flow dim in the gloaming by Yaranyackah;

The Koppio sorrows for lost Wolloway,
　　And sigheth in secret for Murrurundi,
The Whangaroa wombat lamenteth the day
　　That made him an exile from Jerrilderie;

The Teawamute Tumut from Wirrega's glade,
　　The Nangkita swallow, the Wallaroo swan,

They long for the peace of the Timaru shade
   And thy balmy soft airs, O sweet Mittagong!

The Kooringa buffalo pants in the sun,
   The Kondoparinga lies gaping for breath,
The Kongorong Comaum to the shadow has won,
   But the Goomeroo sinks in the slumber of death

In the weltering hell of the Moorooroo plain
   The Yatala Wangary withers and dies,
And the Worrow Wanilla, demented with pain,
   To the Woolgoolga woodlands despairingly flies;

Sweet Nangwarry's desolate, Coonamble wails,
   And Tungkillo Kuitpo in sables is drest,
For the Whangarei winds fall asleep in the sails
   And the Booleroo life-breeze is dead in the west

Myponga, Kapunda, O slumber no more!
   Yankalilla, Parawirra, be warned!
There's death in the air! Killanoola, wherefore
   Shall the prayer of Penola be scorned?

Cootamundra, and Takee, and Wakatipu,
   Toowoomba, Kaikoura are lost!
From Oukaparinga to far Oamaru
   All burn in this hell's holocaust!

Parramatta and Binnum are gone to their rest
   In the vale of Tapanni Taroom,
Kawakawa, Deniliquin—all that was best
   In the earth are but graves and a tomb!

Narrandera mourns, Cameroo answers not
   When the roll of the scathless we cry:
Tongariro, Goondiwindi, Woolundunga, the spot
   Is mute and forlorn where ye lie.

Those are good words for poetry. Among the best I have
ever seen. There are eighty-one in the list. I did not need

them all, but I have knocked down sixty-six of them; which is a good bag, it seems to me, for a person not in the business. Perhaps a poet laureate could do better, but a poet laureate gets wages, and that is different. When I write poetry I do not get any wages; often I lose money by it. The best word in that list, and the most musical and gurgly, is Woolloomooloo. It is a place near Sydney, and is a favorite pleasure resort. It has eight O's in it.

END OF VOL. I